A New China

Intermediate Reader of Modern Chinese

Text
Vocabulary

新 的 中 国
A New China

现 代 汉 语 中 级 读 本
Intermediate Reader of
Modern Chinese

Text
Vocabulary

周质平　　杨　玖　　张家惠
Chih-p'ing Chou　　Joanne Chiang　　Jianna Eagar

Princeton University Press
Princeton, New Jersey

Copyright © 1999 by Princeton University Press
Published by Princeton University Press, 41 William Street,
Princeton, New Jersey 08540
In the United Kingdom: Princeton University Press, Chichester, West Sussex

Library of Congress Catalog Card Number 99-62100

ISBN 0-691-01045-5 (pbk.)

The publisher would like to acknowledge the authors of this volume for providing
the camera-ready copy from which this book was printed

The paper used in this publication meets the minimum requirements of
ANSI/NISO Z39.48-1992 (R1997) (*Permanence of Paper*)

http://pup.princeton.edu

Printed in the United States of America

3 5 7 9 10 8 6 4

目 录

~ Table of Contents ~

序

　　中国最近几年的变化可以说是日新月异。普林斯顿大学对外汉语教研室继《现代汉语中级读本》（1992）、《华夏行》（1995）、《中国啊！中国》（1997）等中级读本之后，编写《新的中国》，正是为了适应这一快速的改变。

　　《新的中国》所体现的，依旧是一个外国学生初到中国时的一些观察和体会，而所介绍的内容和词汇则不出一个留学生的生活日用。《华夏行》所反映的是八十年代初期的中国社会，作者经常拿中国和西方比较。在《新的中国》里，作者不再作中西比较，而是拿当今的中国与改革开放之前的中国比较。在中西比较中，我们看到许多中国不能令人满意的地方；但是在当今和先前的比较中，我们发现中国近二十年来有飞跃的进步，而这个进步也缩小了中西的差距。《新的中国》正是在这个基础上编写出来的一本对外汉语中级读本。和《华夏行》比较，《新的中国》少了一点批评，多了一份"同情的了解"。

在美国对外汉语教学界纷纷编写"商用汉语"读本的今天，我们推出这本一般性的中级读本，也许有其不合时宜的地方。但是我们相信，语文的训练必须从一般的基础下手，所谓"一般"，在内容上指的是生活日用；在结构上，指的是发音和基本语法句构的掌握。《新的中国》特别着重这些基础的训练。

《新的中国》一如我们先前所出的读本，每一课的课文尽量作到不只是简单的叙述或对话，而是在叙述或对话中夹着作者的意见。我们希望能借此引发学生学习和讨论的兴趣。

《新的中国》初稿完成于1997年夏天，1998年我们在普林斯顿大学北京汉语培训班试用，效果很好，并根据老师学生的意见，作了一些增删。在课文的编排上，还是繁简并列，但在词汇的安排上，为了便于学生使用，我们首次采用与本文同页互见的方式。这是形式上的一大改进。与普大前出课本比较，练习部分增添了不少新形式，当有助于实际教学。

本书课文由周质平撰写，词汇、句型和练习是由杨玖、张家惠编写的。

本书之成要特别向 Matthew Eagar 先生和 Kara Wortman, Jennifer Hunt, Robin Workman 三位小姐致谢，他们仔细校看了本书的英文部分，改正了错误。Matthew 并设计了封面，使本书大为增色。普大的同事夏岩、蒋冕华、安延明、戴晓雪四位老师，在最后定稿阶段，参加讨论，提供了许多宝贵意见，在此一并致谢。当然书中若有任何错误或不妥的地方，完全是作者的责任。

周质平、杨玖、张家惠

1999 年 2 月 28 日

Preface

China has experienced rapid changes over the past two decades. The Chinese Language Program at Princeton University is publishing *A New China* to supplement previous textbooks and provide up-to-date material on the changing face of China.

Like some earlier textbooks in our series, *A New China* is written from the perspective of a foreign student who has just arrived in China. Its predecessor *A Trip to China* reflects Chinese society in the early 1980s and compares China to the Western world. In *A New China*, we no longer compare China to the West, but rather compare contemporary China to its pre-reform eras. When we compared China and the West, we found it inevitable that China fell short in many respects. In our comparison between contemporary and pre-reform China, however, we have found great improvements in Chinese society in the recent decade. These improvements have in fact narrowed the gap between China and the western world.

Nowadays in the field of Chinese language instruction in the U. S., it has become very popular to publish textbooks in "business Chinese." We insist, however, that providing a solid foundation in grammar and pronunciation is more essential than teaching vocabulary geared toward specific usage.

As we have done in previous textbooks, we have made every effort in *A New China* to fill each lesson not only with mere description and dialogue, but also with the authors' viewpoints. We hope this will provoke discussion and will inspire students' interest in Chinese.

The draft of *A New China* was written in the summer of 1997 and was field-tested at the 1998 session of *Princeton in Beijing* summer intensive language program. The book was well received by students. As in previous textbooks, we have included both traditional and simplified versions of the text. For the first time, however, we have included vocabulary on the same page as the text. This change should make the book more convenient for students. We have also added several new exercises.

We would sincerely like to thank Matthew Eagar, Kara Wortman, Jennifer Hunt, and Robin Workman, who have taken pains to edit the English glossary and grammar notes. Their efforts have greatly improved the English portions of this book. Matthew also designed the cover which has significantly enhanced the presentation of this text. We would also like to extend thanks to our colleagues, Xia Yan, Chiang Mien-hwa, An Yanming, and Dai Xiaoxue, who have made valuable suggestions for the final revision of the textbook. Any errors are strictly the responsibility of the authors.

Chih-p'ing Chou
Joanne Chiang
Jianna Eagar

Princeton University
February 28, 1999

略语表

~ List of Abbreviations ~

adj.	. . . .	adjective
adv.	. . . .	adverb
AN	. . . .	auxiliary noun
aux.	. . . .	auxiliary
comp.	. . . .	complement
conj.	. . . .	conjunction
idm.	. . . .	idiom
interj.	. . . .	interjection
L.	. . . .	lesson
n.	. . . .	noun
No.	. . . .	number
o.	. . . .	object
postp.	. . . .	postposition
pref.	. . . .	prefix
prep.	. . . .	preposition
pron.	. . . .	pronoun
prov.	. . . .	proverb
p.w.	. . . .	place word
t.w.	. . . .	time word
v.	. . . .	verb
v.-c.	. . . .	verb-complement
v.-o.	. . . .	verb-object

◆ The numbers in parentheses within the lesson text correspond to the grammar notes for that lesson.

第一課
到了北京

　　飛機今天晚上準時降落在(1)北京首都國際機場。學校外事處派來的一位張先生在機場接我們。

　　通過海關的時候ㄦ，我有點ㄦ(2)擔心，因為我帶了幾本ㄦ《花花公子》雜誌給我的中國朋友。據說(3)中國海關對(4)這類雜誌查得很嚴，好在(5)他們根本(6)沒打開箱子就讓(7)我通過了。後來(8)我們坐上

北京	北京	Běijīng		Beijing
飛機	飞机	fēijī	*n.*	airplane
準時	准时	zhǔnshí	*adv.*	punctually; on time
降落	降落	jiàngluò	*v.*	land; descend
首都	首都	shǒudū	*n*	capital
國際	国际	guójì	*adj.*	international
機場	机场	jīchǎng	*n.*	airport
外事處	外事处	wàishìchù	*n.*	foreign affairs office
派	派	pài	*v.*	dispatch; send
張	张	Zhāng		Zhang (a surname)
先生	先生	xiān.shēng	*n.*	Mr.
接	接	jiē	*v.*	meet; welcome
通過	通过	tōngguò	*v.*	pass through; go through

第一课
到了北京

　　飞机今天晚上准时降落在(1)北京首都国际机场。学校外事处派来的一位张先生在机场接我们。

　　通过海关的时候儿，我有点儿(2)担心，因为我带了几本儿《花花公子》杂志给我的中国朋友。据说(3)中国海关对(4)这类杂志查得很严，好在(5)他们根本(6)没打开箱子就让(7)我通过了。后来(8)我们坐上

海關	海关	hǎiguān	*n.*	customs
擔心	担心	dānxīn	*v.*	worry; feel anxious
帶	带	dài	*v.*	take; bring; carry
花花公子	花花公子	Huāhuā Gōngzǐ		*Playboy*
類	类	lèi	*n.*	type
雜誌	杂志	zázhì	*n.*	magazine
據說	据说	jùshuō	*adv.*	it is said; they say
對	对	duì	*prep.*	to; toward
查	查	chá	*v.*	check; inspect
嚴	严	yán	*adj.*	strict; severe; stern
好在	好在	hǎozài	*adv.*	luckily; fortunately
根本	根本	gēnběn	*adv.*	at all; simply
箱子	箱子	xiāngzi	*n.*	chest; trunk; baggage

言襄　　　　　ràng　　　　　　　　allow

3

了一部小麵包車，開了差不多一個小時就到學校了。

北京給我的第一個印象(9)是海關的檢查很鬆，沒有我想的那麼嚴；從機場到城裏的高速公路又(10)寬又平，非常現代化。這和我想像中(11)古老的北京完全不同(12)。

今天很累，可是也很興奮。我們的宿舍很好，房間很大，床也很舒服，不過因為時差的關係(13)，一直到早上三點還沒睡著。

部	部	bù	*an.*	measure word for car
麵包車	面包车	miànbāochē	*n.*	"loaf-of-bread'car"; van; 面包: bread
差不多	差不多	chàbuduō	*adv.*	almost; nearly
印象	印象	yìnxiàng	*n.*	impression
檢查	检查	jiǎnchá	*v.*	check; examine; inspect
鬆	松	sōng	*adj.*	loose; slack
城裏	城里	chéng.lǐ	*p.w.*	inside the city; downtown
高速公路	高速公路	gāosù gōnglù	*n.*	highway
寬	宽	kuān	*adj.*	wide; broad

了一部小面包车，开了差不多一个小时就到学校
了。

　　北京给我的第一个印象 (9) 是海关的检查很
松，没有我想的那么严；从机场到城里的高速公路
又 (10) 宽又平，非常现代化。这和我想象中 (11) 古老
的北京完全不同 (12)。

　　今天很累，可是也很兴奋。我们的宿舍很好，
房间很大，床也很舒服，不过因为时差的关系 (13)，
一直到早上三点还没睡着。

平	平	píng	*adj.*	flat; smooth
現代化	现代化	xiàndàihuà	*adj./n.*	modern, modernization
想像	想象	xiǎngxiàng	*v./n.*	imagine, imagination
古老	古老	gǔlǎo	*adj.*	ancient; age-old
興奮	兴奋	xīngfèn	*adj.*	excited
舒服	舒服	shū.fú	*adj.*	comfortable
不過	不过	búguò	*adv.*	nevertheless
時差	时差	shíchā	*n.*	jet lag; time difference
關係	关系	guān.xì	*n.*	relationships; connections
一直	一直	yìzhí	*adv.*	all the way; all along; continuously
睡著	睡着	shuì-zháo	*v.-c.*	fall asleep

宿舍　~~sù shè~~　dorm

→ 房間　fángjiān　bedroom
　床　chuáng　bed

第二課
給媽媽打電話

女：媽，我已經到了北京了，一切都很順利。

母：那(1)我就放心了！你累不累啊？

女：累是有點儿累(2)，可是很興奮。

母：宿舍怎麼樣啊？是單人房還是雙人房？

女：是雙人房。同屋是個美國學生，我們很談得來(3)。

母：那很好。天氣預報説今年夏天北京特別熱，宿舍裏有空調嗎？

電話	电话	diànhuà	*n.*	telephone; phone call
打電話	打电话	dǎ diànhuà	*v.-o.*	make a phone call; call
一切	一切	yíqiè	*n.*	all; every; everything
順利	顺利	shùnlì	*adj.*	smooth; successful
放心	放心	fàngxīn	*v.*	set one's mind at rest; feel relieved
單人房	单人房	dānrénfáng	*n.*	single room

第二课
给妈妈打电话

女：妈，我已经到了北京了，一切都很顺利。

母：那(1)我就放心了！你累不累啊？

女：累是有点儿累(2)，可是很兴奋。

母：宿舍怎么样啊？是单人房还是双人房？

女：是双人房。同屋是个美国学生，我们很谈得来(3)。

母：那很好。天气预报说今年夏天北京特别热，宿舍里有空调吗？

雙人房	双人房	shuāngrénfáng	n.	double room
同屋	同屋	tóngwū	n.	roommate
談得來	谈得来	tán.délái	v.-c.	get along well
天氣預報	天气预报	tiānqì yùbào	n.	weather forecast
特別	特别	tèbié	adv./adj.	especially, special
空調	空调	kōngtiáo	n.	air conditioning

女：有。不但(4)有空調，還有彩電、電話、熱水

　　　和自己的浴室呢！

母：這樣的條件比(5)你在美國的宿舍還好嘛(6)！

女：是啊！每天還有人給我們換毛巾、整理床鋪、

　　　打掃房間呢！

母：這聽起來(7)簡直(8)像個旅館。學校太照顧外

　　　國學生了。我真擔心你們要被(9)慣壞了。

女：住得舒服點兒才(10)能好好學習呀！

母：校園怎麼樣呢？安全不安全啊？

女：聽説(11)安全得很。而且校園裏又有飯館兒又有

彩電	彩电	cǎidiàn	n.	color TV
浴室	浴室	yùshì	n.	bathroom; washroom
條件	条件	tiáojiàn	n.	condition
換	换	huàn	v.	change
毛巾	毛巾	máojīn	n.	towel
整理	整理	zhěnglǐ	v.	put in order; straigten up
床鋪	床铺	chuángpù	n.	bedding
打掃	打扫	dǎsǎo	v.	sweep; clean
簡直	简直	jiǎnzhí	adv.	simply

女：有。不但(4)有空调，还有彩电、电话、热水
　　和自己的浴室呢！

母：这样的条件比(5)你在美国的宿舍还好嘛(6)！

女：是啊！每天还有人给我们换毛巾、整理床铺、
　　打扫房间呢！

母：这听起来(7)简直(8)像个旅馆。学校太照顾外
　　国学生了。我真担心你们要被(9)惯坏了。

女：住得舒服点儿才(10)能好好学习呀！

母：校园怎么样呢？安全不安全啊？

女：听说(11)安全得很。而且校园里又有饭馆儿又有

旅館	旅馆	lǚguǎn	*n.*	hotel
照顧	照顾	zhào.gù	*v.*	take care of; look after
慣壞	惯坏	guàn-huài	*v.-c.*	spoil
學習	学习	xuéxí	*v.*	study
校園	校园	xiàoyuán	*n.*	campus
安全	安全	ānquán	*adj.*	safe
聽說	听说	tīngshuō	*v.*	be told; hear of; hear
...得很	...得很	....dehěn		very
飯館	饭馆	fànguǎn	*n.*	restaurant

商店，留學生食堂離(12)我的宿舍也很近，方便極了。

母：去了北京，條件又(13)那麼好，要是再(14)學不好中文，可(15)就沒有藉口了。

女：您放心，我會努力學習的。

母：你一方面(16)要努力學習，一方面也得注意健康啊！

女：我知道。媽，國際長途電話太貴了，下星期再給您打吧！

母：好，好。再見再見！

女：再見再見！

商店	商店	shāngdiàn	*n.*	store; shop; 商 : business; 店 : store
留學生	留学生	liúxuéshēng	*n.*	foreign student
食堂	食堂	shítáng	*n.*	dining hall
離	离	lí	*v.*	be away from; from
近	近	jìn	*adj.*	close; near

商店，留学生食堂离(12)我的宿舍也很近，方便极了。

母：去了北京，条件又(13)那么好，要是再(14) 学不好中文，可(15)就没有借口了。

女：您放心，我会努力学习的。

母：你一方面(16)要努力学习，一方面也得注意健康啊！

女：我知道。妈，国际长途电话太贵了，下星期再给您打吧！

母：好，好。再见再见！

女：再见再见！

方便	方便	fāngbiàn	*adj.*	convenient
藉口	借口	jièkǒu	*n.*	excuse
努力	努力	nǔlì	*adv.*	with great effort
注意	注意	zhùyì	*v.*	pay attention to
健康	健康	jiànkāng	*n./adj.*	health; physique, healthy
長途	长途	chángtú	*adj.*	long distance

第 三 課
早 起、 洗 澡

到了北京以後，早上七點半就 (1) 開始上課，我真 (2) 不習慣。我在美國上大學，從來沒 (3) 這麼早起來過。九點鐘的課還 (4) 常常遲到，更 (5) 不用說七點半的課了。

因為我喜歡晚睡，早起對我就特別困難。中國人常說早晨頭腦清楚，是學習最好的時候。可對我來說 (6)，早上剛 (7) 起來的時候頭腦最不清楚，需

早起	早起	zǎoqǐ	v.	get up early
洗澡	洗澡	xǐ-zǎo	v.-o.	have a bath; bathe
習慣	习惯	xíguàn	v./n.	be accustomed to; be used to; habit; custom
上	上	shàng	v.	go to; be engaged (in work, study, etc.) at a fixed time
從來沒 V. 過	从来没 V. 过	cónglái méi... guò		have never V-ed
遲到	迟到	chídào	v.	be late (for a fixed schedule)

12

第三课
早起、洗澡

到了北京以后，早上七点半就(1)开始上课，我真(2)不习惯。我在美国上大学，从来没(3)这么早起来过。九点钟的课还(4)常常迟到，更(5)不用说七点半的课了。

因为我喜欢晚睡，早起对我就特别困难。中国人常说早晨头脑清楚，是学习最好的时候。可对我来说(6)，早上刚(7)起来的时候头脑最不清楚，需

不用說	不用说	búyòng shuō	*conj.*	not to mention; needless to say; let alone
晚睡	晚睡	wǎnshuì	*v.*	go to bed late
困難	困难	kùn.nán	*adj./n.*	difficult; difficulty
早晨	早晨	zǎochén	*n.*	morning
頭腦	头脑	tóunǎo	*n.*	brains; mind
清楚	清楚	qīng.chǔ	*adj.*	clear
剛	刚	gāng	*adv.*	just

要喝兩三杯咖啡才能完全醒過來 (8)。我真不懂為什麼得這麼早上課。

中國人也常說：早睡早起身體好。我卻 (9) 覺得起得早晚跟身體健康沒有什麼關係 (10)。不過，我現在是每天晚睡早起，整天都累得要命 (11)。

除了早起以外 (12)，中國人晚上洗澡的習慣也是我到了北京以後才 (13) 發現的。一般來說 (14)，美國人經常早上洗澡，中國人卻喜歡晚上洗澡，所以中國的學生宿舍多半兒是在晚飯以後、睡覺以前，

需要	需要	xūyào	v./n.	need; want; require
咖啡	咖啡	kāfēi	n.	coffee
醒	醒	xǐng	v.	wake up; sober up
身體	身体	shēntǐ	n.	body; health
卻	却	què	adv.	but; yet; however
整天	整天	zhěngtiān	adv.	the whole day; all day long
…得要命	…得要命	...de yàomìng		awfully; extremely

要喝两三杯咖啡才能完全醒过来(8)。我真不懂为什么得这么早上课。

中国人也常说：早睡早起身体好。我却(9)觉得起得早晚跟身体健康没有什么关系(10)。不过，我现在是每天晚睡早起，整天都累得要命(11)。

除了早起以外(12)，中国人晚上洗澡的习惯也是我到了北京以后才(13)发现的。一般来说(14)，美国人经常早上洗澡，中国人却喜欢晚上洗澡，所以中国的学生宿舍多半儿是在晚饭以后、睡觉以前，

除了...以外	除了...以外	chúle...yǐwài		except for; aside from
才	才	cái	*adv.*	not until
發現	发现	fāxiàn	*v.*	find; discover
一般來說	一般来说	yìbān láishuō	*adv.*	generally speaking
經常	经常	jīngcháng	*adv.*	often; frequently
提供	提供	tígōng	*v.*	offer; provide; supply

提供熱水。我本來 (15) 總是早上洗澡，來了中國以後，不得不 (16) 改成 (17) 晚上洗澡了。

以前我覺得，早上洗完澡，乾乾淨淨的 (18)，開始一天的工作很不錯。現在我認為，晚上洗完澡，舒舒服服地睡覺也很好。

來中國以前，我從來沒想過早上洗澡好還是晚上洗澡好。有許多事情，我本來以為 (19) 一定是這樣做的；到了中國，卻發現中國人不一定這樣做。我學會了從另 (20) 一個角度看事情，這就是到外國去的好處。

本來	本来	běnlái	*adv.*	originally; at first
不得不	不得不	bùdébù	*v.*	have no choice but to; have to
改	改	gǎi	*v.*	change; alter; correct
成	成	chéng	*comp.*	into
乾淨	干净	gānjìng	*adj.*	clean; neat and tidy
認為	认为	rènwéi	*v.*	think; consider; hold

提供热水。我本来(15)总是早上洗澡，来了中国以后，不得不(16)改成(17)晚上洗澡了。

以前我觉得，早上洗完澡，干干净净的(18)，开始一天的工作很不错。现在我认为，晚上洗完澡，舒舒服服地睡觉也很好。

来中国以前，我从来没想过早上洗澡好还是晚上洗澡好。有许多事情，我本来以为(19)一定是这样做的；到了中国，却发现中国人不一定这样做。我学会了从另(20)一个角度看事情，这就是到外国去的好处。

以爲	以为	yǐwéi	v.	mistakenly think
學會	学会	xué-huì	v.-c.	learn
另	另	lìng	adj.	the other; another
角度	角度	jiǎodù	n.	angle; point of view
外國	外国	wàiguó	n.	foreign country
好處	好处	hǎo.chù	n.	benefit; gain; profit; advantage

第 四 課

郵 局 在 哪ㄦ

（一）在宿舍裏

留學生：小姐，請問，附近 (1) 有郵局嗎？

服務員：有是有，可是離這ㄦ比較 (2) 遠。

留學生：走得到嗎？得走多 (3) 長時間？

服務員：得走半個多 (4) 小時呢！你最好 (5) 坐22路

公共汽車去，只有三站地。

留學生：下了車以後，怎麼走呢？

郵局	邮局	yóujú	*n.*	post office
小姐	小姐	xiǎo.jiě	*n.*	Miss; also used for married professional women
附近	附近	fùjìn		nearby; in the vicinity
比較	比较	bǐjiào	*adv./v.*	comparatively, compare
遠	远	yuǎn	*adj.*	distant; far
服務員	服务员	fúwùyuán	*n.*	service personnel 服務: serve; give service to
最好	最好	zuìhǎo	*adv.*	had better; it would be best

第四课

邮局在哪儿

（一）在宿舍里

留学生：小姐，请问，附近(1)有邮局吗？

服务员：有是有，可是离这儿比较(2)远。

留学生：走得到吗？得走多(3)长时间？

服务员：得走半个多(4)小时呢！你最好(5)坐22路

公共汽车去，只有三站地。

留学生：下了车以后，怎么走呢？

路	路	lù	*an.*	route 三路公车: No. 3 bus
公共汽車	公共汽车	gōnggòng qìchē	*n.*	bus; 公共: public; communal
站	站	zhàn	*n.*	station; stop
往	往	wǎng	*prep.*	in the direction of; towards
南	南	nán	*n.*	south
過	过	guò	*v.*	pass; cross
條	条	tiáo	*an.*	measure word for things narrow and long

服務員：下了車以後往南走 (6)，過一條街，再 (7) 往

東，有一個公園儿，郵局就在公園儿對

面。

（二）在郵局裏

留學生：小姐，我要寄一些照片儿到美國去，得去

哪個窗口啊？

服務員：要掛號嗎？

留學生：我怕寄丟了，最好掛號。

服務員：三號窗口辦國際掛號。

留學生：謝謝！

公園	公园	gōngyuán	*n.*	park
對面	对面	duìmiàn	*postp.*	across from; in front of
寄	寄	jì	*v.*	send; mail
照片	照片	zhàopiān	*n.*	photograph; picture
窗口	窗口	chuāngkǒu	*n.*	service window

服务员：下了车以后往南走(6)，过一条街，再(7)往

东，有一个公园儿，邮局就在公园儿对

面。

（二）在邮局里

留学生：小姐，我要寄一些照片儿到美国去，得去

哪个窗口啊？

服务员：要挂号吗？

留学生：我怕寄丢了，最好挂号。

服务员：三号窗口办国际挂号。

留学生：谢谢！

掛號	挂号	guàhào	v.	register; send by registered mail
怕	怕	pà	v.	fear; be afraid of
丢	丢	diū	v.	lose (something)
辦	办	bàn	v.	do; manage; handle

（三號窗口）

留學生：這封信寄到美國，要掛號。

服務員：裏面是什麼？

留學生：洗好的照片儿和一些膠卷儿。要多少錢？

服務員：三十六塊五毛。請您先填這張表，把地址和姓名都寫清楚。

留學生：我還想買些信封、信紙、郵票和幾張風景明信片。

服務員：您要的東西旁邊儿的櫃台都有。

留學生：謝謝！

封	封	fēng	*an.*	measure word for 信
洗	洗	xǐ	*v.*	(in this context) develop (film)
膠卷	胶卷	jiāojuǎn	*n.*	roll of film; film
塊	块	kuài	*n.*	dollor; buck
毛	毛	máo	*n.*	dime
塡	填	tián	*v.*	fill in
表	表	biǎo	*n.*	form; table
地址	地址	dìzhǐ	*n.*	address

（三号窗口 ）

留学生：这封信寄到美国，要挂号。

服务员：里面是什么？

留学生：洗好的照片儿和一些胶卷儿。要多少钱？

服务员：三十六块五毛。请您先填这张表，把地址
和姓名都写清楚。

留学生：我还想买些信封、信纸、邮票和几张风景
明信片。

服务员：您要的东西旁边儿的柜台都有。

留学生：谢谢！

姓名	姓名	xìngmíng	*n.*	full name
信封	信封	xìnfēng	*n.*	envelope
信紙	信纸	xìnzhǐ	*n.*	letter paper
郵票	邮票	yóupiào	*n.*	stamp
風景	风景	fēngjǐng	*n.*	scenery; landscape
明信片	明信片	míngxìnpiàn	*n.*	postcard
櫃台	柜台	guìtái	*n.*	counter

第 五 課
拉肚子，睡不好

學生：王老師，今天我覺得很不舒服，我想請半
　　　天假，在宿舍裏休息休息。

老師：怎麼了(1)？是不是病了？

學生：昨天晚上我吃了一碗牛肉麵，一塊西瓜。
　　　睡覺以前，肚子很疼，拉了好幾次，後來
　　　還吐了。

老師：也許你吃的東西不太乾淨。發燒了沒有？

學生：燒倒是(2)沒燒，可是沒睡好覺。這幾個星期
　　　我天天都睡不好，累極了。

肚子	肚子	dùzi	n.	stomach; abdomen
拉肚子	拉肚子	lā-dùzi	v.-o.	suffer from diarrhea; have loose bowels
請假	请假	qǐng-jià	v.-o.	ask for leave
休息	休息	xiū.xí	v.	rest; have a rest
病	病	bìng	v.	be sick; be ill
碗	碗	wǎn	n./an.	bowl
牛肉		niúròu		beef

第 五 课

拉肚子，睡不好

学生：王老师，今天我觉得很不舒服，我想请半

　　　天假，在宿舍里休息休息。

老师：怎么了(1)？是不是病了？

学生：昨天晚上我吃了一碗牛肉面，一块西瓜。

　　　睡觉以前，肚子很疼，拉了好几次，后来

　　　还吐了。

老师：也许你吃的东西不太干净。发烧了没有？

学生：烧倒是(2)没烧，可是没睡好觉。这几个星期

　　　我天天都睡不好，累极了。

麵	面	miàn	*n.*	noodle
塊	块	kuài	*an.*	piece; lump; chunk
西瓜	西瓜	xīguā	*n.*	watermelon
疼	疼	téng	*v./adj.*	ache; sore, painful
吐	吐	tù	*v.*	vomit
發燒	发烧	fā-shāo	*v.-o.*	have a fever
也許		yěxǔ		peraps

老師：為什麼總睡不好呢？

學生：宿舍裏太熱了。

老師：不是有空調嗎(3)？

學生：我同屋不喜歡開空調，喜歡開窗。結果(4)屋
　　　子裏蚊子多得要命。昨天晚上我被叮了好
　　　幾次。你看，臉上、胳膊上都是(5)。

老師：我不知道你們有這樣的問題。我看，你們得
　　　好好ㄦ談談。

學生：談過好幾次了。但是她總是把窗子開開，
　　　把空調關掉(6)。我們的關係越來越(7)緊張
　　　了。

老師：這件事，我真不知道(8)該怎麼幫你的忙。你
　　　先到學校的醫院去，讓大夫看看吧！

結果	結果	jiéguǒ	*adv./n.*	as a result, result
蚊子	蚊子	wénzi	*n.*	mosquito
叮	叮	dīng	*v.*	sting; bite
胳膊	胳膊	gē.bó	*n.*	arm
關掉	关掉	guān-diào	*v.-c.*	turn off

老师：为什么总睡不好呢？

学生：宿舍里太热了。

老师：不是有空调吗(3)？

学生：我同屋不喜欢开空调，喜欢开窗。结果(4)屋
　　　子里蚊子多得要命。昨天晚上我被叮了好
　　　几次。你看，脸上、胳膊上都是(5)。

老师：我不知道你们有这样的问题。我看，你们得
　　　好好儿谈谈。

学生：谈过好几次了。但是她总是把窗子开开，
　　　把空调关掉(6)。我们的关系越来越(7)紧张
　　　了。

老师：这件事，我真不知道(8)该怎么帮你的忙。你
　　　先到学校的医院去，让大夫看看吧！

緊張	紧张	jǐnzhāng	*adj.*	tense; intense; strained
該	该	gāi	*aux.*	应该
幫忙	帮忙	bāng-máng	*v.-o.*	help
醫院	医院	yīyuàn	*n.*	hospital
大夫	大夫	dài.fū	*n.*	physician; doctor

第 六 課
睡 午 覺、喝 熱 水

　　中國人多半儿在中飯以後睡個午覺。剛到北京的時候，我很不習慣。怎麼(1)白天睡覺呢？不是太浪費時間了嗎？但是兩個星期以後，我自己(2)也睡起午覺來(3)了。

　　我們早上七點半就開始上課，中飯以後已經(4)很累了。休息半個小時，讓(5)我下午和晚上都比較有精神，怪不得(6)中國人大多有睡午覺的習慣。

　　一般說來，中國人喜歡喝熱茶，很少喝冰水。夏天喝熱水，對我來說，簡直是受罪！但是因為

午覺	午觉	wǔjiào	*n.*	afternoon nap
白天	白天	báitiān	*n.*	daytime; day
浪費	浪费	làngfèi	*v.*	waste; squander
自己	自己	zìjǐ	*pron.*	oneself
精神	精神	jīng.shén	*n.*	vigor; vitality; spirit
有精神	有精神	yǒu jīng.shén	*adj.*	vigorous; spirited

28

第 六 课
睡午觉、喝热水

中国人多半儿在中饭以后睡个午觉。刚到北京的时候，我很不习惯。怎么(1)白天睡觉呢？不是太浪费时间了吗？但是两个星期以后，我自己(2)也睡起午觉来(3)了。

我们早上七点半就开始上课，中饭以后已经(4)很累了。休息半个小时，让(5)我下午和晚上都比较有精神，怪不得(6)中国人大多有睡午觉的习惯。

一般说来，中国人喜欢喝热茶，很少喝冰水。夏天喝热水，对我来说，简直是受罪！但是因为

怪不得	怪不得	guài.bù.dé	conj.	no wonder; so that's why
大多	大多	dàduō	adv.	for the most part; mostly
冰水	冰水	bīngshuǐ	n.	ice water; 冰: ice
夏天	夏天	xiàtiān	n.	summer
受罪	受罪	shòu-zuì	v.-o.	endure hardships, tortures, rough conditions, etc.; have a hard time; 受: receive; suffer 罪: sin; hardship

中國的自來水不能直接喝,要喝到涼開水並 (7) 不容易,每天買礦泉水不但貴也不方便,所以最近我學著 (8) 喝熱水瓶裏的熱水,有時也泡茶。沒想到 (9) 喝了幾天以後,我也習慣了,而且覺得熱水並不難喝呢!

各地有各地的習慣,這都是有原因的。我們到了一個新地方,不應該再堅持自己原來的生活方式,得向 (10) 當地人學習才行。

自來水	自来水	zìláishuǐ	*n.*	tap water
直接	直接	zhíjiē	*adv.*	directly
涼	凉	liáng	*adj.*	cold; cool
開水	开水	kāishuǐ	*n.*	boiled water
礦泉水	矿泉水	kuàngquán shuǐ	*n.*	mineral water 矿泉: mineral spring
最近	最近	zuìjìn	*adv.*	recently
學	学	xué	*v.*	imitate; mimic
熱水瓶	热水瓶	rèshuǐpíng	*n.*	thermos bottle; 瓶 : bottle

中国的自来水不能直接喝，要喝到凉开水并(7)不容易，每天买矿泉水不但贵也不方便，所以最近我学着(8)喝热水瓶里的热水，有时也泡茶。没想到(9)喝了几天以后，我也习惯了，而且觉得热水并不难喝呢！

各地有各地的习惯，这都是有原因的。我们到了一个新地方，不应该再坚持自己原来的生活方式，得向(10)当地人学习才行。

泡茶	泡茶	pào-chá	v.-o.	make tea; 泡 : brew
没想到	没想到	méi xiǎngdào	adv.	unexpectedly
各 n.	各 n.	gè	adj.	each; every
原因	原因	yuányīn	n.	reason; cause
堅持	坚持	jiānchí	v.	insist on; persist in
原來	原来	yuánlái	adj.	original; former
生活	生活	shēng.huó	n.	life
方式	方式	fāngshì	n.	pattern; fashion; way
向	向	xiàng	prep.	from; towards
當地	当地	dāngdì	p.w.	local; in the locality

第七課

去銀行換錢

（一）在出租汽車上

司機：去哪儿啊？

學生：王府井中國銀行。

司機：您要怎麼走啊？二環還是城裏？

學生：走城裏近點儿。

司機：近是近點儿，可是路堵得厲害(1)。走二環快得多。

學生：那就走二環吧！我最怕堵車。在北京常常一堵就是一個小時(2)。在車上什麼都(3)不能做，真急死人。

銀行	银行	yínháng	*n.*	bank
出租汽車	出租汽车	chūzū qìchē	*n.*	taxi; 租: rent
司機	司机	sījī	*n.*	driver
王府井	王府井	Wángfǔjǐng		Wangfujing
二環	二环	Èrhuán		Second Ring Road

第七课

去银行换钱

（一）在出租汽车上

司机：去哪儿啊？

学生：王府井中国银行。

司机：您要怎么走啊？二环还是城里？

学生：走城里近点儿。

司机：近是近点儿，可是路堵得厉害(1)。走二环
　　　快得多。

学生：那就走二环吧！我最怕堵车。在北京常常
　　　一堵就是一个小时(2)。在车上什么都(3)不能
　　　做，真急死人。

堵	堵	dǔ	*v.*	stop up; block up
屬害	厉害	lì.hài	*adv./adj.*	terribly, terrible; severe
堵車	堵车	dǔ-chē	*v.-o.*	have a traffic jam
急	急	jí	*v.*	worry; make anxious; make impatient
...死人	...死人	...sǐrén	*adv.*	extremely; to death

also incredibly (f positive adj)

33

司機：糟糕！今天連二環都(4)堵車。

學生：真沒想到。也許坐車還不如(5)騎自行車快呢！

司機：最近幾年，北京的汽車越來越多，許多人都買了私人汽車，可是北京道路的發展卻趕不上汽車的增加，所以交通堵塞就一天比一天(6)嚴重了。

學生：像今天這樣(7)堵，我寧可(8)走路。

司機：快到了！快到了！

學生：再過半個小時銀行就要關門了！

糟糕	糟糕	zāogāo		how terrible; what bad luck; too bad
連	连	lián	*conj.*	even
騎	骑	qí	*v.*	ride (an animal or bicycle)
不如	不如	bùrú		...not as *adj.* as...
自行車	自行车	zìxíngchē	*n.*	bicycle
私人	私人	sīrén	*adj.*	private; personal
道路	道路	dàolù	*n.*	road; way
發展	发展	fāzhǎn	*v./n.*	develop; development
趕不上	赶不上	gǎn.búshàng	*v.-c.*	cannot catch up with

許多   xǔduō   meny

司机：糟糕！今天连二环都(4)堵车。

学生：真没想到。也许坐车还不如(5)骑自行车快呢！

司机：最近几年，北京的汽车越来越多，许多人都买了私人汽车，可是北京道路的发展却赶不上汽车的增加，所以交通堵塞就一天比一天(6)严重了。

学生：像今天这样(7)堵，我宁可(8)走路。

司机：快到了！快到了！

学生：再过半个小时银行就要关门了！

增加	增加	zēngjiā	v.	increase; raise; add
交通	交通	jiāotōng	n.	traffic
堵塞	堵塞	dǔsè	v.	stop up; block up
交通堵塞	交通堵塞	jiāotōng dǔsè	n.	traffic jam
嚴重	严重	yánzhòng	adj.	(said of illness, situation) serious
寧可	宁可	nìngkě	adv.	would rather; better
走路	走路	zǒu-lù	v.-o.	walk; go on foot
過 + time duration	过+ time duration	guò	v.	after (time duration)
關門	关门	guān-mén	v.-o.	close

司機：過了紅綠燈就是中國銀行了，我看你就在

這儿下車吧！走過去還快一點儿！

學生：好吧(9)好吧！多少錢？

司機：三十二塊八毛。

學生：麻煩您 (10)給張發票。

司機：好的。這是您的發票。您慢走(11)。

（二）在銀行裏

學生：小姐，在哪儿能換人民幣啊？

職員：二樓，五號窗口。

………………

學生：先生，是我先到的，請您排隊。

顧客：隊在哪儿啊？我在這儿等了半天了。

紅綠燈	红绿灯	hónglǜdēng	n.	traffic light
下車	下车	xià-chē	v.-o.	get off (a car)
麻煩	麻烦	má.fán	v.	bother; put somebody to trouble
發票	发票	fāpiào	n.	bill; receipt
人民幣	人民币	rénmínbì	n.	RMB; *Renmimbi*

司机：过了红绿灯就是中国银行了，我看你就在

这儿下车吧！走过去还快一点儿！

学生：好吧(9)好吧！多少钱？

司机：三十二块八毛。

学生：麻烦您(10)给张发票。

司机：好的。这是您的发票。您慢走(11)。

（二）在银行里

学生：小姐，在哪儿能换人民币啊？

职员：二楼，五号窗口。

....

学生：先生，是我先到的，请您排队。

顾客：队在哪儿啊？我在这儿等了半天了。

職員	职员	zhíyuán	*n.*	office worker; staff member
樓	楼	lóu	*n.*	story; floor, a multi-storied building
您	您	nín	*pron.*	you (polite expression)
排隊	排队	pái-duì	*v.-o.*	line up; 排 : to line up 队 : line; a row of people
半天	半天	bàntiān	*n.*	a very long time; half a day

學生：我也等了半天了。您剛才(12)不是在我後頭
　　　嗎？

顧客：我有急事，我得先辦。

學生：誰不急呢？您還是(13)排隊吧！

　　　　　　……………

學生：小姐，我要換五百塊美元。

職員：先填單子。

學生：填好了。這樣兒行嗎？

職員：您要換現金還是旅行支票？

學生：旅行支票。

職員：請您在支票上簽字。有護照嗎？

學生：有。這是我的支票。字也簽好了。

職員：這是您的錢。請您點清楚。

急事	急事	jíshì	n.	urgent matter
美元	美元	měiyuán	n.	U. S. dollar
單子	单子	dānzi	n.	form; list
現金	现金	xiànjīn	n.	cash
旅行	旅行	lǚxíng	v.	travel

学生：我也等了半天了。您刚才(12)不是在我后头

　　　吗？

顾客：我有急事，我得先办。

学生：谁不急呢？您还是(13)排队吧！

··················

学生：小姐，我要换五百块美元。

职员：先填单子。

学生：填好了。这样儿行吗？

职员：您要换现金还是旅行支票？

学生：旅行支票。

职员：请您在支票上签字。有护照吗？

学生：有。这是我的支票。字也签好了。

职员：这是您的钱。请您点清楚。

支票	支票	zhīpiào	*n.*	check
旅行支票	旅行支票	lǚxíng zhīpiào	*n.*	traveler's check
簽字	签字	qiān-zì	*v.-o.*	sign
護照	护照	hùzhào	*n.*	passport
點	点	diǎn	*v.*	check to see if correct

第 八 課
講 價

（一）在古董店裏

甲：這幅山水畫儿多少錢啊？

乙：這幅畫儿是明代的，現在世界上只有這一幅了。

甲：明代的？怎麼看起來這麼新呢？

乙：噢，我們重新(1)整理過，比原來的好多了。

甲：這幅畫儿多少錢呢？

乙：現在明代的畫儿越來越少了，我們只有這一幅了…

甲：我知道這是古畫儿，到底(2)要多少錢呢？

乙：我們對(3)外國朋友總是特別客氣…

講價	讲价	jiǎng-jià	*v.-o.*	bargain; haggle over the price
古董	古董	gǔdǒng	*n.*	antique
甲	甲	jiǎ	*n.*	the first of the ten Heavenly Stems; used as pronoun here meaning "the first person"
乙	乙	yǐ	*n.*	the second of ten Heavenly Stems; the second person
幅	幅	fú	*an.*	measure word for painting

第 八 课
讲 价

（一）在古董店里

甲：这幅山水画儿多少钱啊？

乙：这幅画儿是明代的，现在世界上只有这一幅了。

甲：明代的？怎么看起来这么新呢？

乙：噢，我们重新(1)整理过，比原来的好多了。

甲：这幅画儿多少钱呢？

乙：现在明代的画儿越来越少了，我们只有这一幅了…

甲：我知道这是古画儿，到底(2)要多少钱呢？

乙：我们对(3)外国朋友总是特别客气…

山水畫	山水画	shānshuǐhuà	*n.*	landscape painting
明代	明代	Míngdài		the Ming Dynasty (1368-1644)
世界	世界	shìjiè	*n.*	world
噢	噢	ou	*interj.*	oh (indicates understanding)
重新	重新	chóngxīn	*adv.*	again; anew; afresh
古畫	古画	gǔhuà	*n.*	ancient painting
到底	到底	dàodǐ	*adv.*	after all (used in a question)

甲：你到底要多少錢啊？

乙：這幅畫兒要是(4)在別的店裏，要三千塊。

我賣給你，只要一千塊就行了。

甲：一千塊？太貴了！

乙：一千塊是我的成本，我連一塊錢都不賺。

甲：五百塊，行不行？

乙：開玩笑！要是五百塊賣給你，那我就賠五百塊！

甲：我是個窮學生，根本買不起(5)一千塊錢的

畫兒。再見再見！

乙：來來來來來！別走！別走！你覺得這幅太

貴，我們有比較便宜的。你看這幅人物畫兒…

甲：我不喜歡人物畫兒。我就是(6)要這幅山水畫兒。

要是不便宜一點兒，我只好(7)不買了。

乙：別走！別走！八百塊賣給你了！

甲：太貴了！太貴了！我還有事兒，我得走了！

成本	成本	chéngběn	n.	cost (production)
賺錢	賺钱	zhuàn-qián	v.-o.	make money; make a profit
開玩笑	开玩笑	kāi wánxiào	v.-o.	joke; make fun of
賠錢	赔钱	péi-qián	v.-o.	lose money (in business transactions)
窮	穷	qióng	adj.	poor; poverty-stricken

甲：你到底要多少钱啊？

乙：这幅画儿要是(4)在别的店里，要三千块。

我卖给你，只要一千块就行了。

甲：一千块？太贵了！

乙：一千块是我的成本，我连一块钱都不赚。

甲：五百块，行不行？

乙：开玩笑！要是五百块卖给你，那我就赔五百块！

甲：我是个穷学生，根本买不起(5)一千块钱的

画儿。再见再见！

乙：来来来来来！别走！别走！你觉得这幅太

贵，我们有比较便宜的。你看这幅人物画儿…

甲：我不喜欢人物画儿。我就是(6)要这幅山水画儿。

要是不便宜一点儿，我只好(7)不买了。

乙：别走！别走！八百块卖给你了！

甲：太贵了！太贵了！我还有事儿，我得走了！

買不起	买不起	mǎi.bùqǐ	v.-c.	cannot afford
便宜	便宜	pián.yí	adj.	inexpensive; cheap
人物	人物	rénwù	n.	figure; personage
只好	只好	zhǐhǎo	adv.	have to; be forced to

乙：七百塊怎麼樣？

甲：我只有五百塊錢，多一塊都買不起！

乙：好吧好吧！五百塊錢，賣給你了！

（二）在宿舍裏

甲：我今天逛古董市場，買了一幅山水畫ㄦ，便宜
　　極了。那個老板本來要一千塊錢，後來五百
　　塊就賣給我了。

丙：真巧，我今天也在古董市場買了一幅畫ㄦ。

甲：給我看看！

丙：我最喜歡山水畫ㄦ。你看這幅，真棒！

甲：哎呀！怎麼跟我買的一模一樣？你花了多少
　　錢？

丙：我才 (8) 花了一百塊！

甲：糟糕！又 (9) 上當了！

逛	逛	guàng	v.	stroll; go window-shopping
市場	市场	shìchǎng	n.	market
老闆	老板	lǎobǎn	n.	shopkeeper; boss
丙	丙	bǐng	n.	the third of ten Heavenly Stems, the third person
巧	巧	qiǎo	adj.	coincidental; fortuitous
棒	棒	bàng	adj.	(colloquial) good; excellent

44

乙：七百块怎么样？

甲：我只有五百块钱，多一块都买不起！

乙：好吧好吧！五百块钱，卖给你了！

（二）在宿舍里

甲：我今天逛古董市场，买了一幅山水画儿，便宜极了。那个老闆本来要一千块钱，后来五百块就卖给我了。

丙：真巧，我今天也在古董市场买了一幅画儿。

甲：给我看看！

丙：我最喜欢山水画儿。你看这幅，真棒！

甲：哎呀！怎么跟我买的一模一样？你花了多少钱？

丙：我才(8)花了一百块！

甲：糟糕！又(9)上当了！

哎呀	哎呀	aiya	*interj.*	Oh!; ah! (expresses anger, irritation, contempt, disappointment)
一模一樣	一模一样	yìmú yíyàng	*adj.*	exactly alike
花錢	花钱	huā-qián	*v.-o.*	spend (money)
上當	上当	shàng-dàng	*v.-o.*	be taken in; be fooled

第 九 課
同志、小姐、先生

　　1949年以後，大約有四十年的時間，到中國來的外國人只要⑴學會"同志"這兩個字，就可以稱呼所有的中國人。無論⑵是男的還是女的，老的還是年輕的，認識的還是陌生的，都可以叫他們"同志"。我很喜歡這個稱呼，因為不分男女老少，大家都平等。

1949	1949	yījiǔsìjiǔ		1949
同志	同志	tóngzhì	*n.*	comrade
大約	大约	dàyuē	*adv.*	approximately; about
稱呼	称呼	chēng.hū	*v./n.*	call; address; a form of address
所有	所有	suǒyǒu	*adj.*	all
無論	无论	wúlùn	*conj.*	no matter what, how, etc.; regardless of

第九课

同志、小姐、先生

1949年以后，大约有四十年的时间，到中国来的外国人只要(1)学会"同志"这两个字，就可以称呼所有的中国人。无论(2)是男的还是女的，老的还是年轻的，认识的还是陌生的，都可以叫他们"同志"。我很喜欢这个称呼，因为不分男女老少，大家都平等。

年輕	年轻	niánqīng	*adj.*	young
認識	认识	rèn.shí	*v.*	know; recognize
陌生	陌生	mòshēng	*adj.*	strange; unfamiliar
分	分	fēn	*v.*	divide; seperate; part
男女老少	男女老少	nán nǚ lǎo shào	*n.*	men and women, young and old
平等	平等	píngděng	*adj./n.*	equal, equality

　　但是改革開放以後，這個用了幾十年的老稱呼漸漸地沒有人用了。以前的"男同志"成了(3)"先生"，"女同志"成了"小姐"或"女士"。據說這是受了台灣、香港和海外的影響(4)。

　　其實(5)，"同志"是有中國特色的。用"小姐"和"先生"，表面上(6)是現代化了，但是卻不能表現中國社會的特點了。我很懷念"同志"這個詞。

改革	改革	gǎigé	*v.*	reform
開放	开放	kāifàng	*v.*	open; liberalize
漸漸	渐渐	jiànjiàn	*adv.*	gradually
成了	成了	chéngle	*v.*	have become; became
女士	女士	nǚshì	*n.*	(a polite term for a woman, married or unmarried) lady; madam
台灣	台湾	Táiwān		Taiwan
香港	香港	Xiānggǎng		Hong Kong
海外	海外	hǎiwài	*p.w.*	overseas; abroad
受了	受了	shòule	*v.*	have received
影響	影响	yǐngxiǎng	*n./v.*	influence; effect

但是改革开放以后，这个用了几十年的老称呼渐渐地没有人用了。以前的"男同志"成了(3)"先生"，"女同志"成了"小姐"或"女士"。据说这是受了台湾、香港和海外的影响(4)。

其实(5)，"同志"是有中国特色的。用"小姐"和"先生"，表面上(6)是现代化了，但是却不能表现中国社会的特点了。我很怀念"同志"这个词。

其實	其实	qíshí	*adv.*	in fact; actually
特色	特色	tèsè	*n.*	characteristic; distinguishing feature
表面上	表面上	biǎomiàn .shàng	*adv.*	on the surface 表面: surface; outside
表現	表现	biǎoxiàn	*v.*	show; display
社會	社会	shèhuì	*n.*	society
特點	特点	tèdiǎn	*n.*	characteristic; trait
懷念	怀念	huáiniàn	*v.*	cherish the memory of; think fondly of
詞	词	cí	*n.*	word; term

第 十 課
廁　所

　　來了中國以後，常常是生活上(1)的一些小事讓我覺得特別不方便、不習慣，比方像早起、洗澡、上廁所這些事(2)。

　　中國的廁所很少有坐的馬桶，大多是蹲的。我在美國從來沒上過這樣的廁所；蹲久了，兩條腿真受不了。但是這樣的廁所也有一個好處，就是很衛生。我不必擔心得傳染病。

　　北京街上有不少公共廁所，為(3)市民和行人提

比方	比方	bǐ.fāng		for instance
廁所	厕所	cèsuǒ	n.	toilet; restroom
上廁所	上厕所	shàng cèsuǒ	v.-o.	go to the bathroom
蹲	蹲	dūn	v.	squat on one's heels
馬桶	马桶	mǎtǒng	n.	toilet
久	久	jiǔ	adj.	for a long time
腿	腿	tuǐ	n.	leg

第 十 课
厕 所

来了中国以后，常常是生活上(1)的一些小事让我觉得特别不方便、不习惯，比方像早起、洗澡、上厕所这些事(2)。

中国的厕所很少有坐的马桶，大多是蹲的。我在美国从来没上过这样的厕所；蹲久了，两条腿真受不了。但是这样的厕所也有一个好处，就是很卫生。我不必担心得传染病。

北京街上有不少公共厕所，为(3)市民和行人提

受不了	受不了	shòubùliǎo	*v.-c.*	cannot stand (or endure)
衛生	卫生	wèishēng	*adj.*	hygienic; sanitary
不必	不必	búbì	*adv.*	need not to; not have to
得	得	dé	*v.*	contract (an illness)
傳染病	传染病	chuánrǎnbìng	*n.*	infectious disease 传染 : infect; be contagious
爲	为	wèi	*prep.*	for
市民	市民	shìmín	*n.*	citizen; urban dweller
行人	行人	xíngrén	*n.*	pedestrian

tígōng   supply

51

供了許多方便。有的公共廁所是免費的，這種廁
所既 (4) 沒有衛生紙也沒有洗手台。我常常還沒有
看到廁所就先聞到了一股臭味兒，所以並不難找。
上這種廁所，動作一定得快，大概不會有人在裏頭
看報。這種廁所也常常沒有門，讓我覺得很不好
意思。

　　另一種公共廁所是收費的，一個人大概得花三
毛到五毛錢。這種廁所提供衛生紙，也有洗手
台，而且比較乾淨。雖然要收費，我倒 (5) 寧可上這
種廁所。所以在中國，我上街的時候，一定隨身
帶著 (6) 衛生紙和零錢。

免費	免费	miǎnfèi	adj.	"exempt-charge"; free of charge; free
既…又…	既…又…	jì…yòu…		both… and…
衛生紙	卫生纸	wèishēngzhǐ	n.	toilet paper
洗手台	洗手台	xǐshǒutái	n.	sink (in a restroom)
聞	闻	wén	v.	smell
股	股	gǔ	an.	measure word for strength, smell, etc.
臭味	臭味	chòuwèi	n.	bad smell; stink

供了许多方便。有的公共厕所是免费的，这种厕所既 (4) 没有卫生纸也没有洗手台。我常常还没有看到厕所就先闻到了一股臭味儿，所以并不难找。上这种厕所，动作一定得快，大概不会有人在里头看报。这种厕所也常常没有门，让我觉得很不好意思。

　　另一种公共厕所是收费的，一个人大概得花三毛到五毛钱。这种厕所提供卫生纸，也有洗手台，而且比较干净。虽然要收费，我倒 (5) 宁可上这种厕所。所以在中国，我上街的时候，一定随身带着 (6) 卫生纸和零钱。

動作	动作	dòngzuò	*n.*	movement; notion; action
收費	收费	shōufèi	*v.*	collect a fee; charge
倒	倒	dào	*adv.*	see Grammar Note (5)
上街	上街	shàng-jiē	*v.-o.*	go shopping
隨身	随身	suíshēn	*adv.*	"follow-person"; (carry) on one's person; (take) with
帶著	带着	dàizhe	*v.*	take; bring; carry
零錢	零钱	língqián	*n.*	small change

第 十一 課

坐 火 車

　　在 美 國 生 活 了 十 幾 年，我 從 來 沒 坐 過 長 途 火 車；到 遠 處 去 旅 行，不 是 坐 飛 機 就 是 (1) 開 車。來 了 中 國 以 後，不 到 (2) 三 個 星 期，居 然 已 經 坐 了 兩 次 長 途 火 車 了。一 次 是 到 承 德 去 參 觀 避 暑 山 莊，另 一 次 是 去 山 西 大 同 看 雲 崗 石 窟。去 承 德 那 一 次 坐 的 是 硬 座，去 大 同 那 次 坐 的 是 軟 臥。軟 臥 比 硬 座 舒 服，但 是 也 貴 得 多。

火車	火车	huǒchē	n.	"fire-car"; train
生活	生活	shēnghuó	v.	live
遠處	远处	yuǎnchù	n.	"far-place"; distant place
開車	开车	kāi-chē	v.-o.	drive a car, train, etc.
居然	居然	jūrán	adv.	unexpectedly; to one's surprise
承德	承德	Chéngdé		Chengde (in Hebei Province)
參觀	参观	cānguān	v.	visit; look around

第 十 一 课
坐火车

在美国生活了十几年，我从来没坐过长途火车；到远处去旅行，不是坐飞机就是 (1)开车。来了中国以后，不到 (2) 三个星期，居然已经坐了两次长途火车了。一次是到承德去参观避暑山庄，另一次是去山西大同看云岗石窟。去承德那一次坐的是硬座，去大同那次坐的是软卧。软卧比硬座舒服，但是也贵得多。

避暑 山莊	避暑 山庄	Bìshǔ Shānzhuāng		"avoid-heat-mountain-villa"; (Imperial) Summer Residence
山西	山西	Shānxī		Shanxi Province
大同	大同	Dàtóng		Datong (in Shanxi)
雲崗 石窟	云岗 石窟	Yúngǎng Shíkū		Yungang Caves
硬座	硬座	yìngzuò	n.	hard seat (on a train)
軟臥	软卧	ruǎnwò	n.	soft bunk (on a train)

火車雖然沒有飛機那麼快，但是在車上可以看到路上的風景，在火車站還可以買到當地的特產，嘗到當地的風味儿小吃。坐火車最有趣的是可以在車上跟乘客交談，不但可以練習中文，還可以交到新朋友。

到目前為止 (3)，中國國內長途旅行的主要交通工具還是火車，在火車上有比較多的機會觀察中國人的生活。

路上	路上	lù.shàng	*adv.*	on the way
特產	特产	tèchǎn	*n.*	special local product
嘗	尝	cháng	*v.*	taste
風味	风味	fēngwèi	*n.*	special flavor; local flavor
小吃	小吃	xiǎochī	*n.*	snack; refreshments
有趣	有趣	yǒuqù	*adj.*	interesting
乘客	乘客	chéngkè	*n.*	passenger
交談	交谈	jiāotán	*v.*	talk with each other; converse; chat

火车虽然没有飞机那么快，但是在车上可以看到路上的风景，在火车站还可以买到当地的特产，尝到当地的风味儿小吃。坐火车最有趣的是可以在车上跟乘客交谈，不但可以练习中文，还可以交到新朋友。

到目前为止(3)，中国国内长途旅行的主要交通工具还是火车，在火车上有比较多的机会观察中国人的生活。

交	交	jiāo	v.	make (friends)
到… 為止	到… 为止	dào...wéizhǐ		see Grammar Note (3)
目前	目前	mùqián	t.w.	now; at present
國内	国内	guónèi	adj.	internal; domestic
主要	主要	zhǔyào	adj.	main
工具	工具	gōngjù	n.	tool; instrument
機會	机会	jīhuì	n.	opportunity; chance
觀察	观察	guānchá	v.	observe; watch; survey

第十二課

北京的公園

　　到北京來的中外遊客往往(1)只去參觀幾個有名的景點，像故宮、頤和園、長城這些地方。其實到這些地方去，不但門票很貴，而且任何(2)時候都是人山人海，是看不到北京人的日常生活的。

　　北京城裏有許多小公園兒，那兒沒有有名的古代建築，也沒有華麗的裝飾，可是卻是北京市民休閒的好地方。早晨有許多人在那兒鍛鍊：有的跑

中外	中外	Zhōngwài		China and foreign countries (in China)
遊客	游客	yóukè	n.	visitor (to a park, etc.); tourist
往往	往往	wǎngwǎng	adv.	often; frequently
景點	景点	jǐngdiǎn	n.	scenery spot
故宮	故宫	Gùgōng		the Palace Museum
頤和園	颐和园	Yíhéyuán		the Summer Palace
長城	长城	Chángchéng		the Great Wall
門票	门票	ménpiào	n.	ticket
任何	任何	rènhé	adj.	any; whichever; whatever

第十二课
北京的公园

　　到北京来的中外游客往往(1)只去参观几个有名的景点，像故宫、颐和园、长城这些地方。其实到这些地方去，不但门票很贵，而且任何(2)时候都是人山人海，是看不到北京人的日常生活的。

　　北京城里有许多小公园儿，那儿没有有名的古代建筑，也没有华丽的装饰，可是却是北京市民休闲的好地方。早晨有许多人在那儿锻炼：有的跑

人山人海	人山人海	rénshān rénhǎi	idm.	huge crowds of people
古代	古代	gǔdài	n.	ancient times
建築	建筑	jiànzhù	n.	building
華麗	华丽	huálì	adj.	magnificent; resplendent
裝飾	装饰	zhuāngshì	n.	decoration
休閑	休闲	xiūxián	adj.	recreational
鍛鍊	锻炼	duànliàn	v.	take exercise; have physical training
跑步	跑步	pǎo-bù	v.-o.	jog

日常　rìcháng　everyday
市民　shìmín　citizen

步，有的 (3) 打太極拳，有的跳迪斯科，有的打羽毛
球，還有人遛鳥儿。到了傍晚，又可以看到許多人
在那儿下棋、乘涼和聊天儿。天黑以後，公園儿又成
了情人們談戀愛的好地方。

北京是個有一千多萬人的大城市。平時我們看
到的是忙碌的生活、緊張的工作、擁擠的交通，
只有 (4) 在北京的公園儿裏，才能看到北京人生活中
悠閑的一面。

北京的夏天又悶熱又潮濕，這些小公園儿為忙
碌的北京人提供了休息的好去處。

太極拳	太极拳	tàijíquán	n.	a kind of traditional Chinese shadow boxing 打太极拳 : do taijiquan
跳(舞)	跳(舞)	tiào-wǔ	v.-o.	dance
迪斯科	迪斯科	dísīkē	n.	disco
羽毛球	羽毛球	yǔmáoqiú	n.	badminton
遛鳥	遛鸟	liù-niǎo	v.-o.	take a stroll with one's caged bird
傍晚	傍晚	bàngwǎn	t.w.	evening; dusk
下棋	下棋	xià-qí	v.-o.	play chess
乘涼	乘涼	chéng-liáng	v.-o.	relax in a cool place
聊天	聊天	liáo-tiān	v.-o.	chat

步，有的(3)打太极拳，有的跳迪斯科，有的打羽毛球，还有人遛鸟儿。到了傍晚，又可以看到许多人在那儿下棋、乘凉和聊天儿。天黑以后，公园儿又成了情人们谈恋爱的好地方。

北京是个有一千多万人的大城市。平时我们看到的是忙碌的生活、紧张的工作、拥挤的交通，只有(4)在北京的公园儿里，才能看到北京人生活中悠闲的一面。

北京的夏天又闷热又潮湿，这些小公园儿为忙碌的北京人提供了休息的好去处。

情人	情人	qíngrén	n.	lover
談戀愛	谈恋爱	tán liàn'ài	v.-o.	be in love; have a love affair
...千萬	...千万	qiānwàn		ten million
城市	城市	chéngshì	n.	metropolis; city
平時	平时	píngshí	adv.	ordinarily; normally
忙碌	忙碌	mánglù	adj.	busy
擁擠	拥挤	yōngjǐ	adj.	crowded
悠閑	悠闲	yōuxián	adj.	leisurely and carefree
悶熱	闷热	mēnrè	adj.	hot and suffocating; muggy
潮濕	潮湿	cháoshī	adj.	humid
去處	去处	qùchù	n.	place; site

第 十 三 課

到 時 候 再 説 (1) 吧

在 中 國 話 裏 頭 有 個 詞儿 叫 " 面 子 " ， 英 文 裏 沒 有 一 個 完 全 相 應 的 詞儿。 和 中 國 人 打 交 道 一 定 要 注 意 給 對 方 面 子 ， 尤 其 是 (2) 在 拒 絶 别 人 的 要 求 或 者 不 同 意 别 人 意 見 的 時 候。

比 方 説 ， 有 個 人 想 請 你 下 星 期 和 他 一 塊儿 吃 飯 ， 可 是 你 並 不 想 和 他 一 塊儿 吃 飯 ， 你 又 (3) 不 想 找 個 不 誠 實 的 藉 口。 這 時 候 ， 最 好 的 回 答 是 : " 到 時 候 再 説 吧 ！ " 意 思 是 " 我 們 現 在 不 談 這 件 事。 "

到時候	到时候	dàoshí.hòu		until then; until that time
再說	再说	zàishuō	v.	put off until sometime later
面子	面子	miànzi	n.	face; dignity
相應	相应	xiāngyìng	v.	corresponding; relevant
打交道	打交道	dǎ jiāo.dào	v.-o.	come into contact with; have dealings with
對方	对方	duìfāng	n.	the other side; the other party
給面子	给面子	gěi miànzi	v.-o.	show due respect for somebody's feelings
尤其	尤其	yóuqí	adv.	especially

第十三课

到时候再说(1)吧

在中国话里头有个词儿叫"面子"，英文里没有一个完全相应的词儿。和中国人打交道一定要注意给对方面子，尤其是(2)在拒绝别人的要求或者不同意别人意见的时候。

比方说，有个人想请你下星期和他一块儿吃饭，可是你并不想和他一块儿吃饭，你又(3)不想找个不诚实的借口。这时候，最好的回答是："到时候再说吧！"意思是"我们现在不谈这件事。"

拒絕	拒绝	jùjué	n./v.	reject, rejection
要求	要求	yāoqiú	n./v.	request; demand
同意	同意	tóngyì	n./v.	agreement; approval, agree; approve
意見	意见	yìjiàn	n.	opinion; view
比方說	比方说	bǐ.fāngshuō		for instance; for example
誠實	诚实	chéngshí	adj.	honest
找藉口	找借口	zhǎo jièkǒu	v.-o.	look for an excuse
回答	回答	huídá	n./v.	answer
件	件	jiàn	an.	measure word for clothes, matters, things, jobs, etc.

又比方说，有人請你幫忙，可是你沒有把握，你可以说："問題不大，可是有一定的困難。"你也可以说："我們再研究研究。"要是那個人進一步(4)問你，你可以说："我們一步一步(5)來(6)。"這些話的意思都是说：我現在不能答應你的要求。"

要是有人問一些你個人的私事，像"你一個月賺多少錢啊？""你有沒有女朋友啊？""你多大了？"這類的問題，你可以说："對不起，我不習慣在別人面前談自己的私事，我們換個話題吧！"

教你們说這些話，並不是要你不誠實或不誠懇，而是(7)要你們知道怎麼有禮貌地说"不"。

把握	把握	bǎwò	*n.*	assurance; certainty
一定	一定	yídìng	*adj.*	given; particular; certain
研究	研究	yánjiū	*v.*	consider; discuss; study
進一步	进一步	jìn.yíbù	*adv.*	go a step further; further
一步一步	一步一步	yíbù yíbù	*adv.*	step by step
來	来	lái	*prov.*	see Grammar Note (6)
答應	答应	dā.yìng	*v.*	agree; promise; answer

又比方说，有人请你帮忙，可是你没有把握，你可以说："问题不大，可是有一定的困难。"你也可以说："我们再研究研究。"要是那个人进一步 (4) 问你，你可以说："我们一步一步 (5) 来 (6)。"这些话的意思都是说："我现在不能答应你的要求。"

要是有人问一些你个人的私事，像"你一个月赚多少钱啊？""你有没有女朋友啊？""你多大了？"这类的问题，你可以说："对不起，我不习惯在别人面前谈自己的私事，我们换个话题吧！"

教你们说这些话，并不是要你不诚实或不诚恳，而是 (7) 要你们知道怎么有礼貌地说"不"。

個人	个人	gèrén	n.	individual
私事	私事	sīshì	n.	private affairs
面前	面前	miànqián	postp.	in the face of; in front of
話題	话题	huàtí	n.	topic of conversation
誠懇	诚恳	chéngkěn	adj.	sincere
禮貌	礼貌	lǐmào	n.	courtesy; politeness
有禮貌	有礼貌	yǒu lǐmào	adj.	courteous; polite

第 十 四 課

在 飯 桌 上

　　"來來來，大家隨便坐。"

　　"老張，今天晚上您坐上座。"

　　"不，不！我怎麼能坐上座呢！老李坐上座，
老李坐上座！"

　　"不行，不行！無論是論 (1) 年紀還是論地位，
都該您坐上座。"

　　"哪裏，哪裏 (2)！您是主客，請，請！"

　　"您太客氣了，真不敢當 (3)！"

　　在請客入座的時候，往往可以聽到這樣的一

隨便	随便	suíbiàn	adv.	casually; informally
上座	上座	shàngzuò	n.	seat of honor
論	论	lùn	v.	mention; regard; consider
年紀	年纪	niánjì	n.	age
地位	地位	dìwèi	n.	position; status; standing
哪裏	哪里	nǎ.lǐ		used in a rhetorical question to indicate negation

第十四课

在饭桌上

"来来来，大家随便坐。"

"老张，今天晚上您坐上座。"

"不，不！我怎么能坐上座呢！老李坐上座，老李坐上座！"

"不行，不行！无论是论 (1) 年纪还是论地位，都该您坐上座。"

"哪里，哪里 (2)！您是主客，请，请！"

"您太客气了，真不敢当 (3)！"

在请客入座的时候，往往可以听到这样的一

主客	主客	zhǔkè	n.	guest of honor	zuì zhǔ yào de kè rén
不敢當	不敢当	bùgǎndāng		I really don't deserve this; you flatter me	
請客	请客	qǐng-kè	v.-o.	invite somebody to dinner; entertain guests	
入座	入座	rù-zuò	v.-o.	take one's seat at a banquet, ceremony, etc.	

段對話。中國人很講究飯桌上座位的安排，但是客人的座位並不是主人決定的，而是大家推讓出來的。要是你的年紀很輕，地位又不高，坐在上座是很不合適的。

為了(4)表示熱情，中國主人常常勸菜、勸酒，也就是一再地(5)請客人多(6)吃菜多喝酒。

"來來來，再吃塊肉，再來點儿菜！…"

"我實在(7)吃不下了，謝謝！謝謝！"

"你根本沒吃什麼嘛！再來點儿，再來點儿！"

"這個菜很好吃，我已經吃了很多了！"

段	段	duàn	*an.*	part; segment, paragraph
對話	对话	duìhuà	*n.*	dialogue; conversation
講究	讲究	jiǎng.jiū	*v.*	be particular about; pay attention to; be fastidious about
座位	座位	zuòwèi	*n.*	seat; place (location)
安排	安排	ānpái	*n./v.*	arrangement, arrange
客人	客人	kèrén	*n.*	guest
主人	主人	zhǔrén	*n.*	host
決定	决定	juédìng	*v./n.*	decide; decision
推讓	推让	tuīràng	*v.*	decline (a position, favor, etc, out of modesty)

段对话。中国人很讲究饭桌上座位的安排，但是客人的座位并不是主人决定的，而是大家推让出来的。要是你的年纪很轻，地位又不高，坐在上座是很不合适的。

为了(4)表示热情，中国主人常常劝菜、劝酒，也就是一再地(5)请客人多(6)吃菜多喝酒。

"来来来，再吃块肉，再来点儿菜！…"

"我实在(7)吃不下了，谢谢！谢谢！"

"你根本没吃什么嘛！再来点儿，再来点儿！"

"这个菜很好吃，我已经吃了很多了！"

輕	轻	qīng	*adj.*	small in number, degree, etc.
合適	合适	héshì	*adj.*	proper; appropriate
表示	表示	biǎoshì	*v.*	show; express; indicate
熱情	热情	rèqíng	*n.*	enthusiasm; zeal; warmth
勸菜	劝菜	quàn-cài	*v.-o.*	"advice-dish;" urge (the guest) to eat
勸酒	劝酒	quàn-jiǔ	*v.-o.*	"advise-liquor" ; urge (the guest) to drink
一再	一再	yízài	*adv.*	again and again; repeatedly
實在	实在	shízài	*adv.*	really; honestly; indeed

"吃不下菜,就多喝點儿酒吧!"

"不行不行!我已經快喝醉了,實在不能再喝了!"

"沒關係,不要緊!喝醉了,我送你回家。再喝,再喝!我敬您,乾杯,乾杯!"

類似的對話可以在飯桌上重複好幾次。美國人一般來說是不勸菜也不勸酒的,碰到這種場合,我覺得真不習慣。

"真抱歉,今天沒什麼好菜,不能好好儿招待大家。我愛人做菜的手藝不太好,只是些家常菜。"

吃不下	吃不下	chī.búxià	v.-c.	be unable to eat anymore
喝醉	喝醉	hē-zuì	v.-c.	be drunk
送	送	sòng	v.	walk (somebody); accompany; escort
敬	敬	jìng	v.	offer politely
乾杯	干杯	gān-bēi	v.-o.	drink a toast
類似	类似	lèisì	adj.	similar
重複	重复	chóngfù	v.	repeat

"吃不下菜，就多喝点儿酒吧！"

"不行不行！我已经快喝醉了，实在不能再喝了！"

"没关系，不要紧！喝醉了，我送你回家。再喝，再喝！我敬您，干杯，干杯！"

类似的对话可以在饭桌上重复好几次。美国人一般来说是不劝菜也不劝酒的，碰到这种场合，我觉得真不习惯。

"真抱歉，今天没什么好菜，不能好好儿招待大家。我爱人做菜的手艺不太好，只是些家常菜。"

碰到	碰到	pèng.dào	v.-c.	run into; meet
場合	场合	chǎnghé	n.	occasion; situation
抱歉	抱歉	bàoqiàn	adj.	be sorry; feel apologetic
招待	招待	zhāodài	v.	receive (guests); entertain
愛人	爱人	ài.rén	n.	husband or wife
手藝	手艺	shǒuyì	n.	skill; craftsmanship; workmanship
家常菜	家常菜	jiāchángcài	n.	home cooking; simple meal

"哪裏，哪裏！您太客氣了！這桌菜比飯館ㄦ裏的好多了，在外頭是吃不到的。"

這往往是飯後主人和客人的一段對話。在飯館ㄦ裏，還經常可以看到搶著付賬的情形。這對美國人來說，是很新鮮也是很奇怪的。當然，美國人吃完了飯各付各的(8)，中國人也覺得挺不習慣的。

不同的文化表現在飯桌上的客套和禮節都不相同。我們很難說一種方式比另一種方式好，重要的是"入境隨俗"。

桌	桌	zhuō	*an.*	a entire table of
搶	抢	qiǎng	*v.*	vie for; scramble for
付賬	付账	fù-zhàng	*v.-o.*	pay a bill
新鮮	新鲜	xīnxiān	*adj.*	new; novel; fresh
各付各的	各付各的	gè fù gè de		go Dutch
挺	挺	tǐng	*adv.*	very
文化	文化	wénhuà	*n.*	culture

"哪里，哪里！您太客气了！这桌菜比饭馆儿里的好多了，在外头是吃不到的。"

这往往是饭后主人和客人的一段对话。在饭馆儿里，还经常可以看到抢着付账的情形。这对美国人来说，是很新鲜也是很奇怪的。当然，美国人吃完了饭各付各的 (8)，中国人也觉得挺不习惯的。

不同文化表现在饭桌上的客套和礼节都不相同。我们很难说一种方式比另一种方式好，重要的是"入境随俗"。

客套	客套	kètào	n.	polite remarks; civilities
禮節	礼节	lǐjié	n.	courtesy; etiquette
相同	相同	xiāngtóng	adj.	alike; the same; identical
重要	重要	zhòngyào	adj.	important
入境隨俗	入境随俗	rù jìng suí sú	idm.	"enter-border-follow-custom"; after entering a country, follow its customs; "When in Rome, do as the Romans."

第十五課
點　菜

來北京以前，我以為中國菜都差不多。到了北京以後，才發現各省有不同的風味兒。比方説，川菜和湘菜比較辣，江浙菜比較甜。中國人的飲食習慣也並不完全一樣。一般説來，北方人比較喜歡麵食。他們常吃的主食有饅頭、包子、餃子、麵

點菜	点菜	diǎn-cài	v.-o.	order dishes (in a restaurant)
差不多	差不多	chà.bùduō	adj.	about the same; similar
川	川	Chuān		四川; Sichuan Province
湘	湘	Xiāng		湖南; Hunan Province
辣	辣	là	adj.	peppery; hot
江浙	江浙	Jiāng Zhè		江苏 and 浙江; Jiangsu and Zhejiang Provinces
甜	甜	tián	adj.	sweet
飲食	饮食	yǐnshí	n.	food and drink

74

第十五课
点 菜

来北京以前，我以为中国菜都差不多。到了北京以后，才发现各省有不同的风味儿。比方说，川菜和湘菜比较辣，江浙菜比较甜。中国人的饮食习惯也并不完全一样。一般说来，北方人比较喜欢面食。他们常吃的主食有馒头、包子、饺子、面

一般說來	一般说来	yìbānshuōlái	*adv.*	一般来说
北方人	北方人	běifāngrén	*n.*	Northerner
麵食	面食	miànshí	*n.*	wheat-based food
主食	主食	zhǔshí	*n.*	staple food; principal food
饅頭	馒头	mán.tóu	*n.*	steamed bun
包子	包子	bāozi	*n.*	steamed stuffed bun
餃子	饺子	jiǎozi	*n.*	dumpling
各地		gèdì		each place

條這些東西。南方人的主食大多是米飯。米飯我很喜歡，但是稀飯和粥我真是 (1)吃不慣。北京有中國各地的飯館儿。選擇飯館儿對我來説很不容易，因為從招牌上我常常看不出來 (2)賣的到底是什麼菜。他們把湖南菜叫做 (3)湘菜，廣東菜叫做粤菜，山東館子是齊魯風味儿。對一個外國人來説，要記得中國省名已經很不容易了，為了選擇合適的飯館儿我還得記住許多省名的簡稱，這就更難了。

麵條	面条	miàntiáo	*n.*	noodle
南方人	南方人	nánfāngrén	*n.*	Southerner
米飯	米饭	mǐfàn	*n.*	(cooked) rice
稀飯	稀饭	xīfàn	*n.*	rice or millet gruel; porridge
粥	粥	zhōu	*n.*	gruel
吃不慣	吃不惯	chī.búguàn	*v.-c.*	cannot get used to eating
選擇	选择	xuǎnzé	*v.*	select; choose
招牌	招牌	zhāo.pái	*n.*	shop sign

条这些东西。南方人的主食大多是米饭。米饭我很喜欢，但是稀饭和粥我真是(1)吃不惯。北京有中国各地的饭馆儿。选择饭馆儿对我来说很不容易。因为从招牌上我常常看不出来(2)卖的到底是什么菜。他们把湖南菜叫做(3)湘菜，广东菜叫做粤菜，山东馆子是齐鲁风味儿。对一个外国人来说，要记得中国省名已经很不容易了，为了选择合适的饭馆儿我还得记住许多省名的简称，这就更难了。

湖南	湖南	Hú'nán		Hunan Province
廣東	广东	Guǎngdōng		Guangdong Province
粤	粤	Yuè		another name for Guangdong Province
山東	山东	Shāndōng		Shandong Province
齊魯	齐鲁	Qí Lǔ		ancient names for Shandong
省	省	shěng	n.	province
簡稱	简称	jiǎnchēng	n.	the abbreviated form of a name

在飯館儿點菜，除了需要記住雞、鴨、魚、肉、青菜、豆腐這些東西以外，還得記住幾個基本的做菜方法，像煎、煮、炒、炸、清蒸、紅燒什麼的 (4)。

一般説來，一道菜要是只用一樣材料，往往是動詞賓語的結構，像清蒸魚、紅燒茄子、烤鴨、清炒西蘭花儿。一道菜如果用兩樣材料的話(5)，動

記住	记住	jì.zhù	v.-c.	remember
鴨	鸭	yā	n.	duck
魚	鱼	yú	n.	fish
青菜	青菜	qīngcài	n.	vegetable
豆腐	豆腐	dòu.fu	n.	bean curd
基本	基本	jīběn	adj.	basic; fundamental
方法	方法	fāngfǎ	n.	way; method
煎	煎	jiān	v.	fry in shallow oil
煮	煮	zhǔ	v.	boil, cook
炒	炒	chǎo	v.	stir-fry
炸	炸	zhá	v.	fry in deep fat or oil; deep-fry
清蒸	清蒸	qīngzhēng	v.	steam in clear soup (usually without soy sauce)

在饭馆儿点菜，除了需要记住鸡、鸭、鱼、肉、青菜、豆腐这些东西以外，还得记住几个基本的做菜方法，像煎、煮、炒、炸、清蒸、红烧什么的(4)。

一般说来，一道菜要是只用一样材料，往往是动词宾语的结构，像清蒸鱼、红烧茄子、烤鸭、清炒西兰花儿。一道菜如果用两样材料的话(5)，动

紅燒	红烧	hóngshāo	v.	braise in soy sauce
什麼的	什么的	shénmede		and so on; and what not
道	道	dào	an.	auxilliary noun for dishes
材料	材料	cáiliào	n.	material, ingredient
動詞	动词	dòngcí	n.	verb
賓語	宾语	bīnyǔ	n.	object
結構	结构	jiégòu	n.	structure
茄子	茄子	qiézi	n.	eggplant
烤鴨	烤鸭	kǎoyā	n.	roast duck
清炒	清炒	qīngchǎo	v.	fry in clear sauce
西蘭花	西兰花	xīlánhuā	n.	broccoli

詞往往在兩個名詞中間，像冬筍炒肉絲、腰果炒蝦仁儿、蛋炒飯。當然更常見的是把兩個名詞放在一起，像蝦仁儿豆腐、芥蘭牛肉。其實，這些菜都還容易明白，最麻煩的是有些菜名和實際用的材料完全沒有關係，像"八寶"、"三鮮"、"全家福"之類(6)。我總是避免點這類菜，因為我實在不知道這些菜裏到底有些什麼東西。

只有在北京生活過的人才知道：點中國菜真不是一件容易的事。

名詞	名词	míngcí	*n.*	noun, term
冬筍	冬笋	dōngsǔn	*n.*	bamboo shoot
肉絲	肉丝	ròusī	*n.*	shredded meat
腰果	腰果	yāoguǒ	*n.*	cashew
蝦仁	虾仁	xiārén	*n.*	shelled fresh shrimp
芥蘭	芥兰	jièlán	*n.*	Chinese leaf mustard
牛肉	牛肉	niúròu	*n.*	beef

词往往在两个名词中间，像冬笋炒肉丝、腰果炒虾仁儿、蛋炒饭。当然更常见的是把两个名词放在一起，像虾仁儿豆腐、芥兰牛肉。其实，这些菜都还容易明白，最麻烦的是有些菜名和实际用的材料完全没有关系，像"八宝"、"三鲜"、"全家福"之类(6)。我总是避免点这类菜，因为我实在不知道这些菜里到底有些什么东西。

只有在北京生活过的人才知道：点中国菜真不是一件容易的事。

實際 (上) 实际	shíjì	adv.	actually; in reality
八寶 八宝	bābǎo	n.	eight treasures (choice ingredients of certain special dishes)
三鮮 三鲜	sānxiān	n.	three kinds of fresh delicacies
全家福 全家福	quánjiāfú	n.	"all house happiness": a hodgepodge of ingredients cooked together in one pot
避免 避免	bìmiǎn	v.	avoid; refrain from

第十六課
過馬路真危險

　　學校大門口儿最近建了一座過街天橋，過馬路的時候安全多了。在天橋建成以前，過馬路真危險，因為汽車是不讓人的，行人得在許多車子當中(1)很快地走過去，我真怕會被撞著(2)。在中國，開車的人好像不太照顧走路的人，所以在北京走路一定得時時記得"停""聽""看"這三個字。

　　在美國汽車得讓行人先走，而(3)在中國行人卻得讓汽車。這是我在日常生活中，最不習慣的事。

馬路	马路	mǎlù	n.	road; street; avenue
危險	危险	wēixiǎn	adj.	dangerous
門口	门口	ménkǒu	n.	gate; doorway; entrance
建	建	jiàn	v.	build; construct
座	座	zuò	an.	measure word for bridges, buildings, etc.
過街天橋	过街天桥	guòjiē tiānqiáo	n.	overhead bridge that goes across a street; overpass

82

第十六课
过马路真危险

学校大门口儿最近建了一座过街天桥，过马路的时候安全多了。在天桥建成以前，过马路真危险，因为汽车是不让人的，行人得在许多车子当中(1)很快地走过去，我真怕会被撞着(2)。在中国，开车的人好像不太照顾走路的人，所以在北京走路一定得时时记得"停""听""看"这三个字。

在美国汽车得让行人先走，而(3)在中国行人却得让汽车。这是我在日常生活中，最不习惯的事。

讓	让	ràng	*v.*	give way to; yield (to a person)
當中	当中	dāngzhōng	*postp.*	in the middle
撞	撞	zhuàng	*v.*	collide; bump against; run into
照顧	照顾	zhào.gù	*v.*	give consideration to; show consideration for; look after; care for
時時	时时	shíshí	*adv.*	often; all the time
停	停	tíng	*v.*	stop

在北京雖然也有斑馬線，也有紅綠燈，可是有時好像起不了(4)什麼作用。我真希望北京開車的人都能遵守交通規則，多為行人想想。

北京的天橋和地下通道很多。夏天的傍晚，天橋也是人們乘涼、下棋、打牌的地方，有時甚至(5)有小攤兒賣東西。過街天橋和地下道是北京一個特殊的街景。

北京的交通亂是亂，可是習慣了以後，也能發現一種特有的秩序，中國人把這種情況叫做"亂中有序"。

斑馬線	斑马线	bānmǎ xiàn	*n.*	pedestrian crossing; cross-walk (marked with stripes like those of a zebra)
起	起	qǐ	*v.*	rise; grow
作用	作用	zuòyòng	*n.*	function; effect
起作用	起作用	qǐ (不) zuòyòng	*v.-o.*	be effective; have effect
希望	希望	xīwàng	*v./n.*	hope; wish
遵守	遵守	zūnshǒu	*v.*	observe; abide by
交通規則	交通规则	jiāotōng guīzé	*n.*	traffic regulations
通道	通道	tōngdào	*n.*	passageway

在北京虽然也有斑马线，也有红绿灯，可是有时好像起不了(4)什么作用。我真希望北京开车的人都能遵守交通规则，多为行人想想。

北京的天桥和地下通道很多。夏天的傍晚，天桥也是人们乘凉、下棋、打牌的地方，有时甚至(5)有小摊儿卖东西。过街天桥和地下道是北京一个特殊的街景。

北京的交通乱是乱，可是习惯了以后，也能发现一种特有的秩序，中国人把这种情况叫做"乱中有序"。

地下	地下	dìxià	adj.	underground; subterranean
打牌	打牌	dǎ-pái	v.-o.	play cards
甚至	甚至	shènzhì	adv.	even
小摊	小摊	xiǎotān	n.	vendor's stand; stall
特殊	特殊	tèshū	adj.	special
街景	街景	jiējǐng	n.	street scene
亂	乱	luàn	adj.	in disorder; in a mess
特有	特有	tèyǒu	adj.	peculiar
秩序	秩序	zhìxù	n.	order
情况	情况	qíngkuàng	n.	situation
亂中有序	乱中有序	luànzhōng yǒuxù	idm.	finding order in chaos

第 十 七 課

好好學習，天天向上

　　學校附近有一所小學，小學的大門口儿有一塊很大的牌子，上面有毛主席寫的八個大字："好好學習，天天向上"。大概每個中國小學生都知道這句話。

　　在中國到處(1)都能看到各種各樣的標語，有的教人怎麼做人，有的教人怎麼做事。最常見的是"請勿隨地吐痰"、"高高興興出門去，平平安安回家來"這類和日常生活有關的標語。

向上	向上	xiàngshàng	*v.*	make progress; go upward
小學	小学	xiǎoxué	*n.*	elementary school
牌子	牌子	páizi	*n.*	plate; sign
毛主席	毛主席	Máo Zhǔxí		Chairman Mao
→到處	到处	dàochù	*adv.*	everywhere; at all places
各種各樣	各种各样	gèzhǒng gèyàng	*adj.*	all kinds of
標語	标语	biāoyǔ	*n.*	slogan (usually written on a banner or poster)

第十七课

好好学习，天天向上

学校附近有一所小学，小学的大门口儿有一块很大的牌子，上面有毛主席写的八个大字：" 好好学习，天天向上 "。大概每个中国小学生都知道这句话。

在中国到处(1)都能看到各种各样的标语，有的教人怎么做人，有的教人怎么做事。最常见的是" 请勿随地吐痰 "、" 高高兴兴出门去，平平安安回家来 "这类和日常生活有关的标语。

做人	做人	zuò-rén	*v.-o.*	be an upright person
勿	勿	wù	*adv.*	(written) do not
隨地	随地	suídì	*adv.*	anywhere; everywhere
吐痰	吐痰	tǔ-tán	*v.-o.*	spit; expectorate
出門	出门	chū-mén	*v.-o.*	go out; leave home
平安	平安	píng'ān	*adj.*	safe and sound; without mishap
有關	有关	yǒuguān	*v.*	have something to do with; relate to; concern

和六、七十年代比 (2)，現在政治性 (3) 的標語大大地減少了，而商業性的廣告卻增加了。標語和廣告有個基本的不同：標語大多帶著政治或道德的意義，像天安門前的 "中華人民共和國萬歲；世界人民大團結萬歲"，或者像經常看到的 "為人民服務"、"學習雷鋒" 等等。每個標語都帶著一定的 "教訓"，而廣告只告訴你 "信息"，並沒有什麼教訓的意味。

年代	年代	niándài	*n.*	a decade
政治	政治	zhèngzhì	*n.*	politics
政治性	政治性	zhèngzhìxìng	*adj.*	political
減少	减少	jiǎnshǎo	*v.*	reduce; decrease
商業	商业	shāngyè	*n.*	commerce; trade; business
商業性	商业性	shāngyèxìng	*adj.*	commercial
廣告	广告	guǎnggào	*n.*	advertisement
帶	带	dài	*v.*	bear; have
道德	道德	dàodé	*n.*	morals; morality; ethics
意義	意义	yìyì	*n.*	meaning; significance
天安門	天安门	Tiān'ānmén		Tian An Men; Gate of Heavenly Peace

　　和六、七十年代比(2)，现在政治性(3)的标语大大地减少了，而商业性的广告却增加了。标语和广告有个基本的不同：标语大多带着政治或道德的意义，像天安门前的"中华人民共和国万岁；世界人民大团结万岁"，或者像经常看到的"为人民服务"、"学习雷锋"等等。每个标语都带着一定的"教训"，而广告只告诉你"信息"，并没有什么教训的意味。

中華人民共和國	中华人民共和国	Zhōnghuá Rénmín Gònghéguó		People's Republic of China
萬歲	万岁	wànsuì	v.	long live
團結	团结	tuánjié	v./n.	unite; rally, union
服務	服务	fúwù	v.	serve; give service to
雷鋒	雷锋	Léi Fēng		Lei Feng (1940-1962), a soldier who died on duty and was hailed as a model for the youth of China.
等等	等等	děngděng		and so on; etc.
教訓	教训	jiàoxùn	n.	lesson; moral
信息	信息	xìnxī	n.	information; message
意味	意味	yìwèi	n.	meaning; implication

最近政府在全國提出的一個新標語是"講文明，樹新風"，意思是要大家改掉生活中一些不好的習慣，像隨地吐痰、不排隊、亂(4)倒垃圾、隨便停放自行車等等。

要想進一步了解中國人的生活和思想，我想標語是個非常有趣而且值得(5)研究的題目。

政府	政府	zhèngfǔ	*n.*	government
全 N.	全 N.	quán	*adj.*	whole; entire; total
提出	提出	tí-chū	*v.-c.*	put forward; advance; raise
講	讲	jiǎng	*v.*	stress; pay attention to; be particular about
文明	文明	wénmíng	*n.*	civilization; culture
樹	树	shù	*v.*	(in writing) set up; establish
風	风	fēng	*n.*	(in writing) practice; custom
改掉	改掉	gǎi-diào	*v.-c.*	give up; drop

最近政府在全国提出的一个新标语是"讲文明，树新风"，意思是要大家改掉生活中一些不好的习惯，像随地吐痰、不排队、乱(4)倒垃圾、随便停放自行车等等。

要想进一步了解中国人的生活和思想，我想标语是个非常有趣而且值得(5)研究的题目。

亂 V.	乱 V.	luàn	*adv.*	randomly; arbitrarily
垃圾	垃圾	lājī	*n.*	garbage; rubbish
隨便	随便	suíbiàn	*adv.*	carelessly
停放	停放	tíngfàng	*v.*	park; place
了解	了解	liǎojiě	*v.*	understand
思想	思想	sīxiǎng	*n.*	thinking; thought
值得	值得	zhí.dé	*v.*	be worth; deserve
題目	题目	tímù	*n.*	title; subject; topic

第十八課

普通話和規範字

　　出了學校東門往南走，不到十分鐘就能看到一個很大的標語："說話要說普通話，寫字要寫規範字。"這個標語比許多空洞的政治口號有意義多了。

　　但是，從這個標語也可以看出，中國社會還存在著方言太多和寫字不規範的問題。"南腔北調"這四個字最能說明中國是個多(1)方言的國家。不但北京人聽不懂廣東話，有時在一個省裏，不同的縣

普通	普通	pǔtōng	*adj.*	common; ordinary
普通話	普通话	Pǔtōnghuà	*n.*	*Putonghua* (common speech of the Chinese language)
規範	规范	guīfàn	*n.*	standard; norm (correct)
空洞	空洞	kōngdòng	*adj.*	empty; hollow; devoid of content, meaningless
口號	口号	kǒuhào	*n.*	slogan; watchword (spoken)

第十八课
普通话和规范字

出了学校东门往南走，不到十分钟就能看到一个很大的标语："说话要说普通话，写字要写规范字。"这个标语比许多空洞的政治口号有意义多了。

但是，从这个标语也可以看出，中国社会还存在着方言太多和写字不规范的问题。"南腔北调"这四个字最能说明中国是个多⑴方言的国家。不但北京人听不懂广东话，有时在一个省里，不同的县

存在	存在	cúnzài	v.	exist
方言	方言	fāngyán	n.	dialect
南腔北調	南腔北调	nánqiāng bĕidiào	n.	(speak with) a mixed accent
說明	说明	shuōmíng	v.	explain; show
多-	多-	duō	pref.	multi-
縣	县	xiàn	n.	county

也有不同的方言，這個現象造成了人與人之間(2)溝通上的困難。 中國政府和有遠見的知識份子從二十年代起(3)就提倡説＂國語＂，但是幾十年來，推行普通話的成績並不很理想。

我看電視新聞的時候就注意到，許多人説話的時候，屏幕上打出了字幕。據我的中國老師説，要是沒有字幕，有時甚至連他們也聽不懂。

中國自從(4)五十年代就推行簡體字，可是有一些人一直堅持寫繁體字，或是自己創造出一些不

現象	現象	xiànxiàng	*n.*	phenomenon
造成	造成	zàochéng	*v.*	cause; create; give rise to
與	与	yǔ	*conj.*	and; same as 跟
A與B之間	A与B之间	A yǔ B zhījiān		between A and B
溝通	沟通	gōutōng	*v.*	communicate
遠見	远见	yuǎnjiàn	*n.*	foresight; vision
有遠見	有远见	yǒu yuǎnjiàn	*adj.*	foresightful
知識份子	知识分子	zhīshí fènzǐ	*n.*	intellectual; the intelligentsia
提倡	提倡	tíchàng	*v.*	advocate (political)
國語	国语	Guóyǔ	*n.*	Mandarin Chinese
推行	推行	tuīxíng	*v.*	carry out; practice

也有不同的方言，这个现象造成了人与人之间(2)沟通上的困难。 中国政府和有远见的知识分子从二十年代起 (3)就提倡说"国语"，但是几十年来，推行普通话的成绩并不很理想。

我看电视新闻的时候就注意到，许多人说话的时候，屏幕上打出了字幕。据我的中国老师说，要是没有字幕，有时甚至连他们也听不懂。

中国自从(4)五十年代就推行简体字，可是有一些人一直坚持写繁体字，或是自己创造出一些不

成績	成绩	chéngjī	*n.*	achievement; grade
理想	理想	lǐxiǎng	*adj./n.*	ideal
電視	电视	diànshì	*n.*	television
新聞	新闻	xīnwén	*n.*	news
屏幕	屏幕	píngmù	*n.*	TV screen
打	打	dǎ	*prov.*	(in this context) add subtitles
字幕	字幕	zìmù	*n.*	captions (of motion pictures, etc.); subtitles
自從	自从	zìcóng	*prep.*	since
簡體字	简体字	jiǎntǐzì	*n.*	simplified Chinese characters
繁體字	繁体字	fántǐzì	*n.*	the original complex form of Chinese characters
創造	创造	chuàngzào	*v.*	create; produce; bring about

規範的字來。結果同一個字就有了多種不同的寫法。這不但為漢字的書寫帶來了混亂，也為漢字的辨識帶來了困難。因此(5)，為了要大家都聽得懂、看得懂，我們都應該說普通話，寫規範字。

那麼，什麼是推行普通話和規範字最有效的辦法呢？我認為光(6)靠政府的宣傳是不夠的，最有效的辦法是發展廣播和電視。等到(7)中國農村家家都能收看北京電視和收聽北京廣播的時候，普通話和規範字自然就深入中國各地了。

漢字	汉字	Hànzì	n.	Chinese character
書寫	书写	shūxiě	n./v.	writing, write
混亂	混乱	hùnluàn	n.	confusion; chaos
辨識	辨识	biànshí	v.	differentiate; distinguish
有效	有效	yǒuxiào	adj.	effective
辦法	办法	bànfǎ	n.	way; means; measure
靠	靠	kào	v.	depend on; rely on

规范的字来。结果同一个字就有了多种不同的写法。这不但为汉字的书写带来了混乱，也为汉字的辨识带来了困难。因此(5)，为了要大家都听得懂、看得懂，我们都应该说普通话，写规范字。

那么，什么是推行普通话和规范字最有效的办法呢？我认为光(6)靠政府的宣传是不够的，最有效的办法是发展广播和电视。等到(7)中国农村家家都能收看北京电视和收听北京广播的时候，普通话和规范字自然就深入中国各地了。

宣傳	宣传	xuānchuán	*n./v.*	propaganda, propagandize
廣播	广播	guǎngbō	*n./v.*	radio broadcast, broadcast
農村	农村	nóngcūn	*n.*	countryside; rural area
收看	收看	shōukàn	*v.*	watch (television)
收聽	收听	shōutīng	*v.*	listen to (radio broadcast)
自然	自然	zìrán	*adv./adj.*	naturally, natural
深入	深入	shēnrù	*v./adj.*	go deep into, in depth

97

第十九課

Made in China

　　我從美國買了幾件小禮物來(1)送給中國朋友。到了中國以後，才發現這幾件禮物都是在中國做的。這讓我覺得有些尷尬—從美國買了中國東西來送給中國朋友！

　　人們常說中國是世界上最大的市場，其實中國也是世界上最大的工廠。現在美國許多衣服、鞋子、皮箱、家具和家用電器都是在中國製造的。這主要是因為中國既有豐富的資源，又有比較廉

禮物	礼物	lǐwù	*n.*	present; gift
送	送	sòng	*v.*	give (a present)
尷尬	尴尬	gān'gà	*adj.*	awkward; embarrassed
工廠	工厂	gōngchǎng	*n.*	factory
衣服	衣服	yī.fú	*n.*	clothes; clothing
鞋子	鞋子	xiézi	*n.*	shoes

第十九课

Made in China

　　我从美国买了几件小礼物来(1)送给中国朋友。到了中国以后，才发现这几件礼物都是在中国做的。这让我觉得有些尴尬——从美国买了中国东西来送给中国朋友！

　　人们常说中国是世界上最大的市场，其实中国也是世界上最大的工厂。现在美国许多衣服、鞋子、皮箱、家具和家用电器都是在中国制造的。这主要是因为中国既有丰富的资源，又有比较廉

皮箱	皮箱	píxiāng	n.	leather suitcase
家具	家具	jiājù	n.	furniture
家用電器	家用电器	jiāyòng diànqì	n.	household appliances
製造	制造	zhìzào	v.	manufacture; make
豐富	丰富	fēngfù	adj.	rich; abundant
資源	资源	zīyuán	n.	natural resources

價的勞動力和安定的社會，所以許多美國大公司都把工廠設在中國。一般美國人擔心這個情況會造成美國工人失業。

歐洲和美國的公司把工廠設在發展中國家，一方面當然減少了歐美工人的就業機會，但是另一方面卻降低了商品的成本，使(2)全世界的人都能享受到價廉物美的東西。

中國的改革開放不但提高了中國人的生活水平，對全世界的經濟發展也做出了一定的貢獻。

廉價	廉价	liánjià	*adj.*	low-priced; cheap
勞動力	劳动力	láodònglì	*n.*	labor force
安定	安定	āndìng	*adj.*	stable
公司	公司	gōngsī	*n.*	company; corporation
設	设	shè	*v.*	set up; establish
工人	工人	gōngrén	*n.*	worker; workman
失業	失业	shīyè	*v.*	lose one's job
歐洲	欧洲	Oūzhōu		Europe
發展中	发展中	fāzhǎnzhōng	*adj.*	developing
國家	国家	guójiā	*n.*	country; state; nation

价的劳动力和安定的社会，所以许多美国大公司都把工厂设在中国。一般美国人担心这个情况会造成美国工人失业。

欧洲和美国的公司把工厂设在发展中国家，一方面当然减少了欧美工人的就业机会，但是另一方面却降低了商品的成本，使(2)全世界的人都能享受到价廉物美的东西。

中国的改革开放不但提高了中国人的生活水平，对全世界的经济发展也做出了一定的贡献。

就業	就业	jiùyè	v.	obtain employment
降低	降低	jiàngdī	v.	reduce; drop; lower
商品	商品	shāngpǐn	n.	commodity; merchandise
享受	享受	xiǎngshòu	v.	enjoy
價廉物美	价廉物美	jiàlián wùměi	idm.	excellent quality at low prices-a bargain buy
提高	提高	tígāo	v.	raise; highten; increase
水平	水平	shuǐpíng	n.	level
經濟	经济	jīngjì	n.	economy
貢獻	贡献	gòngxiàn	n./v.	contribution, to contribute

第二十課

從"沒有"到"有"

　　八十年代初期來過中國的人都還記得，那個時候許多外國人所(1)學到的第一句中國話不是"你好"，而是"沒有"。在百貨商場和飯館儿裏，經常可以聽到這樣的對話：

　　"同志，買瓶咖啡。"

　　"沒有。"

　　"同志，買包洗衣粉。"

　　"沒有。"

　　"同志，有洗澡毛巾嗎？"

　　"沒有。"

　　………

初期	初期	chūqī	*n.*	initial stage; early part
記得	记得	jì.dé	*v.*	remember
百貨商場	百货商场	bǎihuò shāngchǎng	*n.*	department store

第二十课
从"没有"到"有"

　　八十年代初期来过中国的人都还记得，那个时候许多外国人所[1]学到的第一句中国话不是"你好"，而是"没有"。在百货商场和饭馆儿里，经常可以听到这样的对话：

　　"同志，买瓶咖啡。"

　　"没有。"

　　"同志，买包洗衣粉。"

　　"没有。"

　　"同志，有洗澡毛巾吗？"

　　"没有。"

　　………

瓶	瓶	píng	*an.*	bottle
包	包	bāo	*an.*	a packet of; a bundle of
洗衣粉	洗衣粉	xǐyīfěn	*n.*	detergent

"來個紅燒魚！"

"沒有！"

"來個腰果雞丁儿！"

"沒有！"

"有水煮牛肉嗎？"

"沒有！"

在那個 "沒有" 的時代裏，不但百貨商場裏的商品少，售貨員臉上的笑容也不多。許多東西只有在友誼商店才買得到。有些家用電器像電冰箱、彩電都是奢侈品，空調和熱水器也不是一般的家庭設備。出租汽車很少，私人汽車更是(2)不常見。可是現在北京的大百貨商場基本上(3)和美國的 mall 沒有什麼不同。

"小姐，我想買個錄像機，哪個牌子的好啊？"

雞丁	鸡丁	jīdīng	n.	diced chicken
時代	时代	shídài	n.	era; times
售貨員	售货员	shòuhuòyuán	n.	salesclerk; shop assistant
臉	脸	liǎn	n.	face
笑容	笑容	xiàoróng	n.	smile; smiling expression
友誼	友谊	yǒuyì	n.	friendship

"来个红烧鱼！"

"没有！"

"来个腰果鸡丁儿！"

"没有！"

"有水煮牛肉吗？"

"没有！"

在那个"没有"的时代里，不但百货商场里的商品少，售货员脸上的笑容也不多。许多东西只有在友谊商店才买得到。有些家用电器像电冰箱、彩电都是奢侈品，空调和热水器也不是一般的家庭设备。出租汽车很少，私人汽车更是(2)不常见。可是现在北京的大百货商场基本上(3)和美国的 mall 没有什么不同。

"小姐，我想买个录像机，哪个牌子的好啊？"

電冰箱	电冰箱	diànbīngxiāng	n.	refrigerator
奢侈品	奢侈品	shēchǐpǐn	n.	luxuries
熱水器	热水器	rèshuǐqì	n.	furnace
家庭	家庭	jiātíng	n.	family; household
基本上	基本上	jīběn.shàng	adv.	basically
錄像機	录像机	lùxiàngjī	n.	VCR
牌子	牌子	páizi	n.	brand; trademark

" 您是要國產的還是進口的 ？ "

" 聽說進口的好點儿 ，先看看進口的吧 ！ "

" 進口的有索尼 、三洋 、松下 …… 您喜歡哪種 ？ "

像這樣一段顧客和售貨員的對話 ，現在聽起來很平常 ，但是在八十年代初期卻是不可能的 。和那個 " 沒有 " 的時代比起來 ，現在的百貨商場裏 ，不但商品增加了 ，服務質量也大大提高了 。

來到中國的美國人常常拿中國和美國比較(4) ，覺得中國有許多地方還相當(5)落後 。這種比較是很自然的 ，也是不可避免的 。但是 ，在拿中國和美國比較的同時(6) ，我們也別忘了拿過去和現在比較 ，我們會發現中國比從前進步多了 ，也開放多了 。

國產	国产	guóchǎn	*adj.*	domestically made
進口	进口	jìnkǒu	*v.*	import
索尼	索尼	Suǒní		Sony
三洋	三洋	Sānyáng		Sanyo
松下	松下	Sōngxià		Panasonic
顧客	顾客	gùkè	*n.*	customer
平常	平常	píngcháng	*adj.*	ordinary; common

"您是要国产的还是进口的？"

"听说进口的好点儿，先看看进口的吧！"

"进口的有索尼、三洋、松下 …… 您喜欢哪种？"

像这样一段顾客和售货员的对话，现在听起来很平常，但是在八十年代初期却是不可能的。和那个"没有"的时代比起来，现在的百货商场里，不但商品增加了，服务质量也大大提高了。

来到中国的美国人常常拿中国和美国比较(4)，觉得中国有许多地方还相当(5)落后。这种比较是很自然的，也是不可避免的。但是，在拿中国和美国比较的同时(6)，我们也别忘了拿过去和现在比较，我们会发现中国比从前进步多了，也开放多了。

可能	可能	kěnéng	*adj./n.*	possible, possibility
質量	质量	zhìliàng	*n.*	quality
相當	相当	xiāngdāng	*adv.*	quite; considerably
落後	落后	luòhòu	*adj.*	backward, lagging behind
同時	同时	tóngshí	*t.w.*	same time, at the same time; simultaneously
過去	过去	guòqù	*n.*	past
進步	进步	jìnbù	*adj.*	improved

第二十一課
脱了褲子放屁

　　中國話裏有許多非常有趣而且生動的俗話、成語和歇後語，這些話用很少的字表示出很深的意思來(1)。有些成語已經有三千多年的歷史了，但還是現在的日常用語。從成語的發展和使用，最能看出中國語言古今並存的有趣現象。

　　中國的俗話和成語成千上萬，我最喜歡的是"脱了褲子放屁"，沒有一句話比它更能生動有趣地表示做了一件多餘的事兒了(2)。當然，這不是一句很高雅的話，在正式的晚飯桌上説這句話是

脱	脱	tuō	v.	take off; cast off
褲子	裤子	kùzi	n.	trousers
放屁	放屁	fàng-pì	v.-o.	pass gas; fart
生動	生动	shēngdòng	adj.	lively; vivid
俗話	俗话	súhuà	n.	common saying; proverb
成語	成语	chéngyǔ	n.	a set phrase; idiom
歇後語	歇后语	xiēhòuyǔ	n.	a two-part allegorical saying
深	深	shēn	adj.	deep; profound
歷史	历史	lìshǐ	n.	history

第二十一课
脱了裤子放屁

　　中国话里有许多非常有趣而且生动的俗话、成语和歇后语，这些话用很少的字表示出很深的意思(1)。有些成语已经有三千多年的历史了，但还是现在的日常用语。从成语的发展和使用，最能看出中国语言古今并存的有趣现象。

　　中国的俗话和成语成千上万，我最喜欢的是"脱了裤子放屁"，没有一句话比它更能生动有趣地表示做了一件多余的事儿了(2)。当然，这不是一句很高雅的话，在正式的晚饭桌上说这句话是

用語	用语	yòngyǔ	n.	wording; choice of words
使用	使用	shǐyòng	v./n.	use; make use of; apply
語言	语言	yǔyán	n.	language
並存	并存	bìngcún	v.	exist simultaneously
成千上萬	成千上万	chéngqiān shàngwàn	idm.	thousands upon thousands
它	它	tā	pron.	it
多餘	多余	duōyú	adj.	unnecessary; surplus
高雅	高雅	gāoyǎ	adj.	refined; elegant

109

不太合適的。這時你可以改用"畫蛇添足"，這就高雅多了，可也就不那麼有趣了。

　　歇後語的意思是只說上半句，下半句讓聽的人自己去理解。這種話有點儿像謎語，對外國人來說，非常難懂。但是只要聽懂了，就不容易忘記。譬如"狗拿耗子"就是一句常用的歇後語，意思是"多管閑事"。"捉耗子"是貓的責任，而狗去做貓該做的事，這不是多管閑事嗎？當然，這句話也不太客氣，除非(3)是對非常熟的朋友，要不然是不能用的。

　　用成語和俗話，要是用得不合適就會鬧笑話，得特別小心。

改用	改用	gǎiyòng	v.	use (something else) instead
畫蛇添足	画蛇添足	huà shé tiān zú		draw a snake and add feet to it-- ruin the effect by adding something superflous
理解	理解	lǐjiě	v.	understand; comprehend
謎語	谜语	míyǔ	n.	riddle; conundrum
忘記	忘记	wàngjì	v.	forget
譬如	譬如	pìrú		for example; such as
拿	拿	ná	v.	seize; capture
耗子	耗子	hàozi	n.	mouse; rat

不太合适的。这时你可以改用"画蛇添足"，这就高雅多了，可也就不那么有趣了。

歇后语的意思是只说上半句，下半句让听的人自己去理解。这种话有点儿像谜语。对外国人来说，非常难懂。但是只要听懂了，就不容易忘记。譬如"狗拿耗子"就是一句常用的歇后语，意思是"多管闲事"。"捉耗子"是猫的责任，而狗去做猫该做的事，这不是多管闲事吗？当然，这句话也不太客气，除非(3)是对非常熟的朋友，要不然是不能用的。

用成语和俗话，要是用得不合适就会闹笑话，得特别小心。

多管闲事	多管闲事	duōguǎn xiánshì	v.	poke one's nose into others' business
捉	捉	zhuō	v.	catch; capture
貓	猫	māo	n.	cat
責任	责任	zérèn	n.	responsibility
除非	除非	chúfēi	conj.	only if; only when; unless
熟	熟	shú	adj.	familiar
要不然	要不然	yào.bùrán	conj.	otherwise; or else
鬧笑話	闹笑话	nào xiào.huà	v.-o.	make a fool of oneself

第二十二課

"鐵飯碗"打破了

在北京設立辦事處的外國公司越來越多了。從飛機到(1)計算機，從電話到快餐，美國的大公司在北京幾乎(2)都有辦公室。這些公司為北京人也為在北京的外國人提供了許多工作機會。這次我來北京，一方面是為了提高我的漢語水平，另一方面也是想找個工作。外國人在北京找工作，幾年前還很困難，現在已經是很平常的事兒了。我有幾個朋友都在北京找到了理想的工作。

鐵飯碗	铁饭碗	tiěfànwǎn	n.	"iron rice bowl"-- a secure job
打破	打破	dǎ-pò	v.-c.	break; smash
設立	设立	shèlì	v.	establish
辦事處	办事处	bànshìchù	n.	office; agency
計算機	计算机	jìsuànjī	n.	computer

第二十二课

"铁饭碗"打破了

　　在北京设立办事处的外国公司越来越多了。从飞机到(1)计算机，从电话到快餐，美国的大公司在北京几乎(2)都有办公室。这些公司为北京人也为在北京的外国人提供了许多工作机会。这次我来北京，一方面是为了提高我的汉语水平，另一方面也是想找个工作。外国人在北京找工作，几年前还很困难，现在已经是很平常的事儿了。我有几个朋友都在北京找到了理想的工作。

快餐	快餐	kuàicān	n.	fast food
幾乎	几乎	jīhū	adv.	almost; nearly
辦公室	办公室	bàngōngshì	n.	office
找	找	zhǎo	v.	look for; try to find; seek

　　從前中國的大學畢業生都是靠學校為他們分配工作，現在他們也得自己找工作了。這幾年改革開放的政策不但促進了中國的經濟發展，也漸漸打破了"鐵飯碗"的觀念。

　　"鐵飯碗"的制度雖然為大家提供了穩定的工作，但是卻減少了各行各業的競爭。現在中國的年輕人都已經認識到只有努力工作才能為自己帶來成功。"鐵飯碗"、"大鍋飯"已經不再(3)是中國的特色了。

畢業	毕业	bìyè	v.	graduate
分配	分配	fēnpèi	v.	distribute; allot; assign
政策	政策	zhèngcè	n.	policy
促進	促进	cùjìn	v.	promote; accelerate
觀念	观念	guānniàn	n.	concept; notion; idea
制度	制度	zhìdù	n.	system
穩定	稳定	wěndìng	adj.	stable

　　从前中国的大学毕业生都是靠学校为他们分配工作，现在他们也得自己找工作了。这几年改革开放的政策不但促进了中国的经济发展，也渐渐打破了"铁饭碗"的观念。

　　"铁饭碗"的制度虽然为大家提供了稳定的工作，但是却减少了各行各业的竞争。现在中国的年轻人都已经认识到只有努力工作才能为自己带来成功。"铁饭碗"、"大锅饭"已经不再(3)是中国的特色了。

各行各業	各行各业	gèháng gèyè	n.	all trades and professions
競爭	竞争	jìngzhēng	n.	competition
成功	成功	chénggōng	n.	success
大鍋飯	大锅饭	dàguōfàn	n.	food prepared in a large pot 吃大锅饭: "eat out of the same pot"-- reap the same benefits regardless of who works more

第二十三課

乒乓外交

　　在校園裏經常可以看到幾個孩子圍著一張水泥的乒乓球桌子打乒乓球。雖然設備非常簡陋，但是他們的球技卻很好。這使我想起(1)了 1972 年中國第一次派出乒乓球隊到美國去訪問的事，這就是有名的 "乒乓外交"。"乒乓外交" 打破了中美之間二十幾年敵對的局面，從此以後(2)，兩國開始了多方面的交流。

　　在過去這二十幾年裏(3)，中美兩國的人民和政府從體育、學術到經濟、政治都進行了大規模的

乒乓	乒乓	pīngpāng	*n.*	table tennis; ping-pong
外交	外交	wàijiāo	*n.*	diplomacy; foreign affairs
孩子	孩子	háizi	*n.*	children; kid
圍	围	wéi	*v.*	surround; enclose
水泥	水泥	shuǐní	*n.*	cement
設備	设备	shèbèi	*n.*	equipment; facilities
簡陋	简陋	jiǎnlòu	*adj.*	simple and crude
球技	球技	qiújì	*n.*	ball-playing skills
球隊	球队	qiúduì	*n.*	ball team
訪問	访问	fǎngwèn	*v.*	visit (formally)

第二十三课
乒乓外交

在校园里经常可以看到几个孩子围着一张水泥的乒乓球桌子打乒乓球。虽然设备非常简陋，但是他们的球技却很好。这使我想起(1)了1972年中国第一次派出乒乓球队到美国去访问的事，这就是有名的"乒乓外交"。"乒乓外交"打破了中美之间二十几年敌对的局面，从此以后(2)，两国开始了多方面的交流。

在过去这二十几年里 (3)，中美两国的人民和政府从体育、学术到经济、政治都进行了大规模的

敵對	敌对	díduì	*v.*	hostile; antagonistic
局面	局面	júmiàn	*n.*	aspect; situation
從此以後	从此以后	cóngcǐ yǐhòu		from then on; from now on
多方面	多方面	duōfāngmiàn	*adj.*	many-sided; in many ways
交流	交流	jiāoliú	*v.*	exchange; interaction
人民	人民	rénmín	*n.*	people
體育	体育	tǐyù	*n.*	physical education; sports
學術	学术	xuéshù	*n.*	learning, academic
進行	进行	jìnxíng	*v.*	carry on; carry out; conduct
規模	规模	guīmó	*n.*	scale; scope; dimensions

交流。然而(4)，由於(5)兩國隔離的時間太久，社會制度和語言文化又有很大的差異，在交流的過程中(6)常常出現一些困難和障礙，尤其在"人權"這個問題上，雙方都比較堅持自己的看法，到今天還沒法達成協議。

兩國進行交流的時候，由於歷史和文化背景的不同，矛盾和衝突是不能完全避免的。這時最需要的是相互(7)的尊重和理解，而不是一國強迫另一國接受自己的標準。

我相信隨著(8)中美兩國政府和人民交流的增加，雙方都會更進一步地了解對方。

然而	然而	ránér	*conj.*	yet; but; however
由於	由于	yóuyú	*prep.*	owing to; as a result of
隔離	隔离	gélí	*v.*	keep apart; isolate; segregate
差異	差异	chāyì	*n.*	difference; divergence
過程	过程	guòchéng	*n.*	course; process
出現	出现	chūxiàn	*v.*	appear; arise; emerge
障礙	障碍	zhàng'ài	*n.*	obstacle; barrier
人權	人权	rénquán	*n.*	human rights
看法	看法	kànfǎ	*n.*	view; a way of looking at a thing
達成	达成	dáchéng	*v.*	reach (an agreement)

交流。然而(4)，由于(5)两国隔离的时间太久，社会制度和语言文化又有很大的差异，在交流的过程中(6)常常出现一些困难和障碍，尤其在"人权"这个问题上，双方都比较坚持自己的看法，到今天还没法达成协议。

两国进行交流的时候，由于历史和文化背景的不同，矛盾和冲突是不能完全避免的。这时最需要的是相互(7)的尊重和理解，而不是一国强迫另一国接受自己的标准。

我相信随着(8)中美两国政府和人民交流的增加，双方都会更进一步地了解对方。

協議	协议	xiéyì	n.	agreement
背景	背景	bèijǐng	n.	background
矛盾	矛盾	máodùn	n.	contradiction; conflict
衝突	冲突	chōngtū	v.	conflict; clash
相互	相互	xiānghù	adj.	mutual; each other
尊重	尊重	zūnzhòng	n.	respect; value; esteem
強迫	强迫	qiǎngpò	v.	force; compel; coerce
接受	接受	jiēshòu	v.	accept
標準	标准	biāozhǔn	n.	standard; criterion
隨著	随着	suízhe	adv.	along with; in the wake of

第二十四課
高 考

　　每年七月，中國各地同時舉行大學的入學考試，中國人把這個考試叫做高考。這是全國高中生最重要的一個考試。這個考試不但決定他們進入哪所大學，同時也決定了他們以後四年的專業是什麼。

　　我和幾位北京的老師聊天兒，發現中國整個兒的高中教育幾乎都是在為高考做準備，學生很少有機會發展自己的興趣。高考這個制度固然(1)有些負面的影響，使許多高中學生只知道死記硬背，而(2)缺乏分析和理解的訓練，但是這個考試制度卻

高考	高考	gāokǎo	*n.*	the entrance examination for colleges and universities
舉行	举行	jǔxíng	*v.*	hold (a meeting, ceremony, etc.)
入學	入学	rùxué	*v.-o.*	start school; enter school
考試	考试	kǎoshì	*n./v.*	test; examination, take a test
進入	进入	jìnrù	*v.*	enter; get into
所	所	suǒ	*an.*	measure word for house
專業	专业	zhuānyè	*n.*	special field of study; major
整個	整个	zhěnggè	*adj.*	whole; entire

第二十四课
高 考

每年七月，中国各地同时举行大学的入学考试，中国人把这个考试叫做高考。这是全国高中生最重要的一个考试。这个考试不但决定他们进入哪所大学，同时也决定了他们以后四年的专业是什么。

我和几位北京的老师聊天儿，发现中国整个儿的高中教育几乎都是在为高考做准备，学生很少有机会发展自己的兴趣。高考这个制度固然(1)有些负面的影响，使许多高中学生只知道死记硬背，而(2)缺乏分析和理解的训练，但是这个考试制度却

教育	教育	jiàoyù	n.	education
準備	准备	zhǔnbèi	n./v.	preparation, prepare
興趣	兴趣	xìngqù	n.	interest
固然	固然	gùrán	conj.	no doubt; it is true
負面	负面	fùmiàn	adj.	negative
死記硬背	死记硬背	sǐjì yìngbèi	v.	rote memorizing
缺乏	缺乏	quēfá	v.	lack; be short of
分析	分析	fēnxī	v./n	analyse, analysis
訓練	训练	xùnliàn	n./v.	training, train

體現了公平競爭的精神。一個生長在農村的年輕人，只要通過考試，就可以跟別人一樣(3)進入北京大學。我認為這種公平競爭的精神是非常有意義的。不靠關係，不走後門，完全靠自己的本事，通過考試，進入大學。在我看來(4)，這個考試的優點比缺點多得多。

有些人批評中國的教育制度過分強調記憶而不重視分析，這也許有道理；但是在美國的中國留學生，一般來說，表現都很好。顯然中國教育給他們的訓練是很不錯的。

體現	体现	tǐxiàn	v.	embody; incarnate; reflect
公平	公平	gōngpíng	adj.	fair; just
生長	生长	shēngzhǎng	v.	grow up; be brought up
通過	通过	tōngguò	v.	pass
北京大學	北京大学	Běijīng dàxué		Peking University
有意義	有意义	yǒu yìyì	adj.	meaningful
後門	后门	hòumén	n.	back door
本事	本事	běn.shì	n.	ability; capability
在....看來	在....看来	zài .... kànlái		in (one's) opinion
優點	优点	yōudiǎn	n.	good point; merit

体现了公平竞争的精神。一个生长在农村的年轻
人，只要通过考试，就可以跟别人一样(3)进入北京
大学。我认为这种公平竞争的精神是非常有意义
的。不靠关系，不走后门，完全靠自己的本事，
通过考试，进入大学。在我看来(4)，这个考试的优
点比缺点多得多。

　　有些人批评中国的教育制度过分强调记忆而不
重视分析，这也许有道理；但是在美国的中国留
学生，一般来说，表现都很好。显然中国教育给
他们的训练是很不错的。

缺點	缺点	quēdiǎn	n.	shortcoming; defect; weakness
批評	批评	pīpíng	v.	criticize
過分	过分	guòfèn	adv.	excessively; over-
強調	强调	qiángdiào	v.	emphasize; stress
記憶	记忆	jìyì	n.	memory
重視	重视	zhòngshì	v.	think highly of; value; take something seriously
道理	道理	dào.li	n.	reason; sense
有道理	有道理	yǒu dào.li	adj.	reasonable
表現	表现	biǎoxiàn	n.	performance
顯然	显然	xiǎnrán	adv.	obviously; clearly

第二十五課

北京的書店

　　北京是中國的政治中心，也是文化中心。北京的書店、出版社、博物館和文化活動都比中國其他城市多得多。到了北京以後，我去看過幾次話劇和電影，雖然不能全懂，但是對於(1)北京老百姓日常的文化活動還是有了一定的了解。

　　到了周末，我常去逛北京的書店，尤其喜歡逛琉璃廠。琉璃廠可以説是北京的文化街。除了書店以外，還有許多賣字畫儿、古董的鋪子；那儿的建築和街道也保持著幾十年前的老樣子。清末民初

中心	中心	zhōngxīn	n.	center
出版社	出版社	chūbǎnshè	n.	publishing house
博物館	博物馆	bówùguǎn	n.	museum
活動	活动	huódòng	n.	activity
其他	其他	qítā	adj.	other; else
話劇	话剧	huàjù	n.	modern drama; stage play
電影	电影	diànyǐng	n.	movie
全	全	quán	adv.	完全；comepletely; entirely
周末	周末	zhōumò	n.	weekend

第 二十五 课
北京的书店

　　北京是中国的政治中心，也是文化中心。北京的书店、出版社、博物馆和文化活动都比中国其他城市多得多。到了北京以后，我去看过几次话剧和电影，虽然不能全懂，但是对于(1)北京老百姓日常的文化活动还是有了一定的了解。

　　到了周末，我常去逛北京的书店，尤其喜欢逛琉璃厂。琉璃厂可以说是北京的文化街。除了书店以外，还有许多卖字画儿、古董的铺子；那儿的建筑和街道也保持着几十年前的老样子。清末民初

琉璃廠	琉璃厂	Liúlíchǎng		Liulichang
鋪子	铺子	pùzi	*n.*	(archaic) store; shop
街道	街道	jiēdào	*n.*	street
保持	保持	bǎochí	*v.*	keep; maintain; preserve
老樣子	老样子	lǎoyàngzi	*n.*	the way a thing or person used to look
清	清	Qīng		清代; the Qing Dynasty (1644-1911)
末	末	mò	*n.*	end; last stage
民	民	Mín		民国; the Republic of China (1912-)

古老的商店

的許多大學者都到琉璃廠來找他們的研究材料。
據說那時琉璃廠書店裏的職員都精通中國文學歷
史的書目和版本，他們都是最有經驗的圖書館員。

最近幾年北京的出版事業非常發達。從一般的
小說到嚴肅的學術著作，從古典的詩歌到電子計
算機的教材，幾乎每天都有新書出版。有許多重
要的中國古代經典，也都在整理之後出了簡體字
的版本。我在美國的時候，老師常說：只學簡體

初	初	chū	n.	the beginning of
學者	学者	xuézhě	n.	scholar; learned man
材料	材料	cáiliào	n.	data; material
精通	精通	jīngtōng	v.	be proficient in; have a good command of
文學	文学	wénxué	n.	literature
書目	书目	shūmù	n.	catalogue of titles; booklist
版本	版本	bǎnběn	n.	edition
經驗	经验	jīngyàn	n.	experience
有經驗	有经验	yǒu jīngyàn	adj.	experienced
圖書館員	图书馆员	túshūguǎn yuán	n.	librarian
出版	出版	chūbǎn	v.	publish; come out

的许多大学者都到琉璃厂来找他们的研究材料。据说那时琉璃厂书店里的职员都精通中国文学历史的书目和版本，他们都是最有经验的图书馆员。

最近几年北京的出版事业非常发达。从一般的小说到严肃的学术著作，从古典的诗歌到电子计算机的教材，几乎每天都有新书出版。有许多重要的中国古代经典，也都在整理之后出了简体字的版本。我在美国的时候，老师常说：只学简体

事業	事业	shìyè	n.	enterprise; facilities
發達	发达	fādá	adj.	developed; flourishing
小說	小说	xiǎoshuō	n.	fiction; novel
嚴肅	严肃	yánsù	adj.	serious; solemn
著作	著作	zhùzuò	n.	work; book; writing
古典	古典	gǔdiǎn	adj.	classical
詩歌	诗歌	shīgē	n.	poems and songs; poetry
電子計算機	电子计算机	diànzǐ jìsuànjī	n.	computer
教材	教材	jiàocái	n.	teaching material
經典	经典	jīngdiǎn	n.	classics
...之後	...之后	zhīhòu		after...

字是看不懂中國古書的。其實，只要常去北京的書店看看，就知道用簡體字印的古書真不少。看不懂古書和會不會繁體字實在沒有什麼關係。

　　許多解放(1949)以後被禁的著作，最近幾年又重新出版了，這是一個非常可喜(2)的現象。這說明了思想的解放和言論自由的放寬。雖然現在還有一些問題是不能隨便批評的，但是和七十年代比較，中國在這方面的進步是應該受到(3)肯定的。

印	印	yìn	v.	print
解放	解放	jiěfàng	n.	the liberation of China (in 1949)
禁	禁	jìn	v.	prohibit; forbid; ban
可喜	可喜	kěxǐ	adj.	gratifying; heartening
解放	解放	jiěfàng	v.	liberate; emancipate

字是看不懂中国古书的。其实，只要常去北京的书
店看看，就知道用简体字印的古书真不少。看不懂
古书和会不会繁体字实在没有什麼关系。

　　许多解放(1949)以后被禁的著作，最近几年又
重新出版了，这是一个非常可喜(2)的现象。这说明
了思想的解放和言论自由的放宽。虽然现在还有
一些问题是不能随便批评的，但是和七十年代比
较，中国在这方面的进步是应该受到(3)肯定的。

言論	言论	yánlùn	n.	opinion on public affairs; speech
自由	自由	zìyóu	n./adj.	freedom
放寬	放宽	fàngkuān	v./n.	relax (restrictions); relaxation
受到	受到	shòudào	v.	receive (usually take a verb as object)
肯定	肯定	kěndìng	v.	affirm; confirm; approve; regard as positive

第二十六課
愛人、先生、太太

　　自從八十年代初期，中國大陸和台灣有了來往以後，海峽兩岸語言上的不同就成了大家討論的話題。但是我覺得在討論這個問題的時候，大家過分強調兩岸語言的不同，而忽略了它們只是在大同之中(1)有一點儿小異。

　　談兩岸語言問題的人大多是因為覺得兩岸的不同相當有趣，很少是因為這個不同造成了相互的不了解。譬如在台灣和海外的中國人用"先生、太

太太	太太	tàitai	*n.*	wife
大陸	大陆	dàlù		mainland China
來往	来往	láiwǎng	*n.*	communication; relations
海峽	海峡	hǎixiá	*n.*	strait

海峽兩岸　　　　　　　　mainland & Taiwan

第二十六课
爱人、先生、太太

　　自从八十年代初期，中国大陆和台湾有了来往以后，海峡两岸语言上的不同就成了大家讨论的话题。但是我觉得在讨论这个问题的时候，大家过分强调两岸语言的不同，而忽略了它们只是在大同之中(1)有一点儿小异。

　　谈两岸语言问题的人大多是因为觉得两岸的不同相当有趣，很少是因为这个不同造成了相互的不了解。譬如在台湾和海外的中国人用"先生、太

岸	岸	àn	n.	coast
忽略	忽略	hūlüè	v.	neglect
大同小異	大同小异	dàtóng xiǎoyì	idm.	largely identical but with minor differences

131

太"來表示"husband and wife",在大陸只說"愛人"。"愛人"可以是先生,也可以是太太。台灣的人剛聽見"愛人",可能不太習慣,可是只要多談幾次,立刻就能懂它的意思。大陸的人聽見"先生、太太"也毫無(2)問題,不會產生任何誤會。其實,從男女平等的角度來看(3),"愛人"這個詞是很好的。為什麼王小姐跟張先生結了婚就一定得變成張太太,而張先生不能變成王先生呢?另外(4)還有些詞也是這樣,雖然不同,但是一看就懂;像計程車就是出租汽車,冷氣就是空調,電腦就是電子計算機等等。

毫	毫	háo	*adv.*	in the least; at all
無	无	wú	*v.*	(written) there is no
產生	产生	chǎnshēng	*v.*	produce
誤會	误会	wùhuì	*n./v.*	misunderstanding, misunderstand

太"来表示"husband and wife"，在大陆只说"爱人"。"爱人"可以是先生，也可以是太太。台湾的人刚听见"爱人"，可能不太习惯，可是只要多听几次，立刻就能懂它的意思。大陆的人听见"先生、太太"也毫无(2)问题，不会产生任何误会。其实，从男女平等的角度来看(3)，"爱人"这个词是很好的。为什么王小姐跟张先生结了婚就一定得变成张太太，而张先生不能变成王先生呢？另外(4)还有些词也是这样，虽然不同，但是一看就懂；像计程车就是出租汽车，冷气就是空调，电脑就是电子计算机等等。

變成	变成	biànchéng	v.	become
計程車	计程车	jìchéng chē	n.	taxi
冷氣	冷气	lěngqì	n.	air conditioning
電腦	电脑	diànnǎo	n.	computer

台灣在1949年以後和大陸隔離了幾十年，因此有些用語往往是過去的說法，"國語"這個詞就是個很好的例子。現在大陸上標準的說法是"普通話"。在"繁體字"和"簡體字"、"注音符號"和"漢語拼音"這兩方面(5)，台灣也都是保留了1949年以前的形式。

學中文的外國人經常接觸到兩岸和海外的中國人，也常看到各地的中文報紙，對各地的用語都應該有些了解。兩岸用語的不同，對中國人來說相當有趣，但是對外國人來說，卻造成了學習上一定的困難。不過，我相信，這些不同一定會隨著兩岸人民交往的增加而漸漸減少的。

說法	说法	shuōfǎ	*n.*	wording; way of saying a thing
例子	例子	lìzi	*n.*	example
注音符號	注音符号	zhùyīn fúhào	*n.*	the national phonetic alphabet (in use before the Chinese phonetic alphabet was implemented)
漢語拼音	汉语拼音	Hànyǔ pīnyīn	*n.*	the Chinese phonetic alphabet

　　台湾在1949年以后和大陆隔离了几十年，因此有些用语往往是过去的说法，"国语"这个词就是个很好的例子。现在大陆上标准的说法是"普通话"。在"繁体字"和"简体字"、"注音符号"和"汉语拼音"这两方面(5)，台湾也都是保留了1949年以前的形式。

　　学中文的外国人经常接触到两岸和海外的中国人，也常看到各地的中文报纸，对各地的用语都应该有些了解。两岸用语的不同，对中国人来说相当有趣，但是对外国人来说，却造成了学习上一定的困难。不过，我相信，这些不同一定会随着两岸人民交往的增加而渐渐减少的。

方面	方面	fāngmiàn	*n.*	aspect; respect
保留	保留	bǎoliú	*v.*	retain; continue to have
形式	形式	xíngshì	*n.*	form
接觸	接触	jiēchù	*v.*	come into contact with
相信	相信	xiāngxìn	*v.*	believe
交往	交往	jiāowǎng	*n.*	contact; association

第二十七課

離 婚

甲：電視上的新聞報導說中國離婚的人越來越多了。這是不是表示中國人的道德水平正在下降？

乙：離婚的人增加的確造成了一些社會問題。但是與其說這是道德水平的下降，不如(1)說是婦女地位的提高。

甲：離婚和婦女地位的提高有什麼關係呢？

乙：以前女人在經濟上完全依靠男人。如果離了婚，他們就失去了生活的保障；所以即使(2)

離婚	离婚	lí-hūn	v.-o.	divorce
報導	报道	bàodǎo / bàodào	n./v.	report, broadcast
下降	下降	xiàjiàng	v.	descend; drop
的確	的确	díquè	adv.	indeed; really
與其 A，不如 B	与其 A，不如 B	yǔqí..., bùrú...	conj.	A is not so much ... as B; A is less desirable than B

136

第二十七课
离 婚

甲：电视上的新闻报道说中国离婚的人越来越多了。这是不是表示中国人的道德水平正在下降？

乙：离婚的人增加的确造成了一些社会问题。但是与其说这是道德水平的下降，不如(1)说是妇女地位的提高。

甲：离婚和妇女地位的提高有什麽关系呢？

乙：以前女人在经济上完全依靠男人。如果离了婚，他们就失去了生活的保障；所以即使(2)

婦女	妇女	fùnǔ	*n.*	woman (as a collective noun)
依靠	依靠	yīkào	*v.*	depend on
失去	失去	shīqù	*v.*	lose
保障	保障	bǎozhàng	*n./v.*	safety net, guarantee; safeguard
即使	即使	jíshǐ	*conj.*	even though; even if

沒有愛情，婚姻還是得維持下去(3)。現在可不是這樣了。有的家庭裏，妻子的收入比丈夫還高。要是夫妻之間沒有愛情，他們不必再忍受下去。再說(4)，現在男女的交往越來越公開，越來越平等，發生婚外關係的可能也就大大地增加了。因此，在我看來，離婚人數的增多正(5)說明中國婦女有了更多的婚姻自由。

甲：我很同意你的看法。離婚是個法律和經濟的問題，而不是(6)道德問題。但是離婚的人太

愛情	爱情	àiqíng	n.	romantic love
婚姻	婚姻	hūnyīn	n.	marriage
維持	维持	wéichí	v.	maintain, persist, endure
妻子	妻子	qīzi	n.	wife
收入	收入	shōurù	n.	income
丈夫	丈夫	zhàng.fū	n.	husband
夫妻	夫妻	fūqī	n.	married couple

没有爱情，婚姻还是得维持下去(3)。现在可不是这样了。有的家庭里，妻子的收入比丈夫还高。要是夫妻之间没有爱情，他们不必再忍受下去。再说(4)，现在男女的交往越来越公开，越来越平等，发生婚外关系的可能也就大大地增加了。因此，在我看来，离婚人数的增多正(5)说明中国妇女有了更多的婚姻自由。

甲：我很同意你的看法。离婚是个法律和经济的问题，而不是(6)道德问题。但是离婚的人太

忍受	忍受	rěnshòu	*v.*	endure; bear
再說	再说	zàishuō	adv.	moreover
公開	公开	gōngkāi	*adj.*	public; open
婚外關係	婚外关系	hūnwài guān.xì	*n.*	extra-marital relationship
人數	人数	rénshù	*n.*	the number of people
法律	法律	fǎlǜ	*n.*	law

多，還是會造成社會問題，對不對？

乙：沒錯儿。離婚人數的增加造成很多單親家庭，而在單親家庭長大的孩子產生問題的可能也比較大。

甲：其實，離婚的時候，孩子所受到的傷害往往比夫妻受到的傷害更大。

乙：是啊！有些夫婦要不是(7)為了孩子，早就(8)離婚了。孩子小的時候他們勉強生活在一起；孩子長大了，不必依靠父母了，他們的婚姻也就不必再維持下去了。

單親家庭	单亲家庭	dānqīn jiātíng	n.	single-parent family
長大	长大	zhǎngdà	v.	grow up
傷害	伤害	shānghài	v.	injure; harm (in an abstract sense)
夫婦	夫妇	fūfù	n.	married couple
勉強	勉强	miǎnqiǎng	adv.	reluctantly; grudgingly

多，还是会造成社会问题，对不对？

乙：没错儿。离婚人数的增加造成很多单亲家庭，而在单亲家庭长大的孩子产生问题的可能也比较大。

甲：其实，离婚的时候，孩子所受到的伤害往往比夫妻受到的伤害更大。

乙：是啊！有些夫妇要不是(7)为了孩子，早就(8)离婚了。孩子小的时候他们勉强生活在一起；孩子长大了，不必依靠父母了，他们的婚姻也就不必再维持下去了。

第二十八課

從 " 發福 " 到 " 減肥 "

　　從前，兩個中國人一段時間沒見面，再見面的
時候常説對方 " 發福了 " ，意思是 " 你胖了一點儿(1)，
近來一定過得不錯，真有福氣。" 説 " 發福了 " 是恭
維別人的客套話。現在可不行了。打開北京的報紙
和電視，減肥的廣告到處都是，在街上胖子也一天
比一天多，尤其是小孩儿；不到十歲卻有五、六十公
斤重(2)的孩子到處可以看到。

發福	发福	fāfú	v.-o.	gain weight
減肥	减肥	jiǎnféi	v.	go on a diet to lose weight
段	段	duàn	an.	a period (of time)
見面	见面	jiàn-miàn	v.-o.	meet (somebody); A 跟 B 见面
胖	胖	pàng	v./adj.	become fat; fat
近來	近来	jìnlái	adv.	recently
過	过	guò	v.	spend (time); pass (time)

第二十八课

从"发福"到"减肥"

　　从前，两个中国人一段时间没见面，再见面的时候常说对方"发福了"，意思是"你胖了一点儿(1)，近来一定过得不错，真有福气。"说"发福了"是恭维别人的客套话。现在可不行了。打开北京的报纸和电视，减肥的广告到处都是，在街上胖子也一天比一天多，尤其是小孩儿；不到十岁却有五、六十公斤重(2)的孩子到处可以看到。

福氣	福气	fúqì	*n.*	good fortune
恭維	恭维	gōngwéi	*v.*	compliment
客套話	客套话	kètàohuà	*n.*	polite expressions; civilities; social decorum
胖子	胖子	pàngzi	*n.*	fatty
小孩	小孩	xiǎohái	*n.*	kid; children
歲	岁	suì		(age unit) ... years old
公斤	公斤	gōngjīn		kilogram

143

　　五、六十年代，許多中國人都有營養不良的問題，可是現在肥胖成了城市居民的煩惱，大家都想方設法要減肥。有的不吃肉，有的不吃飯，有的練氣功，有的爬高山；可是好像無論做什麼都沒有用，胖子還是一天比一天多。所以，現在中國人見了面不但不說 " 發福了 "，反而(3)說 " 最近你好像瘦了點儿，看起來健康多了！"

　　中國的小胖子越來越多，可能是因為父母過分愛護他們的獨生子女的緣故(4)，總給他們吃最

營養	营养	yíngyǎng	*n.*	nutrition
不良	不良	bùliáng	*adj.*	mal-; bad
肥胖	肥胖	féipàng	*n.*	obese
居民	居民	jūmín	*n.*	resident
煩惱	烦恼	fánnǎo	*n.*	worriment; vexation
想方設法	想方设法	xiǎngfāng shèfǎ	*v.*	conjure up all kinds of methods
爬	爬	pá	*v.*	climb
氣功	气功	qìgōng	*n.*	*qigong,* a system of deep breathing exercises

　　五、六十年代，许多中国人都有营养不良的问题，可是现在肥胖成了城市居民的烦恼，大家都想方设法要减肥。有的不吃肉，有的不吃饭，有的练气功，有的爬高山；可是好像无论做什么都没有用，胖子还是一天比一天多。所以，现在中国人见了面不但不说"发福了"，反而(3)说"最近你好像瘦了点儿，看起来健康多了！"

　　中国的小胖子越来越多，可能是因为父母过分爱护他们的独生子女的缘故(4)，总给他们吃最

練氣功	练气功	liàn qìgōng	*v.-o.*	practice *qigong*
反而	反而	fǎn'ér	*conj.*	on the contrary; instead
瘦	瘦	shòu	*v./adj.*	thin
愛護	爱护	àihù	*v.*	cherish; treasure
獨生子女	独生子女	dúshēng zǐnǚ	*n.*	only child
緣故	缘故	yuángù	*n.*	cause; reason (generally takes a noun phrase modifier)

好的；但是美國食物也許也得負點ㄦ責任。漢堡包、炸薯條、巧克力糖、冰激凌、可口可樂，哪一個(5)不是又甜又膩又有害健康的食物？可是這些都是小孩子們最愛吃的東西。美國商人，尤其是香煙商人，在賺中國人錢的時候，也應該為中國人的健康想想。

　　最近中國因為改革開放，不但大家的生活水平提高了，人和人之間的關係，以及(6)人們對許多事情的看法也和過去不同了。因此，我相信經濟的改變是所有改變的基礎。

食物	食物	shíwù	n.	food
負責任	负责任	fù zérèn	v.-o.	be responsible for sth.
漢堡包	汉堡包	hànbǎobāo	n.	hamburger
炸薯條	炸薯条	zhá shǔtiáo	n.	french fries
巧克力	巧克力	qiǎokèlì	n.	chocolate
糖	糖	táng	n.	candy; sugar
冰激凌	冰激凌	bīngjīlíng	n.	ice cream
可口可樂	可口可乐	Kěkǒukělè	n.	Coca Cola

好的；但是美国食物也许也得负点儿责任。汉堡包、炸薯条、巧克力糖、冰激凌、可口可乐，哪一个(5)不是又甜又腻又有害健康的食物？可是这些都是小孩子们最爱吃的东西。美国商人，尤其是香烟商人，在赚中国人钱的时候，也应该为中国人的健康想想。

最近中国因为改革开放，不但大家的生活水平提高了，人和人之间的关系，以及(6)人们对许多事情的看法也和过去不同了。因此，我相信经济的改变是所有改变的基础。

腻	腻	nì	*adj.*	satiating
有害	有害	yǒuhài	*v.*	harmful
商人	商人	shāngrén	*n.*	businessman; merchant
香煙	香烟	xiāngyān	*n.*	cigarette
以及	以及	yǐjí	*conj.*	and (used in writing)
改變	改变	gǎibiàn	*v.*	change
基礎	基础	jīchǔ	*n.*	foundation

第二十九課

從 " 溫飽 " 到 " 小康 "

　　" 溫飽 " 就是 " 吃得飽、穿得暖 " 的意思；" 小康 " 是一種在溫飽以上(1)的生活水平；比 " 小康 " 更好的生活叫做 " 富裕 " 。

　　中國過去二十年來(2)，人民生活的改變可以説是從 " 溫飽 " 漸漸變到 " 小康 " 的一個過程。在這個改變的過程當中，最明顯的是老百姓消費結構的改變。

　　在七十年代，人們的花費主要是用在吃的東西上；但現在，對城市居民來説，食物上的花費

溫飽	温饱	wēnbǎo	*adj.*	adequately fed and clothed 溫: warm; 飽: full (from eating)
小康	小康	xiǎokāng	*adj.*	(said of a family or society) comparatively well-off
飽	饱	bǎo	*adj.*	full (from eating)
暖	暖	nuǎn	*adj.*	warm
...以上	...以上	...yǐshàng	*postp.*	above (a given point or line)

第二十九课
从"温饱"到"小康"

　　"温饱"就是"吃得饱、穿得暖"的意思；"小康"是一种在温饱以上⑴的生活水平；比"小康"更好的生活叫做"富裕"。

　　中国过去二十年来⑵，人民生活的改变可以说是从"温饱"渐渐变到"小康"的一个过程。在这个改变的过程当中，最明显的是老百姓消费结构的改变。

　　在七十年代，人们的花费主要是用在吃的东西上；但现在，对城市居民来说，食物上的花费

富裕	富裕	fùyù	*adj.*	rich; wealthy; prosperous
變	变	biàn	*v.*	change; turn into
明顯	明显	míngxiǎn	*adj.*	evident; obvious
老百姓	老百姓	lǎobǎixing	*n.*	the common people
消費	消费	xiāofèi	*v./n.*	consume; consumption
花費	花费	huāfèi	*n.*	expenses

已經不再是生活費用當中最主要的部分了，人們對食物質量的要求也一天一天地提高。二十年前，只要吃飽就行，現在人人都講究營養、味道和方便。在食物的消耗上，主食和蔬菜的分量減少，魚、肉和雞蛋的分量增加。消費品的定量配給制度早已成了歷史。

多年來，一般中國家庭都希望有所謂(3)"四大件儿"－－自行車、縫紉機、手錶和收音機。二十幾年前，擁有這四件日用品被認為是生活達到一定水平的表現，而現在這四大件儿已經被彩電、洗衣

費用	費用	fèiyòng	n.	expenses; costs
部分	部分	bù.fèn	n.	a portion; a part
味道	味道	wèi.dào	n.	taste
消耗	消耗	xiāohào	v.	consume; expend; exhaust
蔬菜	蔬菜	shūcài	n.	vegetable
分量	分量	fèn.liàng	n.	amount
消費品	消费品	xiāofèipǐn	n.	consumer goods
定量	定量	dìngliàng	n.	fixed amount/quantity
配給	配给	pèijǐ	v.	distribute in rations; allocate

已经不再是生活费用当中最主要的部分了。人们
对食物质量的要求也一天一天地提高。二十年前，
只要吃饱就行，现在人人都讲究营养、味道和方
便。在食物的消耗上，主食和蔬菜的分量减少，
鱼、肉和鸡蛋的分量增加。消费品的定量配给制度
早已成了历史。

多年来，一般中国家庭都希望有所谓 (3) " 四大
件儿 " --自行车、缝纫机、手表和收音机。二十几
年前，拥有这四件日用品被认为是生活达到一定
水平的表现，而现在这四大件儿已经被彩电、洗衣

一般	一般	yìbān	*adj.*	general; common
所謂	所谓	suǒwèi	*adj.*	so-called
四大件	四大件	sìdàjiàn	*n.*	the four big things
縫紉機	缝纫机	féngrènjī	*n.*	sewing machine
手錶	手表	shǒubiǎo	*n.*	watch
收音機	收音机	shōuyīnjī	*n.*	radio
擁有	拥有	yōngyǒu	*v.*	own; possess
日用品	日用品	rìyòngpǐn	*n.*	daily necessities
達到	达到	dádào	*v.*	achieve (a goal)

機、電冰箱、音響等家用電器取代了。電話、空調、家用電腦和汽車也漸漸進入了部分家庭。

　　住房的緊張一直是城市居民最大的煩惱。最近幾年，政府也採取了新的措施。商品房上市，房子有了買賣的可能，這確實是中國老百姓生活中的一大改變。

　　從中國人民生活水平提高的歷史進程來看，可以說八十年代主要是解決溫飽問題；到了九十年代，溫飽問題基本上得到了解決，開始由 (4) 溫飽過渡到小康。

音響	音响	yīnxiǎng	n.	stereo
取代	取代	qǔdài	v.	replace
住房	住房	zhùfáng	n.	housing
緊張	紧张	jǐnzhāng	adj.	(said of a financial market) tight; tense; high demand
採取	采取	cǎiqǔ	v.	adopt
措施	措施	cuòshī	n.	(political, financial, etc.) measure; step
商品房	商品房	shāngpǐnfáng	n.	commercialized housing
上市	上市	shàngshì	v.	(said of seasonal goods or new products) go on the market

机、电冰箱、音响等家用电器取代了。电话、空调、家用电脑和汽车也渐渐进入了部分家庭。

住房的紧张一直是城市居民最大的烦恼。最近几年，政府也采取了新的措施。商品房上市，房子有了买卖的可能，这确实是中国老百姓生活中的一大改变。

从中国人民生活水平提高的历史进程来看，可以说八十年代主要是解决温饱问题；到了九十年代，温饱问题基本上得到了解决，开始由(4)温饱过渡到小康。

買賣	买卖	mǎimài	*n.*	buy and sell; trade
確實	确实	quèshí	*adj.*	real; true; certain
一大 n.	一大 n.	yídà		one big ...
進程	进程	jìnchéng	*n.*	course; process; progress
解決	解决	jiějué	*v.*	solve
得到	得到	dédào	*v.*	succeed in obtaining
由	由	yóu	*prep.*	从; from
過渡	过渡	guòdù	*v./n.*	transit, transition

第三十課
老年人的生活

甲：在中國流行著一句話，說美國是 " 兒童的天堂，中年人的戰場，老年人的墳場。" 這句話能不能大概地反映這三種年齡的人在美國的生活？

乙：美國是 " 兒童的天堂，中年人的戰場 "，這句話大致是對的。美國的教育制度，一般來說，比較注重個人發展，孩子們也沒有什麼升學或考試的壓力。至於 (1) 中年人，在那個競爭激烈的社會裏，必須盡最大的努力去工作，才能不

老年人	老年人	lǎoniánrén	*n.*	old people; the elderly
流行	流行	liúxíng	*v.*	prevalent; be popular
兒童	儿童	értóng	*n.*	children
天堂	天堂	tiāntáng	*n.*	heaven; paradise
中年人	中年人	zhōngniánrén	*n.*	middle-aged person
戰場	战场	zhànchǎng	*n.*	battlefield; battleground
墳場	坟场	fénchǎng	*n.*	graveyard; cemetery
大概	大概	dàgài	*adv.*	(here) generally
反映	反映	fǎnyìng	*v.*	reflect

第三十课
老年人的生活

甲：在中国流行着一句话，说美国是"儿童的天堂，中年人的战场，老年人的坟场。"这句话能不能大概地反映这三种年龄的人在美国的生活？

乙：美国是"儿童的天堂，中年人的战场"，这句话大致是对的。美国的教育制度，一般来说，比较注重个人发展，孩子们也没有什么升学或考试的压力。至於 (1) 中年人，在那个竞争激烈的社会里，必须尽最大的努力去工作，才能不

年齡	年龄	niánlíng	*n.*	age
大致	大致	dàzhì	*adv.*	roughly; more or less
注重	注重	zhùzhòng	*v.*	lay stress on; pay attention to
升學	升学	shēng-xué	*v.-o.*	enter a higher school
或	或	huò	*conj.*	or
壓力	压力	yālì	*n.*	pressure
至於	至于	zhìyú	*prep.*	as for; as to
激烈	激烈	jīliè	*adj.*	intense; sharp; fierce
盡	尽	jìn	*v.*	exert; exhaust

被淘汰。可是我並不同意＂美國是老年人的
墳場＂這個説法。

甲：聽説美國的老年人都得住老人院，孩子也不
常去看他們。這樣的生活不是和等死差不多
嗎？

乙：這倒不見得(2)。我的祖父母都住在老人院裏，
而且他們是自願去住老人院的，他們對那儿的
生活也相當滿意。他們覺得和子女住在一起，
不但失去了獨立和尊嚴，還加重了子女的負
擔，對孩子是不公平的。

甲：我的祖父母就(3)和我們住在一起。中國人把
這樣的生活叫做＂三代同堂＂，老年人一般
都覺得這是比較理想的晚年生活。我父母也

淘汰	淘汰	táotài	v.	eliminate through selection or competition; die out; fall into disuse
老人院	老人院	lǎorényuàn	v.	nursing home
不見得	不见得	bújiàn.dé		not necessarily; not likely
祖父母	祖父母	zǔfùmǔ	n.	grandparents
自願	自愿	zìyuàn	adv.	of one's own free will
滿意	满意	mǎnyì	adj.	satisfied; pleased

被淘汰。可是我并不同意美国是"老年人的
坟场"这个说法。

甲：听说美国的老年人都得住老人院，孩子也不
常去看他们。这样的生活不是和等死差不多
吗？

乙：这倒不见得⑵。我的祖父母都住在老人院里，
而且他们是自愿去住老人院的，他们对那儿的
生活也相当满意。他们觉得和子女住在一起，
不但失去了独立和尊严，还加重了子女的负
担，对孩子是不公平的。

甲：我的祖父母就⑶和我们住在一起。中国人把
这样的生活叫做"三代同堂"，老年人一般
都觉得这是比较理想的晚年生活。我父母也

獨立	独立	dúlì	n.	independence
尊嚴	尊严	zūnyán	n.	dignity; honor
加重	加重	jiāzhòng	v.	make or become heavier; increase the weight of
負擔	负担	fùdān	n.	burden; load
三代同堂	三代同堂	sāndài tóngtáng		three generations living under the same roof (part of the "big family" system in old China)
晚年	晚年	wǎnnián	n.	one's later years

不願意讓祖父母住進敬老院，他們覺得孝順
的孩子應該照顧父母的生活。

乙：美國的孩子並不是不孝順，我們也很愛我們
的父母，也願意照顧他們，但是我們覺得住
在一起並不是孝順最好的辦法。我的祖父母
一再表示他們不願意把他們的晚年變成孩子
的負擔，所以他們寧可住老人院。

甲：當然三代同堂也有三代同堂的問題。在中國
的城市裏，住房一向(4)比較緊張。三代人擠
在一個小單元裏，更增加了產生矛盾和摩擦
的可能。隨著工業化和現代化的快速發展，
我相信，以夫婦為(5)中心的小家庭一定會漸漸
取代三代同堂的大家庭。

願意	愿意	yuànyì	*v.*	be willing
敬老院	敬老院	jìnglǎoyuàn	*n.*	nursing home
孝順	孝顺	xiàoshùn	*v.*	show filial obedience
愛	爱	ài	*v.*	love
一向	一向	yíxiàng	*adv.*	always; all along
擠	挤	jǐ	*v.*	crowd; pack; cram

不愿意让祖父母住进敬老院，他们觉得孝顺的孩子应该照顾父母的生活。

乙：美国的孩子并不是不孝顺，我们也很爱我们的父母，也愿意照顾他们，但是我们觉得住在一起并不是孝顺最好的办法。我的祖父母一再表示他们不愿意把他们的晚年变成孩子的负担，所以他们宁可住老人院。

甲：当然三代同堂也有三代同堂的问题。在中国的城市里，住房一向(4)比较紧张。三代人挤在一个小单元里，更增加了产生矛盾和摩擦的可能。随着工业化和现代化的快速发展，我相信，以夫妇为(5)中心的小家庭一定会渐渐取代三代同堂的大家庭。

單元	单元	dānyuán	n.	unit
摩擦	摩擦	mócā	n.	clash (between two parties); friction
工業化	工业化	gōngyèhuà	n.	industrialization
快速	快速	kuàisù	adj.	fast; high-speed
以 A 爲 B	以 A 为 B	yǐ...wéi...		take A as B; regard A as B

第三十一課
中國的交通建設

最近幾年，中國政府在交通建設上做了很大的努力，投資的數量也相當高。鐵路方面，京九線的完成是一件大事。京九線把首都和南方的九龍連接起來(1)，對南北客運和貨運都是很重大的改進。公路方面，許多高速公路縮短了城市之間的距離。航空方面，新建了許多機場，使偏遠地區的人們，在一天之內(2)就能到達北京、上海等大城市。同時，中國也向歐美各國購買了許多新飛機。中

建設	建设	jiànshè	*n.*	construction
投資	投资	tóuzī	*v./n.*	invest, investment
數量	数量	shùliàng	*n.*	number; quantity
鐵路	铁路	tiělù	*n.*	railroad
京九線	京九线	Jīngjiǔxiàn		Beijing-Kowloon railway
完成	完成	wánchéng	*n./v.*	completion, complete
九龍	九龙	Jiǔlóng		Jiulong; Kowloon
連接	连接	liánjiē	*v.*	connect
客運	客运	kèyùn	*n.*	passenger transportation
貨運	货运	huòyùn	*n.*	cargo transportation

第三十一课
中国的交通建设

最近几年，中国政府在交通建设上做了很大的努力，投资的数量也相当高。铁路方面，京九线的完成是一件大事。京九线把首都和南方的九龙连接起来(1)，对南北客运和货运都是很重大的改进。公路方面，许多高速公路缩短了城市之间的距离。航空方面，新建了许多机场，使偏远地区的人们，在一天之内(2)就能到达北京、上海等大城市。同时，中国也向欧美各国购买了许多新飞机。中

重大	重大	zhòngdà	*adj.*	significant
改進	改进	gǎijìn	*v./n.*	improve, improvement
縮短	缩短	suōduǎn	*v.*	shorten
距離	距离	jùlí	*n.*	distance; disparity
航空	航空	hángkōng	*n.*	aviation
偏遠	偏远	piānyuǎn	*adj.*	remote; faraway
地區	地区	dìqū	*n.*	district; area
...之內	...之內	...zhīnèi		within...
到達	到达	dàodá	*v.*	arrive
購買	购买	gòumǎi	*v.*	purchase

國是美國波音公司最大的買主之一(3)。

　　中國的土地面積和美國的差不多一樣大，要把東南西北各個地區聯繫起來，非有現代化的交通不可(4)。城鄉的差距一直是中國經濟和文化發展上的一個大問題，而縮短城鄉差距最有效的方法，就是加強交通建設。

　　有了快速的現代交通，再加上(5)電話、電視、廣播深入農村，不但城鄉的距離可以縮小，對提倡普通話也很有幫助(6)。我真希望中國每一個地方的人都能說標準的普通話。這樣(7)，我離開北京到別的地方的時候，就不必擔心聽不懂當地的話了。

波音	波音	Bōyīn		Boeing
買主	买主	mǎizhǔ	n.	buyer
…之一	…之一	…zhīyī		one of …
土地	土地	tǔdì	n.	land
面積	面积	miànjī	n.	area (the product of the length times the width)
東南西北	东南西北	dōng nán xī běi		the east, the south, the west, and the north; every direction

国是美国波音公司最大的买主之一(3)。

中国的土地面积和美国的差不多一样大，要把东南西北各个地区联系起来，非有现代化的交通不可(4)。城乡的差距一直是中国经济和文化发展上的一个大问题，而缩短城乡差距最有效的方法，就是加强交通建设。

有了快速的现代交通，再加上(5)电话、电视、广播深入农村，不但城乡的距离可以缩小，对提倡普通话也很有帮助(6)。我真希望中国每一个地方的人都能说标准的普通话。这样(7)，我离开北京到别的地方的时候，就不必担心听不懂当地的话了。

聯繫	联系	liánxì	v.	intergrate; link
城鄉	城乡	chéngxiāng	adj.	urban and rural
差距	差距	chājù	n.	gap; disparity
加強	加强	jiāqiáng	v.	strengthen; enhance
再加上	再加上	zài jiā.shàng	conj.	on top of that; in addition
幫助	帮助	bāngzhù	v.	help
有幫助	有帮助	yǒu bāngzhù	adj.	helpful
離開	离开	líkāi	v.	leave

第三十二課

從大哥大到電子郵件

北京人真愛打電話！

無論在哪兒，無論在什麼時候，都可以看到北京人在打電話！開車的時候，走路的時候，吃飯的時候，甚至於在公園兒裏跟女朋友談戀愛的時候，都有人拿著手機，忙著和別人説話。

手機也叫做"大哥大"，是最近幾年才流行起來的。手機除了為人們提供通訊的便利以外，在一定程度上(1)也代表了那個人的身份和地位。

大哥大	大哥大	dàgēdà	n.	cellular phone
電子郵件	电子邮件	diànzǐ yóujiàn	n.	e-mail
甚至於	甚至于	shènzhìyú	conj.	even
手機	手机	shǒujī	n.	cellular phone
通訊	通讯	tōngxùn	n.	communication; correspondence

164

第三十二课
从大哥大到电子邮件

北京人真爱打电话！

无论在哪儿，无论在什么时候，都可以看到北
京人在打电话！开车的时候，走路的时候，吃饭
的时候，甚至于在公园儿里跟女朋友谈恋爱的时
候，都有人拿着手机，忙着和别人说话。

手机也叫做"大哥大"，是最近几年才流行
起来的。手机除了为人们提供通讯的便利以外，
在一定程度上(1)也代表了那个人的身分和地位。

便利	便利	biànlì	n.	convenience
程度	程度	chéngdù	n.	extent; degree
代表	代表	dàibiǎo	v.	represent
身份	身分	shēn.fèn	n.	status; identity; capacity

只有成功和重要的人才用得著 (2) 手機。改革開放
以後，很多人做生意賺了不少錢，用手機的人也
就越來越多了。

　有一次，我請了幾個朋友去飯館儿吃飯，在飯
桌上不是他們給朋友打電話，就是朋友給他們打
電話，結果我簡直沒什麼機會跟他們談話。他們
這麼忙，我真同情他們。

　除了大哥大，BP 機在北京也很普遍。BP 機也
叫 "呼機"。據 (3) 一個在摩托羅拉工作的朋友告訴

用得著	用得着	yòng.dézháo	v.-c.	find something useful; need
生意	生意	shēng.yì	n.	business
同情	同情	tóngqíng	v.	sympathize
...機	...机	...jī	suff.	... machine; ... gadget

只有成功和重要的人才用得着 (2) 手机。改革开放以后，很多人做生意赚了不少钱，用手机的人也就越来越多了。

有一次，我请了几个朋友去饭馆儿吃饭，在饭桌上不是他们给朋友打电话，就是朋友给他们打电话，结果我简直没什么机会跟他们谈话。他们这么忙，我真同情他们。

除了大哥大，BP机在北京也很普遍。BP机也叫"呼机"。据 (3) 一个在摩托罗拉工作的朋友告诉

BP 機	BP 机	...jī	*n.*	beeper
普遍	普遍	pǔbiàn	*adj.*	widespread; general; common
據	据	jù	*prep.*	according to
摩托羅拉	摩托罗拉	Mótuōluólā		Motorola

我，他們在全世界賣 BP 機，以 (4) 在中國賣出去的為最多。一個好的 BP 機不但可以用來 (5) 呼人，還可以看最新的氣象報告和股票行情，難怪 (6) 這麼受歡迎。

隨著中國和國際上聯繫的增加，我的許多北京朋友也已經有了電子郵件。這種最新的通訊方法，已經把全世界聯繫在一起了，使全世界成了一個 " 地球村 " 。不但中國走進了世界，世界也走進了中國。

呼人	呼人	hū-rén	v.-o.	call people; to page
氣象報告	气象报告	qìxiàng bàogào	n.	weather report
股票	股票	gǔpiào	n.	stock
行情	行情	hángqíng	n.	quotations (on the market); prices

我，他们在全世界卖 BP 机，以(4)在中国卖出去的为最多。一个好的 BP 机不但可以用来(5)呼人，还可以看最新的气象报告和股票行情，难怪(6)这么受欢迎。

随着中国和国际上联系的增加，我的许多北京朋友也已经有了电子邮件。这种最新的通讯方法，已经把全世界联系在一起了，使全世界成了一个"地球村"。不但中国走进了世界，世界也走进了中国。

難怪	难怪	nánguài	*conj.*	no wonder
歡迎	欢迎	huānyíng	*v.*	welcome
受歡迎	受欢迎	shòu huānyíng	*adj.*	be well received
地球村	地球村	dìqiúcūn	*n.*	the global village

第三十三課
開放留學政策

　　校園的佈告牌上貼著許多托福和GRE考試的廣告，大多是補習班教人怎麼預備這兩個考試的信息。據說每年有幾十萬大學本科生和研究生為了申請美國大學和研究生院而⑴參加這兩個考試。

　　我有個中國朋友很擔心地告訴我，要是中國的留學政策繼續開放下去，中國最優秀的人才都會到美國去了，這對中國的發展是不利的⑵。所以他主張中國政府限制學生出國，讓他們畢業以後留

佈告牌	布告牌	bùgàopái	*n.*	bulletin board
貼	貼	tiē	*v.*	paste; stick; glue
托福	托福	Tuōfú	*n.*	TOEFL
補習班	补习班	bǔxíbān	*n.*	cram school
預備	预备	yùbèi	*v.*	prepare
幾十萬	几十万	jǐshíwàn	*n.*	hundreds of thousands
本科生	本科生	běnkēshēng	*n.*	undergraduate student
研究生	研究生	yánjiūshēng	*n.*	graduate student
申請	申请	shēnqǐng	*v.*	apply for

第三十三课
开放留学政策

校园的布告牌上贴着许多托福和 GRE 考试的广告，大多是补习班教人怎么预备这两个考试的信息。据说每年有几十万大学本科生和研究生为了申请美国大学和研究生院而⑴参加这两个考试。

我有个中国朋友很担心地告诉我，要是中国的留学政策继续开放下去，中国最优秀的人才都会到美国去了，这对中国的发展是不利的⑵。所以他主张中国政府限制学生出国，让他们毕业以后留

研究生院	研究生院	yánjiū shēng yuàn	n.	graduate school
參加	参加	cānjiā	v.	attend
繼續	继续	jìxù	v.	continue
優秀	优秀	yōuxiù	adj.	outstanding; execllent
人才	人才	réncái	n.	a person of ability; a talented person
不利	不利	búlì	adj.	disadvantageous; harmful
主張	主张	zhǔzhāng	v.	advocate; maintain
限制	限制	xiànzhì	v.	limit
出國	出国	chū-guó	v.-o.	go abroad

在中國，為中國服務。這個説法當然不是完全沒有道理。許多發展中國家都面臨著"人才外流"的問題。二十年前的台灣、香港和新加坡也都討論過這個問題。但是現在這三個地區從海外回去的留學生越來越多了，他們都願意為自己的家鄉服務。所謂"人才外流"只是一個暫時的現象。我們不能因為人才暫時的流失就永遠不開放留學政策。

再説，不放寬留學政策只能限制大學生出國，並不能吸引已經在國外的留學生回國。只有開放的留學政策，再加上發達的經濟，才能吸引留學生回國。

只要中國在政治上繼續開放，在經濟上繼續發展，留學生回國，只是一個時間上的問題。

面臨	面临	miànlín	v.	be faced with; be confronted with
外流	外流	wàiliú	v.	outflow; drain
新加坡	新加坡	Xīnjiāpō		Singapore
討論	讨论	tǎolùn	v.	discuss
家鄉	家乡	jiāxiāng	n.	hometown

在中国，为中国服务。这个说法当然不是完全没有道理。许多发展中国家都面临着"人才外流"的问题。二十年前的台湾、香港和新加坡也都讨论过这个问题。但是现在这三个地区从海外回去的留学生越来越多了，他们都愿意为自己的家乡服务。所谓"人才外流"只是一个暂时的现象。我们不能因为人才暂时的流失就永远不开放留学政策。

再说，不放宽留学政策只能限制大学生出国，并不能吸引已经在国外的留学生回国。只有开放的留学政策，再加上发达的经济，才能吸引留学生回国。

只要中国在政治上继续开放，在经济上继续发展，留学生回国，只是一个时间上的问题。

暂時	暂时	zànshí	*adj.*	temporary; transient
流失	流失	liúshī	*v.*	run off; to be washed away
永遠	永远	yǒngyuǎn	*adv.*	forever
吸引	吸引	xīyǐn	*v.*	attract
回國	回国	huí-guó	*v.-o.*	return to one's country

第三十四課
下　崗

　　自從改革開放以來，下崗職工成了中國一個新的社會問題。下崗，在美國人看來，是失業或者提早退休；這兩個問題在任何一個市場經濟的社會中都存在，並不是新話題，可是對中國人來說，卻是一個新的挑戰。

　　中國老百姓過去幾十年來，總是把就業的責任放在政府或單位身上 (1)。從工作到住房，從保險到孩子的教育，都依靠政府或者單位的安排。現在因為改革開放，漸漸由計劃經濟轉向市場競爭，

下崗	下岗	xiàgǎng	v.	be laid off; be fired 下: step down, 岗: a post
職工	职工	zhígōng	n.	staff and workers
提早	提早	tízǎo	v.	shift to an earlier time; be earlier than planned or expected
退休	退休	tuìxiū	v.	retire
市場經濟	市场经济	shìchǎng jīngjì	n.	market economy
挑戰	挑战	tiǎozhàn	n./v.	challenge

第三十四课
下 岗

　　自从改革开放以来，下岗职工成了中国一个
新的社会问题。下岗，在美国人看来，是失业或者
提早退休；这两个问题在任何一个市场经济的社
会中都存在，并不是新话题，可是对中国人来说，
却是一个新的挑战。

　　中国老百姓过去几十年来，总是把就业的责任
放在政府或单位身上(1)。从工作到住房，从保险
到孩子的教育，都依靠政府或者单位的安排。现在
因为改革开放，渐渐由计划经济转向市场竞争，

單位	单位	dānwèi	*n.*	(work) unit
在…身上	在…身上	zài…shēn.shàng		on one's body
保險	保险	bǎoxiǎn	*n.*	insurance
或者	或者	huòzhě	*conj.*	或; or
計劃經濟	计划经济	jìhuà jīngjì	*n.*	planned economy
轉向	转向	zhuǎnxiàng	*v.*	转: turn, 向: towards

許多單位必須解雇過多的工作人員來減輕負擔；這也就是美國人所説的 " layoff "，在美國是常有的事。

在中國，一方面有下崗職工的問題，另一方面卻普遍存在 " 有人沒活儿幹，有活儿沒人幹 " 的矛盾現象。" 活儿 " 就是工作，" 幹 " 就是 " 做 "。換一句話説(2)，就是 " 有的人找不到工作，而有的工作卻找不到人。" 這一方面説明許多想找工作的人缺乏專業訓練，另一方面也表現了中國人自古以來看不起(3)體力工作的傳統。

中國人自古就把工作分成用腦力和用體力的

必須	必须	bìxū	v.	must
解雇	解雇	jiěgù	v.	lay off; fire
過 adj.	过 adj.	guò...		too; exceedingly
人員	人员	rényuán	n.	staff
減輕	减轻	jiǎnqīng	v.	alleviate
活儿	活儿	huór	n.	(colloquial) work
幹	干	gàn	v.	(colloquial) do

许多单位必须解雇过多的工作人员来减轻负担；这也就是美国人所说的 "layoff"，在美国是常有的事。

在中国，一方面有下岗职工的问题，另一方面却普遍存在 "有人没活儿干，有活儿没人干" 的矛盾现象。"活儿" 就是工作，"干" 就是 "做"。换一句话说(2)，就是 "有的人找不到工作，而有的工作却找不到人。" 这一方面说明许多想找工作的人缺乏专业训练，另一方面也表现了中国人自古以来看不起(3)体力工作的传统。

中国人自古就把工作分成用脑力和用体力的

專業	专业	zhuānyè	adj.	professional
自古以來	自古以来	zì gǔ yǐlái		since ancient times
看不起	看不起	kàn.bùqǐ	v.-c.	look down upon; despise
體力	体力	tǐlì	n.	physical strength
傳統	传统	chuántǒng	n.	tradition
分成	分成	fēnchéng	v.-c.	divide into
腦力	脑力	nǎolì	n.	brains; mental capability 脑: brain

兩類。用腦力的人往往是所謂的"知識份子"，而
用體力的主要是農民和工人。知識份子總認為用體
力來維持生活是一件不體面的事。有時他們寧可
下崗，也不去當工人。因此，要解決下崗職工再 (4)
就業的問題，還得從改變人們對工作的想法開始；
得讓人們覺得，所有的工作都是值得尊敬的，不
勞而獲才是可恥的。

　　許多人對下崗問題非常擔心，認為這是改革開
放中的一個危機，我卻不這樣想。我認為下崗所
反映的是中國過去經濟結構的不合理，而不是市
場經濟所帶來的不穩定。中國政府有勇氣面對這
個問題，堅持走改革開放的道路，是非常可喜的。

類	类	lèi	n.	category
農民	农民	nóngmín	n.	farmer
體面	体面	tǐ.miàn	adj./n.	honorable, dignity; face
當	当	dāng	v.	be; work as; serve as
尊敬	尊敬	zūnjìng	v.	respect a person (because of his age, status, or deeds)

两类。用脑力的人往往是所谓的"知识分子"，而用体力的主要是农民和工人。知识分子总认为用体力来维持生活是一件不体面的事。有时他们宁可下岗，也不去当工人。因此，要解决下岗职工再(4)就业的问题，还得从改变人们对工作的想法开始；得让人们觉得，所有的工作都是值得尊敬的，不劳而获才是可耻的。

许多人对下岗问题非常担心，认为这是改革开放中的一个危机，我却不这样想。我认为下岗所反映的是中国过去经济结构的不合理，而不是市场经济所带来的不稳定。中国政府有勇气面对这个问题，坚持走改革开放的道路，是非常可喜的。

不勞而獲	不劳而获	bù láo ér huò	*idm.*	gain without effort
可恥	可耻	kěchǐ	*adj.*	shameful
危機	危机	wēijī	*n.*	crisis; precarious point
合理	合理	hélǐ	*adj.*	reasonable
勇氣	勇气	yǒngqì	*n.*	courage
面對	面对	miànduì	*v.*	face; confront

第三十五課
北京的 " 古今中外 "

　　從元代 (1279-1368) 開始，北京就是中國的國都。由於這個特殊的歷史原因，在北京我們還可以看到許多保存完好的古代建築，像故宮、天壇、頤和園等。此外(1)，也有許多寺廟是明 (1368-1644) 清 (1644-1911) 兩朝的建築。北京城裏的街道也大致保持了原來的設計，以天安門為中心，向 (2) 四方伸展出去。正因為這種整齊的設計，北京人大都有很清楚的

元代	元代	Yuándài		Yuan Dynasty
國都	国都	guódū	*n.*	the national capital
保存	保存	bǎocún	*v.*	preserve
完好	完好	wánhǎo	*adj.*	intact; whole
天壇	天坛	Tiāntán		the Temple of Heaven
此外	此外	cǐwài	*adv.*	besides; moreover
寺廟	寺庙	sìmiào	*n.*	temple

第三十五课
北京的"古今中外"

  从元代 (1279-1368) 开始，北京就是中国的国都。由于这个特殊的历史原因，在北京我们还可以看到许多保存完好的古代建筑，像故宫、天坛、颐和园等。此外(1)，也有许多寺庙是明 (1368-1644) 清 (1644-1911) 两朝的建筑。北京城里的街道也大致保持了原来的设计，以天安门为中心，向 (2) 四方伸展出去。正因为这种整齐的设计，北京人大都有很清楚的

朝	朝	cháo	*n.*	dynasty
設計	设计	shèjì	*n./v.*	design
向	向	xiàng	*prep.*	toward
四方	四方	sìfāng	*n.*	four directions
伸展	伸展	shēnzhǎn	*v.*	extend; stretch
整齊	整齐	zhěngqí	*adj.*	orderly
大都	大都	dàdōu	*adv.*	for the most part; mostly

方向感。他們在說明方向的時候，很少說向左、向右，而是說往東、往西，或往南、往北。這當然要(3)比前後左右精確得多。

　　在北京可以看到五六百年前的建築，也可以看到最現代的摩天大樓。幾百年來變化不大的四合院儿和小胡同儿往往就保留在寬闊的環城公路旁邊儿。在衣食住行各方面，北京都是古今中外同時並存。最有趣的是時間上的古今和地理上的中外並存得非常協調。最現代的歐洲轎車和人力三輪

方向感	方向感	fāngxiànggǎn	n.	sense of direction
精確	精确	jīngquè	adj.	precise
摩天大樓	摩天大楼	mótiān dàlóu	n.	skyscraper
變化	变化	biànhuà	n./v.	change
四合院	四合院	sìhéyuàn	n.	a traditional Chinese-style compound with rooms around a courtyard
胡同儿	胡同儿	hútòngr	n.	traditional alleys in Beijing
寬闊	宽阔	kuānkuò	adj.	wide

方向感。他们在说明方向的时候，很少说向左、向右，而是说往东、往西，或往南、往北。这当然要(3)比前后左右精确得多。

在北京可以看到五六百年前的建筑，也可以看到最现代的摩天大楼。几百年来变化不大的四合院儿和小胡同儿往往就保留在宽阔的环城公路旁边儿。在衣食住行各方面，北京都是古今中外同时并存。最有趣的是时间上的古今和地理上的中外并存得非常协调。最现代的欧洲轿车和人力三轮

環城公路	环城公路	huánchéng gōnglù	n.	the roads circling the city
衣食住行	衣食住行	yī shí zhù xíng	idm.	"food, clothing, shelter and transportation" -- basic necessities of life
地理	地理	dìlǐ	n.	geography
協調	协调	xiétiáo	adj.	coordinate; harmonious
轎車	轿车	jiàochē	n.	sedan
人力	人力	rénlì	n.	human labor
三輪車	三轮车	sānlúnchē	n.	three-wheel cart

車同時在長安街上行駛；北京烤鴨和肯德基炸雞出現在同一幢樓裏；一方面能欣賞到地道的京劇和相聲，一方面又能看到正在上映的最新的美國電影。我還發現許多美國的電視影片都用中文配了音。在我看來，有一點兒彆扭，在中國人看來卻是再自然不過了(4)。

　　正是這種古今中外協調並存的現象，給北京增添了許多趣味和活力。

長安街	长安街	Cháng'ān Jiē		Chang'an Street
行駛	行驶	xíngshǐ	*v.*	(of a vehicle, ship, etc.) go; travel
肯德基	肯德基	Kěndéjī		Kentucky
炸雞	炸鸡	zhájī	*n.*	fried chicken
幢	幢	zhuàng	*an.*	measure word for building
欣賞	欣赏	xīnshǎng	*v.*	appreciate; enjoy
地道	地道	dì.dào	*adj.*	pure; typical
京劇	京剧	Jīngjù	*n.*	the Beijing Opera

车同时在长安街上行驶；北京烤鸭和肯德基炸鸡出现在同一幢楼里；一方面能欣赏到地道的京剧和相声，一方面又能看到正在上映的最新的美国电影。我还发现许多美国的电视影片都用中文配了音。在我看来，有一点儿别扭，在中国人看来却是再自然不过了(4)。

正是这种古今中外协调并存的现象，给北京增添了许多趣味和活力。

相聲	相声	xiàng.shēng	*n.*	traditional Chinese comic dialogue
上映	上映	shàngyìng	*v.*	show (a film)
影片	影片	yǐngpiān	*n.*	film
配音	配音	pèiyīn	*v.-o.*	dubb; synchronize
彆扭	别扭	biè.niǔ	*adj.*	awkward
增添	增添	zēngtiān	*v.*	add; increase
趣味	趣味	qùwèi	*n.*	fun; interest
活力	活力	huólì	*n.*	vigour; energy

第三十六課

各有所長

甲：中國最近十幾年來，汽車工業的發展非常快，私人汽車的數量和八十年代比起來增加了好幾倍。這是老百姓生活水平提高最好的證明。

乙：私人汽車增加當然很方便，可是也會帶來許多問題。中國人口多，都市很擁擠。如果人人都有汽車，不但停車是個問題，空氣污染也會更嚴重。所以我認為中國應該多發展公共交通建設，像鐵路、公路和飛機。這麼做，對大多數中國人可能更有幫助。

各有所長	各有所长	gè yǒu suǒ cháng	*idm.*	each has his own strong points
證明	证明	zhèngmíng	*n./v.*	proof, prove
人口	人口	rénkǒu	*n.*	population
都市	都市	dūshì	*n.*	city; metropolis

第三十六课
各有所长

甲：中国最近十几年来，汽车工业的发展非常
快，私人汽车的数量和八十年代比起来增加
了好几倍。这是老百姓生活水平提高最好的
证明。

乙：私人汽车增加当然很方便，可是也会带来许
多问题。中国人口多，都市很拥挤。如果人
人都有汽车，不但停车是个问题，空气污染
也会更严重。所以我认为中国应该多发展公
共交通建设，像铁路、公路和飞机。这麽做，
对大多数中国人可能更有帮助。

停車	停车	tíng-chē	v.-o.	park (one's car)
空氣	空气	kōngqì	n.	the air
污染	污染	wūrǎn	n.	pollution
大多數	大多数	dàduōshù	n.	great majority

甲：其實，中國的公共交通建設是相當不錯的，
尤其是在大城市裏，都有非常便宜的公共汽
車、電車或地鐵。不過，現在大家的收入增
加了，在生活上也想有點ㄦ享受，過點ㄦ舒服
日子。買輛汽車，裝個空調，不算是 (1) 奢侈浪
費。美國哪個家庭沒有汽車、空調啊？

乙：中國和美國的情形不一樣。美國的土地不比
中國小 (2)，可是人口只有中國的五分之一 (3)；
中國不比美國大，可是人口卻是美國的五倍。
所以中國的發展方式不能跟美國的完全一樣。

甲：發展的方式不能完全一樣，這我同意。但是
舒適不舒適是有個客觀的標準的。汽車比

電車	电车	diànchē	*n.*	tram
地鐵	地铁	dìtiě	*n.*	subway
享受	享受	xiǎngshòu	*n.*	ease and comfort; enjoyment
過日子	过日子	guò rìzi	*v.-o.*	lead a life
輛	辆	liàng	*an.*	measure word for cars
裝	装	zhuāng	*v.*	set up; install
算是	算是	suàn.shì	*v.*	be considered as; be regarded as

甲：其实，中国的公共交通建设是相当不错的，
尤其是在大城市里，都有非常便宜的公共汽
车、电车或地铁。不过，现在大家的收入增
加了，在生活上也想有点儿享受，过点儿舒服
日子。买辆汽车，装个空调，不算是(1)奢侈浪
费。美国哪个家庭没有汽车、空调啊？

乙：中国和美国的情形不一样。美国的土地不比
中国小(2)，可是人口只有中国的五分之一(3)；
中国不比美国大，可是人口却是美国的五倍。
所以中国的发展方式不能跟美国的完全一样。

甲：发展的方式不能完全一样，这我同意。但是
舒适不舒适是有个客观的标准的。汽车比

奢侈	奢侈	shēchǐ	adj.	luxurious; extravagant
情形	情形	qíng.xíng	n.	situation
五分之一	五分之一	wǔ fēn zhī yī		one fifth
倍	倍	bèi	n.	times; -fold
舒适	舒适	shūshì	adj./n.	comfortable; comfort
客观	客观	kèguān	adj.	objective

自行車方便，有空調的屋子比沒有空調的舒服，抽水馬桶比傳統的廁所衛生，這不都是很明顯的嗎？

乙：你總是說舒服、方便。你要知道，舒服方便的東西不一定對健康有幫助。我真羨慕中國人能騎自行車上下班。這不但解決了交通堵塞的問題，還為個每人提供了運動的機會。在美國許多大城市裏，並沒有為自行車預備的車道，就是(4)要騎車上下班也做不到。

甲：當然，每一種制度、每一種生活方式都有長處也都有短處。這就叫做 " 各有所長，各有所短 "。短處應該改進，長處應該保持。

抽水馬桶	抽水马桶	chōushuǐ mǎtǒng	n.	flushing toilet
羨慕	羡慕	xiànmù	v.	envy
上下班	上下班	shàngxià bān	v.-o.	go back and forth to work; 上班 : go to work 下班 : get off work

自行车方便，有空调的屋子比没有空调的舒服，抽水马桶比传统的厕所卫生，这不都是很明显的吗？

乙：你总是说舒服、方便。你要知道，舒服方便的东西不一定对健康有帮助。我真羡慕中国人能骑自行车上下班。这不但解决了交通堵塞的问题，还为每个人提供了运动的机会。在美国许多大城市里，并没有为自行车预备的车道，就是(4)要骑车上下班也做不到。

甲：当然，每一种制度、每一种生活方式都有长处也都有短处。这就叫做"各有所长，各有所短"。短处应该改进，长处应该保持。

運動	运动	yùndòng	v.	exercise
車道	车道	chēdào	n.	(traffic) lane
長處	长处	cháng.chù	n.	strong point; good point
短處	短处	duǎn.chù	n.	shortcoming; weakness

第三十七課
懷　舊

　　今天我去琉璃廠買了一本 1969 年出版的《毛主席語錄》。我發現只有外國人在那家書店裏翻看文革時期的雜誌和當年的一些宣傳畫儿。

　　外國人來到中國，常常帶著一定的懷舊情緒。他們在找一個過去的中國。早一點儿的是明代（1368-1644）清代（1644-1911）的中國，晚一點儿的是文革時期（1966-1976）的中國。

　　這次來到北京以後，我才發現外國專家學者在美國所經常討論的話題，並不見得是一般中國人最感興趣(1)的題目。例如 "文化大革命"，在美國，

懷舊	怀旧	huáijiù	v.	a sense of nostalgia; nostalgic sentiments; recollect the good old days
語錄	语录	yǔlù	n.	recorded utterance; quotation
翻看	翻看	fānkàn	v.	browse; glance over; leaf through
文革	文革	Wéngé		an abbreviation of 文化大革命; Cultural Revolution

第三十七课
怀 旧

今天我去琉璃厂买了一本 1969 年出版的《毛主席语录》。我发现只有外国人在那家书店里翻看文革时期的杂志和当年的一些宣传画儿。

外国人来到中国，常常带着一定的怀旧情绪。他们在找一个过去的中国。早一点儿的是明代（1368-1644）清代（1644-1911）的中国，晚一点儿的是文革时期（1966-1976）的中国。

这次来到北京以后，我才发现外国专家学者在美国所经常讨论的话题，并不见得是一般中国人最感兴趣 (1) 的题目。例如"文化大革命"，在美国，

時期	时期	shíqī	*n.*	(time) period
當年	当年	dāngnián	*t.w.*	in those years (days)
情緒	情绪	qíngxù	*n.*	feeling; sentiments
專家	专家	zhuānjiā	*n.*	expert
感興趣	感兴趣	gǎn xìngqù	*v.*	be interested in

到今天還是 "當代中國" 研究的主要議題，但是現在談 "文革" 的中國人實在並不很多了。

"文革" 對中國人來說，是過去的歷史。現在他們對 "外資企業"、"合資企業" 和 "商品房" 的興趣遠遠超過對 "文革" 的興趣。對一個二十幾歲的年輕人來說，"文革" 只剩下一個模糊的印象；就像越南戰爭，對美國大學生來說，已經是他們出生以前的歷史了。

有些外國人，一提起中國，就聯想到 "農業社會"、"大家庭"、"小老婆"、"纏腳"、

當代	当代	dāngdài	*adj.*	contemporary
議題	议题	yìtí	*n.*	subject under discussion; issue
外資	外资	wàizī	*n.*	foreign capital
合資	合资	hézī	*adj.*	joint venture
遠遠	远远	yuǎnyuǎn	*adv.*	far (in degree); by far
超過	超过	chāoguò	*v.*	exceed
剩下	剩下	shèng.xià	*v.*	be left (over); remain
模糊	模糊	mó.hú	*adj.*	vague; blurred

到今天还是"当代中国"研究的主要议题，但是现在谈"文革"的中国人实在并不很多了。

"文革"对中国人来说，是过去的历史。现在他们对"外资企业"、"合资企业"和"商品房"的兴趣远远超过对"文革"的兴趣。对一个二十几岁的年轻人来说，"文革"只剩下一个模糊的印象；就像越南战争，对美国大学生来说，已经是他们出生以前的历史了。

有些外国人，一提起中国，就联想到"农业社会"、"大家庭"、"小老婆"、"缠脚"、

越南	越南	Yuènán		Vietnam
戰爭	战争	zhànzhēng	n.	war
出生	出生	chūshēng	v.	be born
提起	提起	tí-qǐ	v.-c.	mention; speak of
聯想	联想	liánxiǎng	v.	associate; connect in the mind
農業	农业	nóngyè	n.	agriculture
小老婆	小老婆	xiǎolǎo.pó	n.	mistress; concubine
纏腳	缠脚	chánjiǎo	v.-o.	foot-binding

"舞龍"、"舞獅"這些所謂的中國傳統。其實這些 "中國特色" 不是早已不存在，就是正在快速地消失。

一個在現代中國城市裏長大的孩子，從小喝可口可樂，吃麥當勞，看美國電視片，穿牛仔褲、T恤，騎山地車，玩電子遊戲，他們和美國孩子的不同越來越小了。要想在現代的北京找到古代的中國，恐怕不是很容易了。

在中國看不到舞龍、舞獅，老外難免 (2) 有點儿失望，但是高興也好，失望也好 (3)，中國的現代化是擋不住的。

舞龍	舞龙	wǔ-lóng	v.-o.	Chinese dragon dance
舞獅	舞狮	wǔ-shī	v.-o.	Chinese lion dance
消失	消失	xiāoshī	v.	disappear
從小	从小	cóngxiǎo		from childhood
麥當勞	麦当劳	Màidāngláo		McDonald's
牛仔褲	牛仔裤	niúzǎikù	n.	jeans
T恤	T恤	tī xù	n.	T-shirt
山地車	山地车	shāndìchē	n.	mountain bike

"舞龙"、"舞狮"这些所谓的中国传统。其实这些"中国特色"不是早已不存在，就是正在快速地消失。

一个在现代中国城市里长大的孩子，从小喝可口可乐，吃麦当劳，看美国电视片，穿牛仔裤、T恤，骑山地车，玩电子遊戏，他们和美国孩子的不同越来越小了。要想在现代的北京找到古代的中国，恐怕不是很容易了。

在中国看不到舞龙、舞狮，老外难免(2)有点儿失望，但是高兴也好，失望也好(3)，中国的现代化是挡不住的。

電子遊戲	电子遊戏	diànzǐ yóuxì	n.	video game; 电子: electronic; 遊戏: game
恐怕	恐怕	kǒngpà	adv.	be afraid
老外	老外	lǎowài	n.	(colloquial) foreigner
難免	难免	nánmiǎn	adv./adj.	hard to avoid, inevitable
失望	失望	shīwàng	v.	be disappointed
高興	高兴	gāoxìng	adj.	happy
擋不住	挡不住	dǎng.bú zhù	v.-c.	be unable to (be) resist(ed); be unable to (be) stop(ped)

第三十八課
學習外語

　　每天早晨，在校園裏都能看到許多中國學生在專心地學習英文，有的念課本，有的聽收音機。我還在報上看見天津一家百貨商場在商場裏設了一個"英語橋"，要以(1)這個用英語交流的場所來吸引顧客。果然(2)，這個場地一出現，立刻引起了大家的注意，"英語橋"上熱鬧得不得了(3)。許多人覺得一邊兒買東西，一邊兒(4)練習英語實在是一舉兩得。北京的公園兒、街頭、校園也常有所謂"英語角"，任何人都可以到這樣的地方來用英語互

外語	外语	wàiyǔ	*n.*	foreign language
專心	专心	zhuānxīn	*adv./adj.*	concentrate one's attention; be absorbed
課本	课本	kèběn	*n.*	textbook
天津	天津	Tiānjīn		Tianjin
橋	桥	qiáo	*n.*	bridge
以	以	yǐ		用; use
場所	场所	chǎngsuǒ	*n.*	place; arena (for certain activities)
果然	果然	guǒrán	*adv.*	as expected; sure enough

第三十八课
学习外语

　　每天早晨，在校园里都能看到许多中国学生在专心地学习英文，有的念课本，有的听收音机。我还在报上看见天津一家百货商场在商场里设了一个"英语桥"，要以(1)这个用英语交流的场所来吸引顾客。果然(2)，这个场地一出现，立刻引起了大家的注意，"英语桥"上热闹得不得了(3)。许多人觉得一边儿买东西，一边儿(4)练习英语实在是一举两得。北京的公园儿、街头、校园也常有所谓"英语角"，任何人都可以到这样的地方来用英语互

場地	场地	chǎngdì	n.	site; space; place
引起	引起	yǐnqǐ	v.	raise; arouse
熱鬧	热闹	rè.nào	v.	a scene of bustle and excitement
不得了	不得了	bùdéliǎo	adv.	extremely; exceedingly
一舉兩得	一举两得	yì jǔ liǎng dé	idm.	kill two birds with one stone
街頭	街头	jiētóu	p.w.	street corner; street
角	角	jiǎo	n.	corner

相 (5) 交談。

　　中國孩子一進初中就必須學習英語，有的甚至從小學就開始了，中年人學英語的也很多。這一方面當然是因為英語是世界上最通行的一種語言，另一方面也反映了中國人對學習外來事物的熱情。

　　美國中文教學的歷史相當短。一般大學到了七十年代才開始教中文。第二次世界大戰以前，只有少數大學開中文課。美國大學的文學、歷史和語言課程一向是以歐美為中心；一直到朝鮮戰爭以後，美國才漸漸認識到太平洋地區—尤其是中國和日本，在國際事務上的重要性。

互相	互相	hùxiāng	*adv.*	mutually; with each other
初中	初中	chūzhōng	*n.*	middle school
通行	通行	tōngxíng	*adj.*	current; general
外來	外来	wàilái	*adj.*	outside; external; foreign
事物	事物	shìwù	*n.*	thing; object
第二次世界大戰	第二次世界大战	Dì'èr Cì Shìjiè Dàzhàn		the Second World War (1939-1945)

相 (5) 交谈。

中国孩子一进初中就必须学习英语，有的甚至从小学就开始了，中年人学英语的也很多。这一方面当然是因为英语是世界上最通行的一种语言，另一方面也反映了中国人对学习外来事物的热情。

美国中文教学的历史相当短。一般大学到了七十年代才开始教中文。第二次世界大战以前，只有少数大学开中文课。美国大学的文学、历史和语言课程一向是以欧美为中心；一直到朝鲜战争以后，美国才渐渐认识到太平洋地区—尤其是中国和日本，在国际事务上的重要性。

少數	少数	shǎoshù	*adj.*	small number; few
開	开	kāi	*v.*	offer (a course, chiefly in college)
課程	课程	kèchéng	*n.*	course; curriculum
朝鮮戰爭	朝鲜战争	Cháoxiān Zhànzhēng	*n.*	the Korean War (1950-1953)
太平洋	太平洋	Tàipíngyáng	*n.*	the Pacific Ocean
事務	事务	shìwù	*n.*	general affairs
重要性	重要性	zhòngyàoxìng	*n.*	importance

最近幾年，學習亞洲語言的美國學生雖然增加了一些，但畢竟(6)還是少數。隨著中美關係的改善，我相信學習中文的學生也會不斷地增加。

中國學生學習英語也好，美國學生學習中文也好，大多數人都有一個功利的動機，希望學會一種外語，對將來找工作有好處。這當然沒有什麼不對。但是，我之所以(7)學習中文，是希望通過語言的學習來進一步了解中國的社會和中國人的生活。我認為這比找到工作更有意義。

亞洲	亚洲	Yàzhōu	n.	Asia
畢竟	毕竟	bìjìng	adv.	after all
改善	改善	gǎishàn	n./v.	improvement, improve
不斷	不断	búduàn	adv.	constantly; continuously
功利	功利	gōnglì	n.	utility; material gain
動機	动机	dòngjī	n.	motive; intention
將來	将来	jiānglái	t.w./n.	future
之所以	之所以	zhīsuǒyǐ	conj.	the reason that
通過	通过	tōngguò	prep.	by means of; by way of

最近几年，学习亚洲语言的美国学生虽然增加了一些，但毕竟(6)还是少数。随着中美关系的改善，我相信学习中文的学生也会不断地增加。

中国学生学习英语也好，美国学生学习中文也好，大多数人都有一个功利的动机，希望学会一种外语，对将来找工作有好处。这当然没有什么不对。但是，我之所以(7)学习中文，是希望通过语言的学习来进一步了解中国的社会和中国人的生活。我认为这比找到工作更有意义。

第三十九課
看電視

甲：據北京《光明日報》最近的報導，看電視已經成了中國城鎮居民最主要的休閒活動。這是近年來一個新的發展。

乙：這個現象產生的原因是什麼呢？

甲：我想，看電視的人口快速增加和電視機的普及是很有關係的。據統計，1985年中國城鎮居民每(1)一百戶家庭只有17.2台彩色電視機。到了1997年，平均每一戶都至少(2)有一台彩電了。電視機增加得這麼快，看電視的人自然就越來越多了。

乙：我認為，電視機增加，只是看電視人口增加

光明日報	光明日报	Guāngmíng Rìbào	*n.*	Guangming Daily; 光明: light, bright
城鎮	城镇	chéngzhèn	*n.*	city and town
近年來	近年来	jìnniánlái		最近几年来
電視機	电视机	diànshìjī	*n.*	television set
普及	普及	pǔjí	*v.*	be available to all; popularize

第三十九课
看电视

甲：据北京《光明日报》最近的报道，看电视已
　　经成了中国城镇居民最主要的休闲活动。这
　　是近年来一个新的发展。

乙：这个现象产生的原因是什么呢？

甲：我想，看电视的人口快速增加和电视机的普
　　及是很有关系的。据统计，1985年中国城镇
　　居民每(1)一百户家庭只有17.2台彩色电视机。
　　到了1997年，平均每一户都至少(2)有一台彩
　　电了。电视机增加得这么快，看电视的人自
　　然就越来越多了。

乙：我认为，电视机增加，只是看电视人口增加

統計	统计	tǒngjì	*n./v.*	statistics, add up; count
戶	户	hù	*an./n.*	household
17.2	17.2	shíqī diǎn èr		17.2
台	台	tái	*an.*	measure word for machines
彩色	彩色	cǎisè	*adj.*	color
平均	平均	píngjūn	*adv./adj.*	average
至少	至少	zhìshǎo	*adv.*	at least

的原因之一。節目內容的改變影響也很大。

甲：你說得對極了。最近幾年，中國電視在節目內容上有了相當的改變。比方說，政治宣傳減少了，娛樂性和服務性的節目增加了。新聞報導也開始反映一些社會和政治上的問題。這些改變都是老百姓所歡迎的。當然，色情和暴力也漸漸在節目中出現，但比起美國的電視節目來，中國的節目還是乾淨得多。

乙：我覺得中國的電視節目太乾淨了點儿，看起來有點儿無聊。

甲：這是因為我們認為電視節目起著社會教育的作用。為了孩子和社會道德，電視節目應該受到控制。

乙：我對你的看法很不以為然。電視節目應該反

節目	节目	jiémù	n.	(TV, radio, etc.) show; program
內容	内容	nèiróng	n.	content
娛樂	娱乐	yúlè	n.	entertainment
色情	色情	sèqíng	n.	pornography

的原因之一。节目内容的改变影响也很大。

甲：你说得对极了。最近几年，中国电视在节目内容上有了相当的改变。比方说，政治宣传减少了，娱乐性和服务性的节目增加了。新闻报道也开始反映一些社会和政治上的问题。这些改变都是老百姓所欢迎的。当然，色情和暴力也渐渐在节目中出现。但比起美国的电视节目来，中国的节目还是干净得多。

乙：我觉得中国的电视节目太干净了点儿，看起来有点儿无聊。

甲：这是因为我们认为电视节目起着社会教育的作用。为了孩子和社会道德，电视节目应该受到控制。

乙：我对你的看法很不以为然。电视节目应该反

暴力	暴力	bàolì	*n.*	violence
無聊	无聊	wúliáo	*adj.*	boring, silly; stupid
控制	控制	kòngzhì	*v.*	control
對… 不以爲然	对… 不以为然	duì… bù yǐ wéi rán	*v.*	object to; do not approve

映社會現實。無論什麼問題，電視都可以報導。過分保護孩子，反而常常害了孩子，使他們不了解社會上的許多問題。

甲：這我同意。但是像美國那樣色情和暴力泛濫，也不理想啊！

乙：其實，美國並不像你想像的那麼亂。我們也(3)還是有許多法律保護孩子的。好比說在許多州，21歲以下(4)的人不許在公開場合買酒或喝酒。這在中國人看來，就不容易理解了。

甲：每一個國家都有自己的風俗和法律，這叫做"國情不同"。

乙：對了。因為"國情不同"，所以我們得互相尊重。

現實	现实	xiànshí	n.	reality; actuality
保護	保护	bǎohù	v.	protect
害	害	hài	v.	harm
泛濫	泛滥	fànlàn	v.	overrun
好比說	好比说	hǎobǐshuō		for example

映社会现实。无论什么问题，电视都可以报
道。过分保护孩子，反而常常害了孩子，使
他们不了解社会上的许多问题。

甲：这我同意。但是像美国那样色情和暴力泛滥，
也不理想啊！

乙：其实，美国并不像你想像的那么乱。我们也(3)
还是有许多法律保护孩子的。好比说在许多
州，21岁以下(4)的人不许在公开场合买酒或喝
酒。这在中国人看来，就不容易理解了。

甲：每一个国家都有自己的风俗和法律，这叫做
"国情不同"。

乙：对了。因为"国情不同"，所以我们得互相
尊重。

州	州	zhōu	n.	state
...以下	...以下	...yǐxià	postp.	under (a given point or line)
不許	不许	bùxǔ	v.	not allow; must not
風俗	风俗	fēngsú	n.	common customs
國情	国情	guóqíng	n.	state of a nation

第四十課

中國的書法

　　中國的書法是一種技術，也是一種藝術。書法在中國已經有兩三千年的歷史，是傳統教育中很重要的一部分。一個受過良好教育的人應該能寫一手漂亮的字。

　　書法對中國人來説，絕不 (1) 只是寫字。許多人相信書法不但能表現一個人的教育水平，也可以反映一個人的個性。所以在古時候，一個人書法的好壞往往會影響到科舉考試的結果。一個完全不會書法的人很難通過最高學位的考試，也不容

書法	书法	shūfǎ	*n.*	calligraphy
技術	技术	jìshù	*n.*	skill; technique
藝術	艺术	yìshù	*n.*	art
良好	良好	liánghǎo	*adj.*	good
手	手	shǒu	*an.*	measure word for skills or abilities

第四十课
中国的书法

中国的书法是一种技术，也是一种艺术。书法在中国已经有两三千年的历史，是传统教育中很重要的一部分。一个受过良好教育的人应该能写一手漂亮的字。

书法对中国人来说，绝不(1)只是写字。许多人相信书法不但能表现一个人的教育水平，也可以反映一个人的个性。所以在古时候，一个人书法的好坏往往会影响到科举考试的结果。一个完全不会书法的人很难通过最高学位的考试，也不容

絕不	绝不	juébù	*adv.*	absolutely not
個性	个性	gèxìng	*n.*	individual character; personality
科擧	科举	kējǔ	*n.*	imperial examinations
學位	学位	xuéwèi	*n.*	academic degree; degree

易分配到理想的工作。因此，古時候的"舉人""進士"和一般的地方官吏大多能寫一手漂亮的字。

中國人常常把繪畫和書法放在一起，稱作"書畫"。一幅好的中國畫儿少不了作者在畫儿上寫幾個字或作一首詩，書法成了畫儿的一部分。而一個理想的傳統文人除了要能書會畫以外，還得會彈琴和下棋。因此"琴棋書畫"這四個字常常用來描寫一個人多才多藝。由於中國人特別重視書法，因此對筆墨紙硯也非常講究，把這四種東西叫做"文房四寶"。

舉人	举人	jǔrén	*n.*	a successful candidate in the imperial examination at the provincial level in the Ming and Qing dynasties
進士	进士	jìnshì	*n.*	a successful candidate in the highest imperial examination
地方	地方	dìfāng	*adj.*	local
官吏	官吏	guānlì	*n.*	(archaic) government officials
繪畫	绘画	huìhuà	*n.*	drawing; painting
稱作	称作	chēngzuò	*v.*	be called
作者	作者	zuòzhě	*n.*	author; writer
首	首	shǒu	*an.*	measure word for poems, songs

易分配到理想的工作。因此，古时候的"举人""进士"和一般的地方官吏大多能写一手漂亮的字。

中国人常常把绘画和书法放在一起，称作"书画"。一幅好的中国画儿少不了作者在画儿上写几个字或作一首诗，书法成了画儿的一部分。而一个理想的传统文人除了要能书会画以外，还得会弹琴和下棋。因此"琴棋书画"这四个字常常用来描写一个人多才多艺。由于中国人特别重视书法，因此对笔墨纸砚也非常讲究，把这四种东西叫做"文房四宝"。

詩	诗	shī	*n.*	poem; poetry
文人	文人	wénrén	*n.*	man of letters; scholar; literati
彈琴	弹琴	tán-qín	*v.-o.*	play a stringed musical instrument
描寫	描写	miáoxiě	*v.*	describe; depict; portray
多才多藝	多才多艺	duōcái duōyì	*idm.*	versatile; gifted in many ways
墨	墨	mò	*n.*	Chinese ink; ink stick
硯	砚	yàn	*n.*	ink stone; ink slab
文房四寶	文房四宝	wénfáng sìbǎo	*n.*	the four treasures of the study

　　自從鉛筆和鋼筆在二十世紀初年漸漸取代了毛筆以後，中國的書法就不像從前那麼受到重視了。許多人認為寫字的目的只是為了傳達意思，寫得漂亮不漂亮又有什麼關係呢 (2)！而且用毛筆來寫字畢竟沒有用圓珠筆或者鋼筆那麼方便，所以書法漸漸成了只有少數人會做的事了。

　　最近幾年用電腦打字的人越來越多，寫字的人就更少了。打字不但方便，而且比手寫更快、更清楚。

　　一種藝術的興起和衰落不但和當時的政治、教育制度有關係，和一種新工具的發明更是分不開的。

鉛筆	铅笔	qiānbǐ	n.	pencil
鋼筆	钢笔	gāngbǐ	n.	fountain pen
世紀	世纪	shìjì	n.	century
初年	初年	chūnián	n.	initial stage; early years
毛筆	毛笔	máobǐ	n.	writing brush
目的	目的	mùdì	n.	purpose; goal; aim
傳達	传达	chuándá	v.	pass on; communicate

　　自从铅笔和钢笔在二十世纪初年渐渐取代了
毛笔以后，中国的书法就不像从前那么受到重视
了。许多人认为写字的目的只是为了传达意思，
写得漂亮不漂亮又有什么关系呢 (2)！而且用毛笔
来写字毕竟没有用圆珠笔或者钢笔那么方便，所
以书法渐渐成了只有少数人会做的事了。

　　最近几年用电脑打字的人越来越多，写字的
人就更少了。打字不但方便，而且比手写更快、
更清楚。

　　一种艺术的兴起和衰落不但和当时的政治、教
育制度有关系，和一种新工具的发明更是分不开
的。

圓珠筆	圆珠笔	yuánzhūbǐ	*n.*	ballpoint pen
打字	打字	dǎ-zì	*v.-o.*	type
興起	兴起	xīngqǐ	*n./v.*	rise; spring up
衰落	衰落	shuāiluò	*n./v.*	decline
當時	当时	dāngshí	*t.w.*	then; at that time
發明	发明	fāmíng	*n./v.*	invention; invent
分開	分开	fēnkāi	*v.-c.*	separate; part

第四十一課
白話文和文言文

　　許多人以為白話文就是現代漢語，文言文就是古代漢語，而且是兩種完全不同的語言，我認為這個看法是不正確的。

　　文言文是古代漢語的書面形式。從春秋戰國（公元前五世紀）一直到清代末期（二十世紀初年），差不多有兩千五百多年的時間，中國的書面語有個基本的形式，就是文言文。文言文和口語的距離相當大，並不反映任何地方的方言。中國的方言很多，說不同方言的人往往聽不懂對方的話，所以這種不反映口語的書面語言就成了溝通

白話文	白话文	báihuàwén	*n.*	vernacular writing
文言文	文言文	wényánwén	*n.*	classical style of writing
漢語	汉语	Hànyǔ	*n.*	Chinese language
正確	正确	zhèngquè	*adj.*	correct; right
書面	书面	shūmiàn	*adj.*	written; in written form
春秋	春秋	Chūnqiū		the Spring and Autumn Period (770-476 B.C.)

第四十一课
白话文和文言文

　　许多人以为白话文就是现代汉语，文言文就是古代汉语，而且是两种完全不同的语言，我认为这个看法是不正确的。

　　文言文是古代汉语的书面形式。从春秋战国（公元前五世纪）一直到清代末期（二十世纪初年），差不多有两千五百多年的时间，中国的书面语有个基本的形式，就是文言文。文言文和口语的距离相当大，并不反映任何地方的方言。中国的方言很多，说不同方言的人往往听不懂对方的话，所以这种不反映口语的书面语言就成了沟通

戰國	战国	Zhànguó	*n.*	the Warring States Period (475-221 B.C.)
公元	公元	gōngyuán		the Christian era 公元1999年：A.D. 1999 公元前221年：221 B.C.
末期	末期	mòqī	*n.*	last phase; final phase
書面語	书面语	shūmiànyǔ	*n.*	written language
口語	口语	kǒuyǔ	*n.*	spoken language

最好的工具。二十世紀初年，有些提倡白話文的學者説文言文是"死文字"，其實兩千多年以來文言文一直是個非常有效的書面語言。

　　隨著時代的改變，中國和西方的接觸增加了，大量的翻譯名詞進入了日常生活，像科學、民主這些詞都是外來語。有的外來語是從英文直接翻譯成中文的，有的是通過日文再譯成中文的。新詞彙的不斷增加，使文言文不能再適應新時代的需要，於是 (1)白話文就漸漸取代了文言文。

　　白話文普及的另外一個重要原因是二十年代推行國語。因為白話文和口語的距離比文言文小得

文字	文字	wénzì	*n.*	characters; writing
大量	大量	dàliàng	*adj.*	a large number
翻譯	翻译	fānyì	*v.*	translate
科學	科学	kēxué	*n.*	science
民主	民主	mínzhǔ	*n.*	democracy

最好的工具。二十世纪初年，有些提倡白话文的学者说文言文是"死文字"，其实两千多年以来文言文一直是个非常有效的书面语言。

　　随着时代的改变，中国和西方的接触增加了，大量的翻译名词进入了日常生活，像科学、民主这些词都是外来语。有的外来语是从英文直接翻译成中文的，有的是通过日文再译成中文的。新词汇的不断增加，使文言文不能再适应新时代的需要，于是 (1)白话文就渐渐取代了文言文。

　　白话文普及的另外一个重要原因是二十年代推行国语。因为白话文和口语的距离比文言文小得

外來語	外来语	wàiláiyǔ	*n.*	loan words
日文	日文	Rìwén	*n.*	Japanese language
詞彙	词汇	cíhuì	*n.*	vocabulary
適應	适应	shìyìng	*v.*	suit; adapt; fit

多，提倡國語就成了推行白話文一個重要的基礎。但是白話文和文言文並不是完全沒有關係，許多白話的說法其實是從古代沿用下來(2)的，所以要真正學好現代漢語，古代漢語是不可不(3)學的。

要是你去過台灣、香港或新加坡，你可能會發現當地有些報紙或廣告寫的雖然是漢字，你卻看不懂它們的意思。這是因為有時候他們用漢字寫方言而不寫普通話的緣故。這麼一來(4)，不說這個方言的人就完全看不懂了，而且容易引起誤會。因此，我主張中國人都應該用漢字寫普通話。

沿用	沿用	yányòng	*v.*	continue to use (an old method, etc.)
真正	真正	zhēnzhèng	*adv.*	really
這麼一來	这么一来	zhème yìlái		in so doing

多，提倡国语就成了推行白话文一个重要的基础。但是白话文和文言文并不是完全没有关系，许多白话的说法其实是从古代沿用下来(2)的，所以要真正学好现代汉语，古代汉语是不可不(3)学的。

要是你去过台湾、香港或新加坡，你可能会发现当地有些报纸或广告写的虽然是汉字，你却看不懂它们的意思。这是因为有时候他们用汉字写方言而不写普通话的缘故。这么一来(4)，不说这个方言的人就完全看不懂了，而且容易引起误会。因此，我主张中国人都应该用汉字写普通话。

第四十二課
香 港

　　1997 年 7 月 1 日是中國近代史上一個重要的日子。從這一天起，中國對香港恢復行使主權，結束了香港一個半世紀的殖民地歷史。

　　在 1840 年到 1842 年的鴉片戰爭中，中國被英國打敗了。清朝政府除了付給英國大量的賠款以外，還把香港割讓給了英國。鴉片戰爭是帝國主義侵略中國的開始。從此以後的一百多年，中國一再

近代史	近代史	jìndàishǐ	*n.*	modern history
日子	日子	rìzi	*n.*	date; day
恢復	恢复	huīfù	*v.*	resume
行使	行使	xíngshǐ	*v.*	perform; exercise
主權	主权	zhǔquán	*n.*	sovereignty
結束	结束	jiéshù	*v./n.*	finish; conclude, end; conclusion
殖民地	殖民地	zhímíndì	*n.*	colony

第四十二课
香 港

　　1997 年 7 月 1 日是中国近代史上一个重要的日子。从这一天起，中国对香港恢复行使主权，结束了香港一个半世纪的殖民地历史。

　　在 1840 年到 1842 年的鸦片战争中，中国被英国打败了。清朝政府除了付给英国大量的赔款以外，还把香港割让给了英国。鸦片战争是帝国主义侵略中国的开始。从此以后的一百多年，中国一再

鸦片戰爭	鸦片战争	Yāpiàn Zhànzhēng	*n.*	the Opium War
英國	英国	Yīngguó		Britain; England
打敗	打败	dǎbài	*v.*	defeat; beat, be defeated
付	付	fù	*v.*	pay
賠款	赔款	péikuǎn	*n.*	indemnity; reparations
割讓	割让	gēràng	*v.*	cede
帝國主義	帝国主义	dìguó zhǔyì	*n.*	imperialism
侵略	侵略	qīnlüè	*v.*	invade

戰敗，受到了種種不平等的待遇。香港的回歸，象徵著這個恥辱的結束。

　　一百五十年來，在英國人的統治下 (1)，香港在政治、經濟、文化、語言各方面都和中國大陸有了明顯的不同。中國政府為了適應這兩個不同的體制，對香港採取了 "一國兩制" 的政策，使香港在回歸以後能繼續發展。所謂 "港人治港"，就是執行這個政策的結果。

戰敗	战败	zhànbài	*v.*	be defeated
種種	种种	zhǒngzhǒng	*adj.*	all kinds of
待遇	待遇	dàiyù	*n.*	treatment
回歸	回归	huíguī	*n./v.*	return
象徵	象征	xiàngzhēng	*v.*	symbolize
恥辱	耻辱	chǐrǔ	*n.*	humiliation; shame

战败，受到了种种不平等的待遇。香港的回归，象征着这个耻辱的结束。

一百五十年来，在英国人的统治下 (1)，香港在政治、经济、文化、语言各方面都和中国大陆有了明显的不同。中国政府为了适应这两个不同的体制，对香港采取了"一国两制"的政策，使香港在回归以后能继续发展。所谓"港人治港"，就是执行这个政策的结果。

統治	统治	tǒngzhì	*n./v.*	governance, rule; govern
體制	体制	tǐzhì	*n.*	system
一國兩制	一国两制	yìguó liǎngzhì		one country, two systems
港人治港	港人治港	Gǎngrén zhì Gǎng		the Hong Kong citizens govern Hong Kong
執行	执行	zhíxíng	*v.*	execute; carry out

　　上個星期我去了一趟香港。除了特別行政區的區旗以外，真看不出有任何改變！我的香港朋友都說這是一次平穩的過渡。回歸前後(2)，香港的股票和房地產價格也相當穩定。這是香港人對將來充滿信心(3)最好的證明。

　　香港一向以英語為官方語言，而一般人日常生活中常說廣東話。普通話在香港本來是很不普通的。但是我相信，隨著香港的回歸，普通話一定會漸漸成為香港人通用的語言。

趟	趟	tàng	*an.*	measure word for a trip
特別行政區	特別行政区	tèbié xíngzhèngqū	*n.*	special administrative region
區旗	区旗	qūqí	*n.*	regional flag
平穩	平穩	píngwěn	*adj.*	smooth and steady; stable
房地產	房地产	fángdìchǎn	*n.*	real estate

上个星期我去了一趟香港。除了特别行政区的区旗以外，真看不出有任何改变！我的香港朋友都说这是一次平稳的过渡。回归前后⑵，香港的股票和房地产价格也相当稳定。这是香港人对将来充满信心⑶最好的证明。

香港一向以英语为官方语言，而一般人日常生活中常说广东话。普通话在香港本来是很不普通的。但是我相信，随着香港的回归，普通话一定会渐渐成为香港人通用的语言。

價格	价格	jiàgé	*n.*	price
充滿	充满	chōngmǎn	*v.*	be full of; brimming with
信心	信心	xìnxīn	*n.*	confidence
官方	官方	guānfāng	*adj.*	official
通用	通用	tōngyòng	*adj.*	in common use; current

第四十三課

中華民族

　　許多人以為"中國人"就是"漢人"，"中國話"就是"漢語"。這個看法並不完全正確。中國是個多民族的國家，漢族只是中華民族當中最大的一族，大約佔全中國人口的百分之(1)九十五左右(2)。除了漢族以外，中國還有五、六十個少數民族。少數民族的人口雖然不多，但是分布很廣。一般來說，漢族居住在比較適宜農業生產的東南大平原上，少數民族多半分布在東北、西北、西南

中華民族	中华民族	Zhōnghuá Mínzú		the Chinese Nation
漢人	汉人	Hànrén		the Han people
多民族	多民族	duōmínzú	*adj.*	multi-racial
族	族	zú	*n.*	race; nationality
佔	占	zhàn	*v.*	occupy; constitute; make up
左右	左右	zuǒyòu		around (used after a number)
少數民族	少数民族	shǎoshù mínzú	*n.*	minority
分布	分布	fēnbù	*v.*	be distributed (over an area); be scattered

第四十三课
中华民族

　　许多人以为"中国人"就是"汉人"，"中国话"就是"汉语"。这个看法并不完全正确。中国是个多民族的国家，汉族只是中华民族当中最大的一族，大约占全中国人口的百分之(1)九十五左右(2)。除了汉族以外，中国还有五、六十个少数民族。少数民族的人口虽然不多，但是分布很广。一般来说，汉族居住在比较适宜农业生产的东南大平原上，少数民族多半分布在东北、西北、西南

廣	广	guǎng	*adj.*	vast; wide
居住	居住	jūzhù	*v.*	live; reside; dwell
適宜	适宜	shìyí	*v.*	suitable for; appropriate for
生產	生产	shēngchǎn	*n./v.*	production, produce
東南	东南	dōngnán	*n.*	southeast
平原	平原	píngyuán	*n.*	plain; flatlands
東北	东北	dōngběi	*n.*	northeast
西北	西北	xīběi	*n.*	northwest
西南	西南	xīnán	*n.*	southwest

等地和內蒙古、西藏、新疆等自治區。他們有自
己的語言，有的也有自己的文字，他們的宗教信
仰也往往和漢族不同。滿族、藏族、蒙古族和回
族是幾個主要的少數民族，他們都有悠久的歷史
和偉大的傳統；但是有的少數民族因為沒有文字，
文化水平比漢人要低些。

　　蒙古人在十三世紀打敗了宋朝 (960-1279)，建立
了元朝 (1279-1368)。這個蒙古大帝國雖然時間不長，
但是帝國的面積卻是中國歷史上最大的。滿州人
在 1644 年消滅了明朝，建立了清朝。清朝在十九世

內蒙古	內蒙古	Nèi Měnggǔ		Inner Mongolia
西藏	西藏	Xīzàng		Tibet
新疆	新疆	Xīnjiāng		Xinjiang
自治區	自治区	zìzhìqū	n.	autonomous region
宗教	宗教	zōngjiào	n.	religion
信仰	信仰	xìnyǎng	n.	faith; belief; conviction
滿族	滿族	Mǎnzú		the Manchu nationality

等地和内蒙古、西藏、新疆等自治区。他们有自己的语言，有的也有自己的文字，他们的宗教信仰也往往和汉族不同。满族、藏族、蒙古族和回族是几个主要的少数民族，他们都有悠久的历史和伟大的传统；但是有的少数民族因为没有文字，文化水平比汉人要低些。

蒙古人在十三世纪打败了宋朝(960-1279)，建立了元朝(1279-1368)。这个蒙古大帝国虽然时间不长，但是帝国的面积却是中国历史上最大的。满州人在1644年消灭了明朝，建立了清朝。清朝在十九世

回族	回族	Huízú		the Hui nationality
悠久	悠久	yōujiǔ	*adj.*	long; long-standing
偉大	伟大	wěidà	*adj.*	great; mighty
低	低	dī	*adj.*	low
宋朝	宋朝	Sòngcháo		the Song Dynasty
建立	建立	jiànlì	*v.*	establish; set up
滿州	满州	Mǎnzhōu		Manchuria
消滅	消灭	xiāomiè	*v.*	eliminate; abolish; exterminate; wipe out

紀中期以前，在政治、經濟、軍事、文化各方面
都有偉大的成就。1842年鴉片戰爭以後，由於帝國
主義的侵略和政府的腐敗，清朝才漸漸地衰弱了。
滿人和漢人在當時分得很清楚。滿人是統治階級，
漢人是被統治階級，但是現在已經是一家人了。

　　最近幾年因為交通建設的加強和廣播電視深入
每一個地區，漢人和少數民族的距離正在逐漸縮
小，互相通婚的現象也越來越普遍了。中華民族
也是一個 " 大熔爐 " 啊！

中期	中期	zhōngqī	*n.*	middle period (of a dynasty, century, reign)
军事	軍事	jūnshì	*n.*	military affairs
成就	成就	chéngjiù	*n.*	achievement
腐败	腐敗	fǔbài	*n./adj.*	corruption, corrupt; rotten
衰弱	衰弱	shuāiruò	*v./adj.*	weaken, weak; feeble

纪中期以前，在政治、经济、军事、文化各方面都有伟大的成就。1842年鸦片战争以后，由于帝国主义的侵略和政府的腐败，清朝才渐渐地衰弱了。满人和汉人在当时分得很清楚。满人是统治阶级，汉人是被统治阶级，但是现在已经是一家人了。

最近几年因为交通建设的加强和广播电视深入每一个地区，汉人和少数民族的距离正在逐渐缩小，互相通婚的现象也越来越普遍了。中华民族也是一个"大熔炉"啊！

階級	阶级	jiējí	n.	(social) class
一家人	一家人	yìjiārén		of one family or clan
逐漸	逐渐	zhújiàn	adv.	gradually
通婚	通婚	tōnghūn	v.	intermarry
大熔爐	大熔炉	dà rónglú	n.	big melting pot

第四十四課
改變中的中國

　　在中國歷史上，幾個文化最發達、國力最強盛的朝代都是中國大量吸收外來文化的時候。譬如漢朝 (206 B. C. -A. D. 220)，經過絲綢之路引進了大量中亞和西亞的文化。我們現在所吃的葡萄、胡瓜（現在叫做黃瓜），還有胡琴這種樂器，都是那時從中亞、西亞傳進中國來的。胡琴的 " 胡 " 字，就是 " 外國 " 的意思。要是你看到一個詞帶著 " 胡 " 字，像 " 胡琴 " 、 " 胡瓜 " ，十有八九本來都不是中國的東西。這個 " 胡 " 字有點兒像現在的 " 洋 " 字，

國力	国力	guólì	*n.*	national power
強盛	强盛	qiángshèng	*adj.*	powerful and prosperous
朝代	朝代	cháodài	*n.*	dynasty
吸收	吸收	xīshōu	*v.*	absorb
漢朝	汉朝	Hàncháo		the Han Dynasty
經過	经过	jīngguò	*v.*	pass, go through
絲綢之路	丝绸之路	Sīchóu Zhī Lù		the Silk Road
引進	引进	yǐnjìn	*v.*	introduce from elsewhere
中亞	中亚	Zhōngyà		Central Asia

第四十四课
改变中的中国

　　在中国历史上，几个文化最发达、国力最强盛的朝代都是中国大量吸收外来文化的时候。譬如汉朝 (206 B. C. -A. D. 220)，经过丝绸之路引进了大量中亚和西亚的文化。我们现在所吃的葡萄、胡瓜（现在叫做黄瓜），还有胡琴这种乐器，都是那时从中亚、西亚传进中国来的。胡琴的 "胡" 字，就是 "外国" 的意思。要是你看到一个词带着 "胡" 字，像 "胡琴"、"胡瓜"，十有八九本来都不是中国的东西。这个 "胡" 字有点儿像现在的 "洋" 字，

西亞	西亚	Xīyà		Western Asia
葡萄	葡萄	pú.táo	n.	grape
胡瓜	胡瓜	húguā	n.	(archaic name for) cucumber
黃瓜	黄瓜	huángguā	n.	cucumber
胡琴	胡琴	hú.qín	n.	a general term for certain kinds of two-stringed bowed instruments
樂器	乐器	yuèqì	n.	musical instrument
傳	传	chuán	v.	pass; pass on; spread
十有八九	十有八九	shíyǒubājiǔ		in eight or nine cases out of ten; most likely

比方說 " 洋人 " 、 " 洋火 " 、 " 洋布 " 等等。

漢朝初期，印度的佛教傳入中國。佛教的思想一方面對中國起了一定的負面的影響，另一方面也豐富了中國的文學、哲學和藝術。到了後來，佛教竟成了中國文化中不可分割的一部分了。我們現在所看到的歷史文物和名勝古跡，有許多都和佛教在中國的發展有密切的關係。

唐朝 (618-907) 是另一個大量吸收外來文化的時代。佛經的翻譯到了唐代達到了最高的水平。那時中國有不少留學生到印度去留學，而日本也派了很多留學生到中國來學習。中印、中日以及中國和中亞、西亞的交通都是非常發達的。

洋	洋	yáng	*adj.*	western; foreign
洋人	洋人	yángrén	*n.*	foreigner (opposite of Chinese)
洋火	洋火	yánghuǒ	*n.*	(informal) matches; 火柴 huǒchái
洋布	洋布	yángbù	*n.*	foreign cloth
印度	印度	Yìndù		India
佛教	佛教	Fójiào		Buddhism
傳入	传入	chuánrù	*v.*	pass on to; spread into
豐富	丰富	fēngfù	*v.*	enrich
哲學	哲学	zhéxué	*n.*	philosophy

比方说"洋人"、"洋火"、"洋布"等等。

汉朝初期,印度的佛教传入中国。佛教的思想一方面对中国起了一定的负面的影响,另一方面也丰富了中国的文学、哲学和艺术。到了后来,佛教竟成了中国文化中不可分割的一部分了。我们现在所看到的历史文物和名胜古迹,有许多都和佛教在中国的发展有密切的关系。

唐朝 (618-907) 是另一个大量吸收外来文化的时代。佛经的翻译到了唐代达到了最高的水平。那时中国有不少留学生到印度去留学,而日本也派了很多留学生到中国来学习。中印、中日以及中国和中亚、西亚的交通都是非常发达的。

竟	竟	jìng	*adv.*	unexpectedly; to one's surprise
分割	分割	fēn'gē	*v.*	separate; cut up; carve up
文物	文物	wénwù	*n.*	cultural relic; historical relic
名勝古跡	名胜古迹	míngshèng gǔjī	*n.*	famous scenic spot
密切	密切	mìqiè	*adj.*	close
唐朝	唐朝	Tángcháo		the Tang Dynasty
佛經	佛经	fójīng	*n.*	Buddhist sutra

在中國強盛的時候，中國人從來不擔心吸收外來文化會影響到中國本土的文化。相反的，這些外來文化使中國的本土文化更豐富、更多彩多姿。

1842年鴉片戰爭以後，中國開始了一次大規模的西化運動，但是這個向西方學習的運動和漢朝、唐朝甚至於明朝的都有一個基本的不同。十九世紀的西化運動是中國受到了帝國主義侵略以後的一種自衛運動，而漢朝和唐朝是中國的國力和文化向四方擴展的時候，所以漢唐時代和外國文化的交流是自願的，而鴉片戰爭以後的西化卻有一部分是被迫的。

這次我來到中國，看到最近十幾年改革開放的速度和成績，使我想起了中國歷史上的這幾次重大的中外文化交流。我相信這次改革的深度和速度

本土	本土	běntǔ	*adj.*	local; native
相反	相反	xiāngfǎn	*adj.*	opposite
多彩多姿	多彩多姿	duōcǎiduōzī	*idm.*	colorful; diverse
西化	西化	xīhuà	*n.*	westernization
運動	运动	yùndòng	*n.*	movement

在中国强盛的时候，中国人从来不担心吸收外来文化会影响到中国本土的文化。相反的，这些外来文化使中国的本土文化更丰富、更多彩多姿。

1842年鸦片战争以后，中国开始了一次大规模的西化运动，但是这个向西方学习的运动和汉朝、唐朝甚至于明朝的都有一个基本的不同。十九世纪的西化运动是中国受到了帝国主义侵略以后的一种自卫运动，而汉朝和唐朝是中国的国力和文化向四方扩展的时候，所以汉唐时代和外国文化的交流是自愿的，而鸦片战争以后的西化却有一部分是被迫的。

这次我来到中国，看到最近十几年改革开放的速度和成绩，使我想起了中国历史上的这几次重大的中外文化交流。我相信这次改革的深度和速度

自衛	自卫	zìwèi	v.	self-defense
擴展	扩展	kuòzhǎn	v.	expand
被迫	被迫	bèipò	v.	be forced to
速度	速度	sùdù	n.	speed
深度	深度	shēndù	n.	depth

會超過歷史上任何一次西化運動。從飲食、穿著到人際關係、思維方式，中國人都在做快速的調整。這也正是中國人對中國文化充滿信心最好的說明。他們並不擔心中國文化會在現代化的過程中失去它的個性和特色，相反的，一個全新的中國文化正在形成。

許多人一談到"傳統"這兩個字，就認為"傳統"是固定的，是不變的。其實，中國傳統之所以偉大，絕不在於(1)它的固定和不變，而在於它與其他文化交流時能不斷地吸收新成分。

推陳出新，日新月異，正是中國文化偉大的所在(2)。

穿著	穿着	chuānzhuó	*n.*	dress; apparel
人際關係	人际关系	rénjì guān.xì	*n.*	interpersonal relationship
思維	思维	sīwéi	*n.*	thought; thinking
調整	调整	tiáozhěng	*n./v.*	adjustment, adjust
全新	全新	quánxīn	*adj.*	brand-new
形成	形成	xíngchéng	*v.*	form; take shape

会超过历史上任何一次西化运动。从饮食、穿着到人际关系、思维方式，中国人都在做快速的调整。这也正是中国人对中国文化充满信心最好的说明。他们并不担心中国文化会在现代化的过程中失去它的个性和特色，相反的，一个全新的中国文化正在形成。

许多人一谈到"传统"这两个字，就认为"传统"是固定的，是不变的。其实，中国传统之所以伟大，绝不在于(1)它的固定和不变，而在于它与其他文化交流时能不断地吸收新成分。

推陈出新，日新月异，正是中国文化伟大的所在(2)。

固定	固定	gùdìng	*adj.*	fixed; stable
在於	在于	zàiyú	*v.*	lie in; rest with
成分	成分	chéngfèn	*n.*	component
推陳出新	推陈出新	tuī chén chū xīn	*idm.*	weed out the old to bring forth the new
日新月異	日新月异	rìxīn-yuèyì	*idm.*	change with each passing day
所在	所在	suǒzài	*n.*	place; location

Pinyin Index

chūshēng, 出生, 出生, v., be born, L. 37, 195

chūxiàn, 出現, 出现, v., appear; arise; emerge, L. 23, 118

chūzhōng, 初中, 初中, n., middle school, L. 38, 200

chūzū qìchē, 出租汽車, 出租汽车, n., taxi, L. 7, 32

chúfēi, 除非, 除非, conj., only if; only when; unless, L. 21, 111

chúle...yǐwài, 除了…以外, 除了…以外, except for; aside from, L. 3, 15

Chuān, 川, 川, 四川; Sichuan Province, L. 15, 74

chuānzhuó, 穿著, 穿着, n., dress; apparel, L. 44, 240

chuán, 傳, 传, v., pass; pass on; spread, L. 44, 235

chuándá, 傳達, 传达, v., pass on; communicate, L. 40, 214

chuánrǎnbìng, 傳染病, 传染病, n., infectious disease, L. 10, 51

chuánrù, 傳入, 传入, v., pass on to; spread into, L. 44, 236

chuántǒng, 傳統, 传统, n., tradition, L. 34, 177

chuāngkǒu, 窗口, 窗口, n., service window, L. 4, 20

chuángpù, 床鋪, 床铺, n., bedding, L. 2, 8

chuàngzào, 創造, 创造, v., create; produce; bring about, L. 18, 95

Chūnqiū, 春秋, 春秋, the Spring and Autumn Period (770-476 B.C.), L. 41, 216

cí, 詞, 词, n., word; term, L. 9, 49

cíhuì, 詞彙, 词汇, n., vocabulary, L. 41, 219

cǐwài, 此外, 此外, adv., besides; moreover, L. 35, 180

cóngcǐ yǐhòu, 從此以後, 从此以后, from then on; from now on, L. 23, 117

cónglái méi ...guò, 從來沒 V.過, 从来没 V.过, have never V-ed, L. 3, 12

cóngxiǎo, 從小, 从小, from childhood, L. 37, 196

cùjìn, 促進, 促进, v., promote; accelerate, L. 22, 114

cúnzài, 存在, 存在, v., exist, L. 18, 93

cuòshī, 措施, 措施, n., (political, financial, etc.) measure, step, L. 29, 152

dā.yìng, 答應, 答应, v., agree; promise, answer, L. 13, 64

dáchéng, 達成, 达成, v., reach (an agreement), L. 23, 118

dádào, 達到, 达到, v., achieve (a goal), L. 29, 151

dǎ, 打, 打, prov., (in this context) add subtitles, L. 18, 95

dǎbài, 打敗, 打败, v., defeat; be defeated, L. 42, 223

dǎ diànhuà, 打電話, 打电话, v.-o., make a phone call; call, L. 2, 6

dǎ jiāo.dào, 打交道, 打交道, v.-o., come into contact with; have dealings with, L. 13, 62

dǎ-pái, 打牌, 打牌, v.-o., play cards, L. 16, 85

dǎ-pò, 打破, 打破, v.-c., break; smash, L. 22, 112

dǎsǎo, 打掃, 打扫, v., sweep; clean, L. 2, 8

dǎ-zì, 打字, 打字, v.-o., type, L. 40, 215

dàdōu, 大都, 大都, adv., for the most part; mostly, L. 35, 181

dàduō, 大多, 大多, adv., for the most part; mostly, L. 6, 29

dàduōshù, 大多數, 大多数, n., great majority, L. 36, 187

dàgài, 大概, 大概, adv., (here) generally, L. 30, 154

dàgēdà, 大哥大, 大哥大, n., cellular phone, L. 32, 164

dàguōfàn, 大鍋飯, 大锅饭, n., food prepared in a large pot, L. 22, 115

dàliàng, 大量, 大量, adj., a large number, L. 41, 218

dàlù, 大陸, 大陆, mainland China, L. 26, 130

dà rónglú, 大熔爐, 大熔炉, n., big melting pot, L. 43, 233

Dàtóng, 大同, 大同, Datong (in Shanxi), L. 11, 55

dàtóng xiǎoyì, 大同小異, 大同小异, idm., largely identical but with minor differences, L. 26, 131

dàyuē, 大約, 大约, adv., approximately; about, L. 9, 46

dàzhì, 大致, 大致, adv., roughly; more or less, L. 30, 155

dài, 帶, 带, v., take; bring; carry, L. 1, 3

dài, 帶, 带, v., bear; have, L. 17, 88

dàibiǎo, 代表, 代表, v., represent, L. 32, 165

dài.fū, 大夫, 大夫, n., physician; doctor, L. 5, 27

dàiyù, 待遇, 待遇, n., treatment, L. 42, 224

dàizhe, 帶著, 带着, v., take; bring; carry, L. 10, 53

dānqīn jiātíng, 單親家庭, 单亲家庭, n., single-parent family, L. 27, 140

dānrénfáng, 單人房, 单人房, n., single room, L. 2, 6

dānwèi, 單位, 单位, n., (work) unit, L. 34, 175

dānxīn, 擔心, 担心, v., worry; feel anxious, L. 1, 3

dānyuán, 單元, 单元, n., unit, L. 30, 159

dānzi, 單子, 单子, n., form; list, L. 7, 38

dāng, 當, 当, v., be; work as; serve as, L. 34, 178

dāngdài, 當代, 当代, adj., contemporary, L. 37, 194

dāngdì, 當地, 当地, p.w., local; in the locality, L. 6, 31

dāngnián, 當年, 当年, t.w., in those years (days), L. 37, 193

dāngshí, 當時, 当时, t.w., then; at that time, L. 40, 215

dāngzhōng, 當中, 当中, postp., in the middle, L. 16, 83

dǎng.bùzhù, 擋不住, 挡不住, v.-c., be unable to (be) resist(ed); be unable to (be) stop(ped), L. 37, 197

dào, 倒, 倒, adv., see opposite to the expected outcome, L. 10, 53

dào, 道, 道, an., auxilliary noun for dishes, L. 15, 79

dàochù, 到處, 到处, adv., everywhere; at all places, L. 17, 86

dàodá, 到達, 到达, v., arrive, L. 31, 161

dàodé, 道德, 道德, n., morals; morality; ethics, L. 17, 88

dàodǐ, 到底, 到底, adv., after all (used in a question), L. 8, 41

dàolǐ, 道理, 道理, n., reason; sense, L. 24, 123

dàolù, 道路, 道路, n., road; way, L. 7, 34

dàoshí.hòu, 到時候, 到时候, until then; until that time, L. 13, 62

dào...wéizhǐ, 到…爲止, 到…为止, up until..., L. 11, 57

dé, 得, 得, v., contract (an illness), L. 10, 51

fánnǎo, 煩惱, 烦恼, *n.*, worriment; vexation, L. 28, 144

fántǐzì, 繁體字, 繁体字, *n.*, the original complex form of Chinese characters, L. 18, 95

fǎn'ér, 反而, 反而, *conj.*, on the contrary; instead, L. 28, 145

fǎnyìng, 反映, 反映, *v.*, reflect, L. 30, 154

fànguǎn, 飯館, 饭馆, *n.*, restaurant, L. 2, 9

fànlàn, 泛濫, 泛滥, *v.*, overrun, L. 39, 208

fāngbiàn, 方便, 方便, *adj.*, convenient, L. 2, 11

fāngfǎ, 方法, 方法, *n.*, way; method, L. 15, 78

fāngmiàn, 方面, 方面, *n.*, aspect; respect, L. 26, 135

fāngshì, 方式, 方式, *n.*, pattern; fashion; way, L. 6, 31

fāngxiànggǎn, 方向感, 方向感, *n.*, sense of direction, L. 35, 182

fāngyán, 方言, 方言, *n.*, dialect, L. 18, 93

fángdìchǎn, 房地產, 房地产, *n.*, real estate, L. 42, 226

fǎngwèn, 訪問, 访问, *v.*, visit (formally), L. 23, 116

fàngkuān, 放寬, 放宽, *v./n.*, relax (restrictions); relaxation, L. 25, 129

fàng-pì, 放屁, 放屁, *v.-o.*, pass gas; fart, L. 21, 108

fàngxīn, 放心, 放心, *v.*, set one's mind at rest; feel relieved, L. 2, 6

fēijī, 飛機, 飞机, *n.*, airplane, L. 1, 2

féipàng, 肥胖, 肥胖, *n.*, obese, L. 28, 144

fèiyòng, 費用, 费用, *n.*, expenses; costs, L. 29, 150

fēn, 分, 分, *v.*, divide; seperate; part, L. 9, 47

fēnbù, 分布, 分布, *v.*, be distributed (over an area); be scattered, L. 43, 228

fēnchéng, 分成, 分成, *v.-c.*, divide into, L. 34, 177

fēn'gē, 分割, 分割, *v.*, separate; cut up; carve up, L. 44, 237

fēnkāi, 分開, 分开, *v.-c.*, separate; part, L. 40, 215

fēnpèi, 分配, 分配, *v.*, distribute; allot; assign, L. 22, 114

fēnxī, 分析, 分析, *v./n.*, analyse, analysis, L. 24, 121

fénchǎng, 墳場, 坟场, *n.*, graveyard; cemetery, L. 30, 154

fèn.liàng, 分量, 分量, *n.*, amount, L. 29, 150

fēng, 封, 封, *an.*, measure word for 信, L. 4, 22

fēng, 風, 风, *n.*, practice; custom, L. 17, 90

fēngfù, 豐富, 丰富, *adj.*, rich; abundant, L. 19, 99

fēngfù, 豐富, 丰富, *v.*, enrich, L. 44, 236

fēngjǐng, 風景, 风景, *n.*, scenery; landscape, L. 4, 23

fēngsú, 風俗, 风俗, *n.*, common customs, L. 39, 209

fēngwèi, 風味, 风味, *n.*, special flavor; local flavor, L. 11, 56

féngrènjī, 縫紉機, 缝纫机, *n.*, sewing machine, L. 29, 151

fójīng, 佛經, 佛经, *n.*, Buddhist sutra, L. 44, 237

Fójiào, 佛教, 佛教, Buddhism, L. 44, 236

fūfù, 夫婦, 夫妇, *n.*, married couple, L. 27, 140

fūqī, 夫妻, 夫妻, *n.*, married couple, L. 27, 138

fú, 幅, 幅, *an.*, measure word for painting, L. 8, 40

fúqì, 福氣, 福气, *n.*, good fortune, L. 28, 143

fúwù, 服務, 服务, *v.*, serve; give service to, L. 17, 89

fúwùyuán, 服務員, 服务员, *n.*, service personnel, L. 4, 18

fǔbài, 腐敗, 腐败, *n./adj.*, corruption, corrupt; rotten, L. 43, 232

fù, 付, 付, *v.*, pay, L. 42, 223

fùdān, 負擔, 负担, *n.*, burden; load, L. 30, 157

fùjìn, 附近, 附近, nearby; in the vicinity, L. 4, 18

fùmiàn, 負面, 负面, *adj.*, negative, L. 24, 121

fùnǚ, 婦女, 妇女, *n.*, woman (as a collective noun), L. 27, 137

fùyù, 富裕, 富裕, *adj.*, rich; wealthy; prosperous, L. 29, 149

fù zérèn, 負責任, 负责任, *v.-o.*, be responsible for something., L. 28, 146

fù-zhàng, 付賬, 付账, *v.-o.*, pay a bill, L. 14, 72

gāi, 該, 该, *aux.*, 应该, L. 5, 27

gǎi, 改, 改, *v.*, change; alter; correct, L. 3, 16

gǎibiàn, 改變, 改变, *v.*, change, L. 28, 147

gǎi-diào, 改掉, 改掉, *v.-c.*, give up; drop, L. 17, 90

gǎigé, 改革, 改革, *v.*, reform, L. 9, 48

gǎijìn, 改進, 改进, *v./n.*, improve, improvement, L. 31, 161

gǎishàn, 改善, 改善, *n./v.*, improvement, improve, L. 38, 202

gǎiyòng, 改用, 改用, *v.*, use (something else) instead, L. 21, 110

gān-bēi, 乾杯, 干杯, *v.-o.*, drink a toast, L. 14, 70

gān'gà, 尷尬, 尴尬, *adj.*, awkward; embarrassed, L. 19, 98

gānjìng, 乾淨, 干净, *adj.*, clean; neat and tidy, L. 3, 16

gǎn.búshàng, 趕不上, 赶不上, *v.-c.*, cannot catch up with, L. 7, 34

gǎn xìngqù, 感興趣, 感兴趣, *v.*, be interested in, L. 37, 193

gàn, 幹, 干, *v.*, (colloquial) do, L. 34, 176

gāng, 剛, 刚, *adv.*, just, L. 3, 13

gāngbǐ, 鋼筆, 钢笔, *n.*, fountain pen, L. 40, 214

Gǎngrén zhì Gǎng, 港人治港, 港人治港, the Hong Kong citizens govern Hong Kong, L. 42, 225

gāokǎo, 高考, 高考, *n.*, the entrance examination for colleges and universities, L. 24, 120

gāosù gōnglù, 高速公路, 高速公路, *n.*, highway, L. 1, 4

gāoxìng, 高興, 高兴, *adj.*, happy, L. 37, 197

gāoyǎ, 高雅, 高雅, *adj.*, refined; elegant, L. 21, 109

gē.bó, 胳膊, 胳膊, *n.*, arm, L. 5, 26

gēràng, 割讓, 割让, *v.*, cede, L. 42, 223

gélí, 隔離, 隔离, *v.*, keep apart; isolate; segregate, L. 23, 118

gè, 各 *n.*, 各 *n.*, *adj.*, each; every, L. 6, 31

gè fù gè de, 各付各的, 各付各的, go Dutch, L. 14, 72

gèháng gèyè, 各行各業, 各行各业, *n.*, all trades and professions, L. 22, 115

gèrén, 個人, 个人, *n.*, individual, L. 13, 64

gèxìng, 個性, 个性, *n.*, individual character; personality, L. 40, 211 gè yǒu suǒ cháng, 各有所長, 各有所长, *idm.*, each has his own strong points, L. 36, 186

gèzhǒng gèyàng, 各種各樣, 各种各样, *adj.*, all kinds of, L. 17, 86

gěi miànzi, 給面子, 给面子, *v.-o.*, show due respect for somebody's feelings, L. 13, 62

gēnběn, 根本, 根本, *adv.*, at all; simply, L. 1, 3

gōngchǎng, 工廠, 工厂, *n.*, factory, L. 19, 98

gōnggòng qìchē, 公共汽車, 公共汽车, *n.*, bus,, L. 4, 19

gōngjīn, 公斤, 公斤, kilogram, L. 28, 143

gōngjù, 工具, 工具, *n.*, tool; instrument, L. 11, 57

gōngkāi, 公開, 公开, *adj.*, public; open, L. 27, 139

gōnglì, 功利, 功利, *n.*, utility; material gain, L. 38, 202

gōngpíng, 公平, 公平, *adj.*, fair; just, L. 24, 122

gōngrén, 工人, 工人, *n.*, worker; workman, L. 19, 100

gōngsī, 公司, 公司, *n.*, company; corporation, L. 19, 100

gōngwéi, 恭維, 恭维, *v.*, compliment, L. 28, 143

gōngyèhuà, 工業化, 工业化, *n.*, industrialization, L. 30, 159

gōngyuán, 公園, 公园, *n.*, park, L. 4, 20

gōngyuán, 公元, 公元, the Christian era 公元, L. 41, 217

gòngxiàn, 貢獻, 贡献, *v.*, contribution, L. 19, 101

gōutōng, 溝通, 沟通, *v.*, communicate, L. 18, 94

gòumǎi, 購買, 购买, *v.*, purchase, L. 31, 161

gǔ, 股, 股, *an.*, measure word for strength, smell, etc., L. 10, 52

gǔdài, 古代, 古代, *n.*, ancient times, L. 12, 59

gǔdiǎn, 古典, 古典, *adj.*, classical, L. 25, 127

gǔdǒng, 古董, 古董, *n.*, antique, L. 8, 40

gǔhuà, 古畫, 古画, *n.*, ancient painting, L. 8, 41

gǔlǎo, 古老, 古老, *adj.*, ancient; age-old, L. 1, 5

gǔpiào, 股票, 股票, *n.*, stock, L. 32, 168

gùdìng, 固定, 固定, *adj.*, fixed; stable, L. 44, 241

Gùgōng, 故宮, 故宫, the Palace Museum, L. 12, 58

gùkè, 顧客, 顾客, *n.*, customer, L. 20, 106

gùrán, 固然, 固然, *conj.*, no doubt; it is true, L. 24, 121

guàhào, 掛號, 挂号, *v.*, register; send by registered mail, L. 4, 21

guài.bù.dé, 怪不得, 怪不得, *conj.*, no wonder; so that's why, L. 6, 29

guānchá, 觀察, 观察, *v.*, observe; watch; survey, L. 11, 57

guān-diào, 關掉, 关掉, *v.-c.*, turn off, L. 5, 26

guānfāng, 官方, 官方, *adj.*, official, L. 42, 227

guānlì, 官吏, 官吏, *n.*, (archaic) government officials, L. 40, 212

guān-mén, 關門, 关门, *v.-o.*, close, L. 7, 35

guānniàn, 觀念, 观念, *n.*, concept; notion; idea, L. 22, 114

guān.xì, 關係, 关系, *n.*, relationships; connections, L. 1, 5

guàn-huài, 慣壞, 惯坏, *v.-c.*, spoil, L. 2, 9

Guāngmíng Rìbào, 光明日報, 光明日报, *n.*, Guangming Daily, L. 39, 204

guǎng, 廣, 广, *adj.*, vast; wide, L. 43, 229

guǎngbō, 廣播, 广播, *n./v.*, radio broadcast; broadcast, L. 18, 97

Guǎngdōng, 廣東, 广东, Guangdong Province, L. 15, 77

guǎnggào, 廣告, 广告, *n.*, advertisement, L. 17, 88

guàng, 逛, 逛, *v.*, stroll; go window-shopping, L. 8, 44

guīfàn, 規範, 规范, *n.*, standard; norm, L. 18, 92

guīmó, 規模, 规模, *n.*, scale; scope; dimensions, L. 23, 117

guìtái, 櫃台, 柜台, *n.*, counter, L. 4, 23

guóchǎn, 國產, 国产, *adj.*, domestically made, L. 20, 106

guódū, 國都, 国都, *n.*, the national capital, L. 35, 180

guójì, 國際, 国际, *adj.*, international, L. 1, 2

guójiā, 國家, 国家, *n.*, country; state; nation, L. 19, 100

guólì, 國力, 国力, *n.*, national power, L. 44, 234

guónèi, 國內, 国内, *adj.*, internal; domestic, L. 11, 57

guóqíng, 國情, 国情, *n.*, state of a nation, L. 39, 209

Guóyǔ, 國語, 国语, *n.*, Mandarin Chinese, L. 18, 94

guǒrán, 果然, 果然, *adv.*, as expected; sure enough, L. 38, 198

guò, 過, 过, *v.*, pass; cross, L. 4, 19

guò, 過 time duration, 过 time duration, *v.*, after (time duration), L. 7, 35

guò, 過, 过, spend (time); live (life), L. 28, 142

guò..., 過 adj., 过 adj., too; exceedingly, L. 34, 176

guòchéng, 過程, 过程, *n.*, course; process, L. 23, 118

guòdù, 過渡, 过渡, *v./n.*, transit, transition, L. 29, 153

guòfèn, 過分, 过分, *adv.*, excessively; over-, L. 24, 123

guòjiē tiānqiáo, 過街天橋, 过街天桥, *n.*, overhead bridge that goes across a street; overpass, L. 16, 82

guòqù, 過去, 过去, *n.*, past, L. 20, 107

guò rìzi, 過日子, 过日子, *v.-o.*, lead a life, L. 36, 188

háizi, 孩子, 孩子, *n.*, children; kid, L. 23, 116

hǎiguān, 海關, 海关, *n.*, customs, L. 1, 3

hǎiwài, 海外, 海外, *p.w.*, overseas; abroad, L. 9, 48

hǎixiá, 海峽, 海峡, *n.*, strait, L. 26, 130

hài, 害, 害, *v.*, harm, L. 39, 208

hànbǎobāo, 漢堡包, 汉堡包, *n.*, hamburger, L. 28, 146

Hàncháo, 漢朝, 汉朝, the Han Dynasty, L. 44, 234

Hànrén, 漢人, 汉人, the Han people, L. 43, 228

Hànyǔ, 漢語, 汉语, *n.*, Chinese language, L. 41, 216

Hànyǔ pīnyīn, 漢語拼音, 汉语拼音, *n.*, the Chinese phonetic alphabet, L. 26, 134

Hànzì, 漢字, 汉字, *n.*, Chinese character, L. 18, 96

hángkōng, 航空, 航空, *n.*, aviation, L. 31, 161

hángqíng, 行情, 行情, *n.*, quotations (on the market), prices, L. 32, 168

háo, 毫, 毫, *adv.*, in the least; at all, L. 26, 132

hǎobǐshuō, 好比說, 好比说, for example, L. 39, 208

hǎo.chù, 好處, 好处, *n.*, benefit; gain; profit; advantage, L. 3, 17

hǎozài, 好在, 好在, *adv.*, luckily; fortunately, L. 1, 3

hàozi, 耗子, 耗子, *n.*, mouse; rat, L. 21, 110

hē-zuì, 喝醉, 喝醉, v.-c., be drunk, L. 14, 70

hélǐ, 合理, 合理, adj., reasonable, L. 34, 179

héshì, 合適, 合适, adj., proper; appropriate, L. 14, 69

hézī, 合資, 合资, adj., joint venture, L. 37, 194

hónglǜdēng, 紅綠燈, 红绿灯, n., traffic light, L. 7, 36

hóngshāo, 紅燒, 红烧, v., braise in soy sauce, L. 15, 79

hòumén, 後門, 后门, n., back door, L. 24, 122

hūlüè, 忽略, 忽略, v., neglect, L. 26, 131

hū-rén, 呼人, 呼人, v.-o., call people, L. 32, 168

húguā, 胡瓜, 胡瓜, n., (archaic name for) cucumber, L. 44, 235

Hú-nán, 湖南, 湖南, Hunan Province, L. 15, 77

hú.qín, 胡琴, 胡琴, n., a general term for certain kinds of two-stringed bowed instruments, L. 44, 235

hútòngr, 胡同儿, 胡同儿, n., traditional alleys in Beijing, L. 35, 182

hù, 戶, 户, an./n., household, L. 39, 205

hùxiāng, 互相, 互相, adv., mutually; with each other, L. 38, 200

hùzhào, 護照, 护照, n., passport, L. 7, 39

huāfèi, 花費, 花费, n., expenses, L. 29, 149

Huāhuā Gōngzǐ, 花花公子, 花花公子, Playboy, L. 1, 3

huā-qián, 花錢, 花钱, v.-o., spend (money), L. 8, 45

huálì, 華麗, 华丽, adj., magnificent; resplendent, L. 12, 59

huàjù, 話劇, 话剧, n., modern drama; stage play, L. 25, 124

huà shé tiān zú, 畫蛇添足, 画蛇添足, idm., draw a snake and add feet to it--ruin the effect by adding something superflous, L. 21, 110

huàtí, 話題, 话题, n., topic of conversation, L. 13, 65

huáijiù, 懷舊, 怀旧, v., recollect the good old days, L. 37, 192

huáiniàn, 懷念, 怀念, v., cherish the memory of; think fondly of, L. 9, 49

huānyíng, 歡迎, 欢迎, v., welcome, L. 32, 169

huánchéng gōnglù, 環城公路, 环城公路, n., the roads circling the city, L. 35, 183

huàn, 換, 换, v., change, L. 2, 8

huángguā, 黃瓜, 黄瓜, n., cucumber, L. 44, 235

huīfù, 恢復, 恢复, v., resume, L. 42, 222

huídá, 回答, 回答, n./v., answer, L. 13, 63

huíguī, 回歸, 回归, n./v., return, L. 42, 224

huí-guó, 回國, 回国, v.-o., return to one's country, L. 33, 173

Huízú, 回族, 回族, the Hui nationality, L. 43, 231

huìhuà, 繪畫, 绘画, n., drawing; painting, L. 40, 212

hūnwài guān.xì, 婚外關係, 婚外关系, n., extra-marital relationship, L. 27, 139

hūnyīn, 婚姻, 婚姻, n., marriage, L. 27, 138

hùnluàn, 混亂, 混乱, n., confusion; chaos, L. 18, 96

huódòng, 活動, 活动, n., activity, L. 25, 124

huólì, 活力, 活力, n., vigour; energy, L. 35, 185

huǒr, 活儿, 活儿, n., (colloquial) work, L. 34, 176

huǒchē, 火車, 火车, n., train, L. 11, 54

huò, 或, 或, conj., or, L. 30, 155

huòyùn, 貨運, 货运, n., cargo transportation, L. 31, 160

huòzhě, 或者, 或者, conj., 或；or, L. 34, 175

jī, … 機, … 机, suff., ... machine; ... gadget, L. 32, 166

jīběn, 基本, 基本, adj., basic; fundamental, L. 15, 78

jīběn.shàng, 基本上, 基本上, adv., basically, L. 20, 105

jīchǎng, 機場, 机场, n., airport, L. 1, 2

jīchǔ, 基礎, 基础, n., foundation, L. 28, 147

jīdīng, 雞丁, 鸡丁, n., diced chicken, L. 20, 104

jīhū, 幾乎, 几乎, adv., almost; nearly, L. 22, 113

jīhuì, 機會, 机会, n., opportunity; chance, L. 11, 57

jīliè, 激烈, 激烈, adj., intense; sharp; fierce, L. 30, 155

jí, 急, 急, v., worry; make anxious; make impatient, L. 7, 33

jíshǐ, 即使, 即使, conj., even though; even if, L. 27, 138

jíshì, 急事, 急事, n., urgent matter, L. 7, 38

jǐ, 擠, 挤, v., crowd; pack; cram, L. 30, 158

jǐshíwàn, 幾十萬, 几十万, n., hundreds of thousands, L. 33, 170

jì, 寄, 寄, v., send; mail, L. 4, 20

jì...yòu..., 既…又…, 既…又…, both ... and ..., L. 10, 52

jìchéng chē, 計程車, 计程车, n., taxi, L. 26, 133

jì.dé, 記得, 记得, v., remember, L. 20, 102

jìhuà jīngjì, 計劃經濟, 计划经济, n., planned economy, L. 34, 175

jìshù, 技術, 技术, n., skill; technique, L. 40, 210

jìsuànjī, 計算機, 计算机, n., computer, L. 22, 112

jìxù, 繼續, 继续, v., continue, L. 33, 171

jìyì, 記憶, 记忆, n., memory, L. 24, 123

jì.zhù, 記住, 记住, v.-c., remember, L. 15, 78

jiāchángcài, 家常菜, 家常菜, n., home cooking; simple meal, L. 14, 71

jiājù, 家具, 家具, n., furniture, L. 19, 99

jiāqiáng, 加強, 加强, v., strengthen; enhance, L. 31, 163

jiātíng, 家庭, 家庭, n., family; household, L. 20, 105

jiāxiāng, 家鄉, 家乡, n., hometown, L. 33, 172

jiāyòng diànqì, 家用電器, 家用电器, n., household appliances, L. 19, 99

jiāzhòng, 加重, 加重, v., make or become heavier; increase the weight of, L. 30, 157

jiǎ, 甲, 甲, n., the first of the ten Heavenly Stems; used as pronoun here meaning "the first person", L. 8, 40

jiàgé, 價格, 价格, n., price, L. 42, 227

jiàlián wùměi, 價廉物美, 价廉物美, idm., excellent quality at low prices-a bargain buy, L. 19, 101

jiān, 煎, 煎, v., fry in shallow oil, L. 15, 78

jiānchí, 堅持, 坚持, v., insist on; persist in, L. 6, 31

jiǎnchá, 檢查, 检查, v., check; examine; inspect, L. 1, 4

jiǎnchēng, 簡稱, 简称, n., the abbreviated form of a name, L. 15, 77

251

lìshǐ, 歷史, 历史, *n.*, history, L. 21, 108

lìzi, 例子, 例子, *n.*, example, L. 26, 134

lián, 連, 连, *conj.*, even, L. 7, 34

liánjià, 廉價, 廉价, *adj.*, low-priced; cheap, L. 19, 100

liánjiē, 連接, 连接, *v.*, connect, L. 31, 160

liánxì, 聯繫, 联系, *v.*, intergrate; link, L. 31, 163

liánxiǎng, 聯想, 联想, *v.*, associate; connect in the mind, L. 37, 195

liǎn, 臉, 脸, *n.*, face, L. 20, 104

liàn qìgōng, 練氣功, 练气功, *v.-o.*, practice *qigong*, L. 28, 145

liáng, 涼, 凉, *adj.*, cold; cool, L. 6, 30

liánghǎo, 良好, 良好, *adj.*, good, L. 40, 210

liàng, 輛, 辆, *an.*, measure word for cars, L. 36, 188

liáo-tiān, 聊天, 聊天, *v.-o.*, chat, L. 12, 60

liǎojiě, 了解, 了解, *v.*, understand, L. 17, 91

língqián, 零錢, 零钱, *n.*, small change, L. 10, 53

lìng, 另, 另, *adj.*, the other; another, L. 3, 17

Liúlíchǎng, 琉璃廠, 琉璃厂, Liulichang, L. 25, 125

liúshī, 流失, 流失, *v.*, run off; to be washed away, L. 33, 173

liúxíng, 流行, 流行, *v.*, prevalent; be popular, L. 30, 154

liúxuéshēng, 留學生, 留学生, *n.*, foreign student, L. 2, 10

liù-niǎo, 遛鳥, 遛鸟, *v.-o.*, take a stroll with one's caged bird, L. 12, 60

lóu, 樓, 楼, *n.*, story; floor, a multi-storied building, L. 7, 37

lù, 路, 路, *an.*, route 三路公车: No.3 bus, L. 4, 19

lù.shàng, 路上, 路上, *adv.*, on the way, L. 11, 56

lùxiàngjī, 錄像機, 录像机, *n.*, VCR, L. 20, 105

luàn, 亂, 乱, *adj.*, in disorder; in a mess, L. 16, 85

luàn, 亂 V., 乱 V., *adv.*, randomly; arbitrarily, L. 17, 91

luànzhōng yǒuxù, 亂中有序, 乱中有序, *idm.*, finding order in chaos, L. 16, 85

lùn, 論, 论, *v.*, mention; regard; consider, L. 14, 66

luòhòu, 落後, 落后, *adj.*, backward, lagging behind, L. 20, 107

lǚguǎn, 旅館, 旅馆, *n.*, hotel, L. 2, 9

lǚxíng, 旅行, 旅行, *v.*, travel, L. 7, 38

lǚxíng zhīpiào, 旅行支票, 旅行支票, *n.*, traveler's check, L. 7, 39

má.fán, 麻煩, 麻烦, *v.*, bother; put somebody to trouble, L. 7, 36

mǎlù, 馬路, 马路, *n.*, road; street; avenue, L. 16, 82

mǎtǒng, 馬桶, 马桶, *n.*, toilet, L. 10, 50

mǎi.bùqǐ, 買不起, 买不起, *v.-c.*, cannot afford, L. 8, 43

mǎimài, 買賣, 买卖, *n.*, buy and sell; trade, L. 29, 153

mǎizhǔ, 買主, 买主, *n.*, buyer, L. 31, 162

Màidāngláo, 麥當勞, 麦当劳, McDonald's, L. 37, 196

mán.tóu, 饅頭, 馒头, *n.*, steamed bun, L. 15, 75

mǎnyì, 滿意, 满意, *adj.*, satisfied; pleased, L. 30, 156

Mǎnzhōu, 滿州, 满州, Manchuria, L. 43, 231

Mǎnzú, 滿族, 满族, the Manchu nationality, L. 43, 230

mánglù, 忙碌, 忙碌, *adj.*, busy, L. 12, 61

māo, 貓, 猫, *n.*, cat, L. 21, 111

máo, 毛, 毛, *n.*, dime, L. 4, 22

máobǐ, 毛筆, 毛笔, *n.*, writing brush, L. 40, 214

máodùn, 矛盾, 矛盾, *n.*, contradiction; conflict, L. 23, 119

máojīn, 毛巾, 毛巾, *n.*, towel, L. 2, 8

Máo Zhǔxí, 毛主席, 毛主席, Chairman Mao, L. 17, 86

méi xiǎngdào, 沒想到, 没想到, *adv.*, unexpectedly, L. 6, 31

měiyuán, 美元, 美元, *n.*, U. S. dollar, L. 7, 38

mēnrè, 悶熱, 闷热, *adj.*, hot and suffocating; muggy, L. 12, 61

ménkǒu, 門口, 门口, *n.*, gate; doorway; entrance, L. 16, 82

ménpiào, 門票, 门票, *n.*, ticket, L. 12, 58

míyǔ, 謎語, 谜语, *n.*, riddle; conundrum, L. 21, 110

mǐfàn, 米飯, 米饭, *n.*, (cooked) rice, L. 15, 76

mìqiè, 密切, 密切, *adj.*, close, L. 44, 237

miǎnfèi, 免費, 免费, *adj.*, "exempt-charge"; free of charge; free, L. 10, 52

miǎnqiǎng, 勉強, 勉强, *adv.*, reluctantly; grudgingly, L. 27, 140

miàn, 麵, 面, *n.*, noodle, L. 5, 25

miànbāochē, 麵包車, 面包车, *n.*, "loaf-of-bread'car"; van, L. 1, 4

miànduì, 面對, 面对, *v.*, face; confront, L. 34, 179

miànjī, 面積, 面积, *n.*, area (the product of the length times the width), L. 31, 162

miànlín, 面臨, 面临, *v.*, be faced with; be confronted with, L. 33, 172

miànqián, 面前, 面前, *postp.*, in the face of; in front of, L. 13, 65

miànshí, 麵食, 面食, *n.*, wheat-based food, L. 15, 75

miàntiáo, 麵條, 面条, *n.*, noodle, L. 15, 76

miànzi, 面子, 面子, *n.*, face; dignity, L. 13, 62

miáoxiě, 描寫, 描写, *v.*, describe; depict; portray, L. 40, 213

Mín, 民, 民, 民國; the Republic of China (1912-), L. 25, 125

mínzhǔ, 民主, 民主, *n.*, democracy, L. 41, 218

míngcí, 名詞, 名词, *n.*, noun, term, L. 15, 80

Míngdài, 明代, 明代, the Ming Dynasty (1368-1644), L. 8, 41

míngshèng gǔjī, 名勝古跡, 名胜古迹, *n.*, famous scenic spot, L. 44, 237

míngxiǎn, 明顯, 明显, *adj.*, evident; obvious, L. 29, 149

míngxìnpiàn, 明信片, 明信片, *n.*, postcard, L. 4, 23

mócā, 摩擦, 摩擦, *n.*, clash (between two parties); friction, L. 30, 159

mó.hú, 模糊, 模糊, *adj.*, vague, L. 37, 194

mótiān dàlóu, 摩天大樓, 摩天大楼, *n.*, skyscraper, L. 35, 182

Mótuōluólā, 摩托羅拉, 摩托罗拉, Motorola, L. 32, 167

mò, 末, 末, *n.*, end; last stage, L. 25, 125

mò, 墨, 墨, *n.*, Chinese ink; ink stick, L. 40, 213

mòqī, 末期, 末期, *n.*, last phase; final phase, L. 41, 217

mòshēng, 陌生, 陌生, *adj.*, strange; unfamiliar, L. 9, 47

mùdì, 目的, 目的, *n.*, purpose; goal; aim, L. 40, 214

mùqián, 目前, 目前, *t.w.*, now; at present, L. 11, 57

ná, 拿, 拿, *v.*, seize; capture, L. 21, 110

nǎ.li, 哪裏, 哪里, used in a rhetorical question to indicate negation, L. 14, 66

nán, 南, 南, *n.*, south, L. 4, 19

nánfāngrén, 南方人, 南方人, *n.*, Southerner, L. 15, 76

nánguài, 難怪, 难怪, *conj.*, no wonder, L. 32, 169

nánmiǎn, 難免, 难免, *adv./adj.*, hard to avoid, L. 37, 197

nánnǚlǎoshào, 男女老少, 男女老少, *n.*, men and women, young and old, L. 9, 47

nánqiāng běidiào, 南腔北調, 南腔北调, *n.*, (speak with) a mixed accent, L. 18, 93

nǎolì, 腦力, 脑力, *n.*, brains; mental capability, L. 34, 177

nào xiàohua, 鬧笑話, 闹笑话, *v.-o.*, make a fool of oneself, L. 21, 111

Nèi Měnggǔ, 内蒙古, 内蒙古, Inner Mongolia, L. 43, 230

nèiróng, 内容, 内容, *n.*, content, L. 39, 206

nì, 膩, 腻, *adj.*, satiating, L. 28, 147

niándài, 年代, 年代, *n.*, a decade, L. 17, 88

niánjì, 年紀, 年纪, *n.*, age, L. 14, 66

niánlíng, 年齡, 年龄, *n.*, age, L. 30, 155

niánqīng, 年輕, 年轻, *adj.*, young, L. 9, 47

nín, 您, 您, *pron.*, you (polite expression), L. 7, 37

nìngkě, 寧可, 宁可, *adv.*, would rather; better, L. 7, 35

niúròu, 牛肉, 牛肉, *n.*, beef, L. 15, 80

niúzǎikù, 牛仔褲, 牛仔裤, *n.*, jeans, L. 37, 196

nóngcūn, 農村, 农村, *n.*, countryside; rural area, L. 18, 97

nóngmín, 農民, 农民, *n.*, farmer, L. 34, 178

nóngyè, 農業, 农业, *n.*, agriculture, L. 37, 195

nǔlì, 努力, 努力, *adv.*, with great effort, L. 2, 11

nuǎn, 暖, 暖, *adj.*, warm, L. 29, 148

nǚshì, 女士, 女士, *n.*, (a polite term for a woman, married or unmarried) lady; madam, L. 9, 48

Ōuzhōu, 歐洲, 欧洲, Europe, L. 19, 100

ou, 噢, 噢, *interj.*, oh (indicates understanding), L. 8, 41

pá, 爬, 爬, *v.*, climb, L. 28, 144

pà, 怕, 怕, *v.*, fear; be afraid of, L. 4, 21

pái-duì, 排隊, 排队, *v.-o.*, line up, L. 7, 37

páizi, 牌子, 牌子, *n.*, plate; sign, L. 17, 86

páizi, 牌子, 牌子, *n.*, brand; trademark, L. 20, 105

pài, 派, 派, *v.*, dispatch; send, L. 1, 2

pàng, 胖, 胖, *v./adj.*, become fat; fat, L. 28, 142

pàngzi, 胖子, 胖子, *n.*, fatty, L. 28, 143

pǎo-bù, 跑步, 跑步, *v.-o.*, jog, L. 12, 59

pào-chá, 泡茶, 泡茶, *v.-o.*, make tea, L. 6, 31

péikuǎn, 賠款, 赔款, *n.*, indemnity; reparations, L. 42, 223

péi-qián, 賠錢, 赔钱, *v.-o.*, lose money (in business transactions), L. 8, 42

pèijǐ, 配給, 配给, *v.*, distribute in rations, allocate, L. 29, 150

pèiyīn, 配音, 配音, *v.-o.*, dubb; synchronize, L. 35, 185

pèng.dào, 碰到, 碰到, *v.-c.*, run into; meet, L. 14, 71

pīpíng, 批評, 批评, *v.*, criticize, L. 24, 123

píxiāng, 皮箱, 皮箱, *n.*, leather suitcase, L. 19, 99

pìrú, 譬如, 譬如, for example; such as, L. 21, 110

piānyuǎn, 偏遠, 偏远, *adj.*, remote; faraway, L. 31, 161

pián.yí, 便宜, 便宜, *adj.*, inexpensive; cheap, L. 8, 43

pīngpāng, 乒乓, 乒乓, *n.*, table tennis; ping-pong, L. 23, 116

píng, 平, 平, *adj.*, flat; smooth, L. 1, 5

píng, 瓶, 瓶, *an.*, bottle, L. 20, 103

píng'ān, 平安, 平安, *adj.*, safe and sound; without mishap, L. 17, 87

píngcháng, 平常, 平常, *adj.*, ordinary; common, L. 20, 106

píngděng, 平等, 平等, *adj./n.*, equal; equality, L. 9, 48

píngjūn, 平均, 平均, *adv./adj.*, average, L. 39, 205

píngmù, 屏幕, 屏幕, *n.*, TV screen, L. 18, 95

píngshí, 平時, 平时, *adv.*, ordinarily; normally, L. 12, 61

píngwěn, 平穩, 平稳, *adj.*, smooth and steady; stable, L. 42, 226

píngyuán, 平原, 平原, *n.*, plain; flatlands, L. 43, 229

pú.táo, 葡萄, 葡萄, *n.*, grape, L. 44, 235

pǔbiàn, 普遍, 普遍, *adj.*, widespread; general; common, L. 32, 167

pǔjí, 普及, 普及, *v.*, be available to all; popularize, L. 39, 204

pǔtōng, 普通, 普通, *adj.*, common; ordinary, L. 18, 92

Pǔtōnghuà, 普通話, 普通话, *n.*, *Putonghua* (standard Chinese), L. 18, 92

pùzi, 鋪子, 铺子, *n.*, (archaic) store; shop, L. 25, 125

qīzi, 妻子, 妻子, *n.*, wife, L. 27, 138

qí, 騎, 骑, *v.*, ride (an animal or bicycle), L. 7, 34

Qí Lǔ, 齊魯, 齐鲁, ancient name for Shandong, L. 15, 77

qíshí, 其實, 其实, *adv.*, in fact; actually, L. 9, 49

qítā, 其他, 其他, *adj.*, other; else, L. 25, 124

qǐ, 起, 起, *v.*, rise; grow, L. 16, 84

qǐ zuòyòng, 起作用, 起作用, *v.-o.*, be effective; have effect, L. 16, 84

qìgōng, 氣功, 气功, *n.*, *qigong*, a system of deep breathing exercises, L. 28, 144

shòu huānyíng, 受歡迎, 受欢迎, adj., be well received, L. 32, 169

shòuhuòyuán, 售貨員, 售货员, n., salesclerk; shop assistant, L. 20, 104

shòule, 受了, 受了, v., have received, L. 9, 48

shòu-zuì, 受罪, 受罪, v.-o., endure hardships, tortures, rough conditions, etc.; have a hard time, L. 6, 29

shūcài, 蔬菜, 蔬菜, n., vegetable, L. 29, 150

shūfǎ, 書法, 书法, n., calligraphy, L. 40, 210

shū.fú, 舒服, 舒服, adj., comfortable, L. 1, 5

shūmù, 書目, 书目, n., catalogue of titles; booklist, L. 25, 126

shūmiàn, 書面, 书面, adj., written; in written form, L. 41, 216

shūmiànyǔ, 書面語, 书面语, n., written language, L. 41, 217

shūshì, 舒適, 舒适, adj./n., comfortable; comfort, L. 36, 189

shūxiě, 書寫, 书写, n./v., writing, write, L. 18, 96

shú, 熟, 熟, adj., familiar, L. 21, 111

shù, 樹, 树, v., set up; establish, L. 17, 90

shùliàng, 數量, 数量, n., number; quantity, L. 31, 160

shuāiluò, 衰落, 衰落, n./v., decline, L. 40, 215

shuāiruò, 衰弱, 衰弱, v./adj., weaken, weak; feeble, L. 43, 232

shuāngrénfáng, 雙人房, 双人房, n., double room, L. 2, 7

shuǐní, 水泥, 水泥, n., cement, L. 23, 116

shuǐpíng, 水平, 水平, n., level, L. 19, 101

shuì-zháo, 睡著, 睡着, v.-c., fall asleep, L. 1, 5

shùnlì, 順利, 顺利, adj., smooth; successful, L. 2, 6

shuōfǎ, 說法, 说法, n., wording; way of saying a thing, L. 26, 134

shuōmíng, 說明, 说明, v., explain; show, L. 18, 93

Sīchóu Zhī Lù, 絲綢之路, 丝绸之路, the Silk Road, L. 44, 234

sījī, 司機, 司机, n., driver, L. 7, 32

sīrén, 私人, 私人, adj., private; personal, L. 7, 34

sīshì, 私事, 私事, n., private affairs, L. 13, 65

sīwéi, 思維, 思维, n., thought; thinking, L. 44, 240

sīxiǎng, 思想, 思想, n., thinking; thought, L. 17, 91

sǐjì yìngbèi, 死記硬背, 死记硬背, v., rote memorizing, L. 24, 121

...sǐrén, … 死人, … 死人, adv., extremely; to death, L. 7, 33

sìdàjiàn, 四大件, 四大件, n., the four big things, L. 29, 151

sìfāng, 四方, 四方, n., four directions, L. 35, 181

sìhéyuàn, 四合院, 四合院, n., a traditional Chinese-style compound with rooms around a courtyard, L. 35, 182

sìmiào, 寺廟, 寺庙, n., temple, L. 35, 180

sōng, 鬆, 松, adj., loose; slack, L. 1, 4

Sōngxià, 松下, 松下, Panasonic, L. 20, 106

sòng, 送, 送, v., walk (somebody); accompany; escort, L. 14, 70

sòng, 送, 送, v., give (a present), L. 19, 98

Sòngcháo, 宋朝, 宋朝, the Song Dynasty, L. 43, 231

súhuà, 俗話, 俗话, n., common saying; proverb, L. 21, 108

sùdù, 速度, 速度, n., speed, L. 44, 239

suàn.shì, 算是, 算是, v., be considered as; be regarded as, L. 36, 188

suíbiàn, 隨便, 随便, adv., casually; informally, L. 14, 66

suíbiàn, 隨便, 随便, adv., carelessly, L. 17, 91

suídì, 隨地, 随地, adv., anywhere; everywhere, L. 17, 87

suíshēn, 隨身, 随身, adv., "follow-person"; (carry) on one's person; (take) with, L. 10, 53

suízhe, 隨著, 随着, adv., along with; in the wake of, L. 23, 119

suì, 歲, 岁, (age unit) … years old, L. 28, 143

suōduǎn, 縮短, 缩短, v., shorten, L. 31, 161

suǒ, 所, 所, an., measure word for house, L. 24, 120

Suǒní, 索尼, 索尼, Sony, L. 20, 106

suǒwèi, 所謂, 所谓, adj., so-called, L. 29, 151

suǒyǒu, 所有, 所有, adj., all, L. 9, 46

suǒzài, 所在, 所在, n., place; location, L. 44, 241

tā, 它, 它, pron., it, L. 21, 109

tái, 台, 台, an., measure word for machines, L. 39, 205

Táiwān, 台灣, 台湾, Taiwan, L. 9, 48

tàijíquán, 太極拳, 太极拳, n., a kind of traditional Chinese shadow boxing, L. 12, 60

Tàipíngyáng, 太平洋, 太平洋, the Pacific Ocean, L. 38, 201

tàitai, 太太, 太太, n., wife, L. 26, 130

tán.délái, 談得來, 谈得来, v.-c., get along well, L. 2, 7

tán liàn'ài, 談戀愛, 谈恋爱, v.-o., be in love; have a love affair, L. 12, 61

tán-qín, 彈琴, 弹琴, v.-o., play a stringed musical instrument, L. 40, 213

táng, 糖, 糖, n., candy, sugar, L. 28, 146

Tángcháo, 唐朝, 唐朝, the Tang Dynasty, L. 44, 237

tàng, 趟, 趟, an., measure word for a trip, L. 42, 226

táotài, 淘汰, 淘汰, v., eliminate through selection or competition, die out; fall into disuse, L. 30, 156

tǎolùn, 討論, 讨论, v., discuss, L. 33, 172

tèbié, 特別, 特别, adv./adj., especially; special, L. 2, 7

tèbié xíngzhèngqū, 特別行政區, 特别行政区, n., special administrative region, L. 42, 226

tèchǎn, 特產, 特产, n., special local product, L. 11, 56

tèdiǎn, 特點, 特点, n., characteristic; trait, L. 9, 49

tèsè, 特色, 特色, n., characteristic; distinguishing feature, L. 9, 49

tèshū, 特殊, 特殊, adj., special, L. 16, 85

tèyǒu, 特有, 特有, adj., peculiar, L. 16, 85

téng, 疼, 疼, v./adj., ache; sore, painful, L. 5, 25

tī xù, T恤, T恤, n., T-shirt, L. 37, 196

tíchàng, 提倡, 提倡, v., advocate, L. 18, 94

tí-chū, 提出, 提出, v.-c., put forward; advance; raise, L. 17, 90

tígāo, 提高, 提高, v., raise; highten; increase, L. 19, 101

tígōng, 提供, 提供, v., offer; provide; supply, L. 3, 15

tímù, 題目, 题目, n., title; subject; topic, L. 17, 91

tí-qǐ, 提起, 提起, v.-c., mention; speak of, L. 37, 195

tízǎo, 提早, 提早, v., shift to an earlier time; be earlier than planned or expected, L. 34, 174

tǐlì, 體力, 体力, n., physical strength, L. 34, 177

tǐ.miàn, 體面, 体面, adj./n., honorable; dignity; face, L. 34, 178

tǐxiàn, 體現, 体现, v., embody; incarnate; reflect, L. 24, 122

tǐyù, 體育, 体育, n., physical education; sports, L. 23, 117

tǐzhì, 體制, 体制, n., system, L. 42, 225

Tiān'ānmén, 天安門, 天安门, Tian An Men; Gate of Heavenly Peace, L. 17, 88

Tiānjīn, 天津, 天津, Tianjin, L. 38, 198

tiānqì yùbào, 天氣預報, 天气预报, n., weather forecast, L. 2, 7

Tiāntán, 天壇, 天坛, the Temple of Heaven, L. 35, 180

tiāntáng, 天堂, 天堂, n., heaven; paradise, L. 30, 154

tián, 填, 填, v., fill in, L. 4, 22

tián, 甜, 甜, adj., sweet, L. 15, 74

tiáo, 條, 条, an., measure word for things narrow and long, L. 4, 19

tiáojiàn, 條件, 条件, n., condition, L. 2, 8

tiáozhěng, 調整, 调整, n./v., adjustment, adjust, L. 44, 240

tiǎozhàn, 挑戰, 挑战, n./v., challenge, L. 34, 174

tiào-wǔ, 跳(舞), 跳(舞), v.-o., dance, L. 12, 60

tiē, 貼, 贴, v., paste; stick; glue, L. 33, 170

tiěfànwǎn, 鐵飯碗, 铁饭碗, n., "iron rice bowl"--a secure job, L. 22, 112

tiělù, 鐵路, 铁路, n., railroad, L. 31, 160

tōngguò, 通過, 通过, v., pass through, go through, L. 1, 2

tōngguò, 通過, 通过, v., pass, L. 24, 122

tōngguò, 通過, 通过, prep., by means of; by way of, L. 38, 202

tōnghūn, 通婚, 通婚, v., intermarry, L. 43, 233

tōngxíng, 通行, 通行, adj., current; general, L. 38, 200

tōngxùn, 通訊, 通讯, n., communication; correspondence, L. 32, 164

tōngyòng, 通用, 通用, adj., in common use; current, L. 42, 227

tóngqíng, 同情, 同情, v., sympathize, L. 32, 166

tóngshí, 同時, 同时, t.w., same time, at the same time; simultaneously, L. 20, 107

tóngwū, 同屋, 同屋, n., roommate, L. 2, 7

tóngyì, 同意, 同意, n./v., agreement; approval, agree; approve, L. 13, 63

tóngzhì, 同志, 同志, n., comrade, L. 9, 46

tǒngjì, 統計, 统计, n./v., statistics; add up; count, L. 39, 205

tǒngzhì, 統治, 统治, n./v., governance, rule; govern, L. 42, 225

tóunǎo, 頭腦, 头脑, n., brains; mind, L. 3, 13

tóuzī, 投資, 投资, v./n., invest, investment, L. 31, 160

túshūguǎn yuán, 圖書館員, 图书馆员, n., librarian, L. 25, 126

tǔdì, 土地, 土地, n., land, L. 31, 162

tǔ-tán, 吐痰, 吐痰, v.-o., spit; expectorate, L. 17, 87

tù, 吐, 吐, v., vomit, L. 5, 25

tuánjié, 團結, 团结, v./n., unite; rally, union, L. 17, 89

tuī chén chū xīn, 推陳出新, 推陈出新, idm., weed out the old to bring forth the new, L. 44, 241

tuīràng, 推讓, 推让, v., decline (a position, favor, etc, out of modesty), L. 14, 68

tuīxíng, 推行, 推行, v., carry out; practice, L. 18, 94

tuǐ, 腿, 腿, n., leg, L. 10, 50

tuìxiū, 退休, 退休, v., retire, L. 34, 174

tuō, 脫, 脱, v., take off; cast off, L. 21, 108

Tuōfú, 托福, 托福, n., TOEFL, L. 33, 170

wàiguó, 外國, 外国, n., foreign country, L. 3, 17

wàijiāo, 外交, 外交, n., diplomacy; foreign affairs, L. 23, 116

wàilái, 外來, 外来, adj., outside; external; foreign, L. 38, 200

wàiláiyǔ, 外來語, 外来语, n., loan words, L. 41, 219

wàiliú, 外流, 外流, v., outflow; drain, L. 33, 172

wàishìchù, 外事處, 外事处, n., foreign affairs office, L. 1, 2

wàiyǔ, 外語, 外语, n., foreign language, L. 38, 198

wàizī, 外資, 外资, n., foreign capital, L. 37, 194

wánchéng, 完成, 完成, n./v., completion, complete, L. 31, 160

wánhǎo, 完好, 完好, adj., intact; whole, L. 35, 180

wǎn, 碗, 碗, n./an., bowl, L. 5, 24

wǎnnián, 晚年, 晚年, n., one's later years, L. 30, 157

wǎnshuì, 晚睡, 晚睡, v., go to bed late, L. 3, 13

wànsuì, 萬歲, 万岁, long live, L. 17, 89

Wángfǔjǐng, 王府井, 王府井, Wangfujing, L. 7, 32

wǎng, 往, 往, prep., in the direction of; towards, L. 4, 19

wǎngwǎng, 往往, 往往, adv., often; frequently, L. 12, 58

wàngjì, 忘記, 忘记, v., forget, L. 21, 110

wēijī, 危機, 危机, n., crisis; precarious point, L. 34, 179

wēixiǎn, 危險, 危险, adj., dangerous, L. 16, 82

wéi, 圍, 围, v., surround; enclose, L. 23, 116

wéichí, 維持, 维持, v., maintain, L. 27, 138

wěidà, 偉大, 伟大, adj., great; mighty, L. 43, 231

wèi, 爲, 为, prep., for, L. 10, 51

wèi.dào, 味道, 味道, n., taste, L. 29, 150

wèishēng, 衛生, 卫生, adj., hygienic; sanitary, L. 10, 51

wèishēngzhǐ, 衛生紙, 卫生纸, n., toilet paper, L. 10, 52

wēnbǎo, 溫飽, 温饱, adj., adequately fed and clothed, L. 29, 148

wén, 聞, 闻, v., smell, L. 10, 52

wénfáng sìbǎo, 文房四寶, 文房四宝, n., the four treasures of the study, L. 40, 213

Wéngé, 文革, 文革, an abbreviation of 文化大革命; Cultural Revolution, L. 37, 192

wénhuà, 文化, 文化, n., culture, L. 14, 72

wénmíng, 文明, 文明, n., civilization; culture, L. 17, 90

wénrén, 文人, 文人, n., man of letters; scholar; literati, L. 40, 213

wénwù, 文物, 文物, n., cultural relic; historical relic, L. 44, 237

wénxué, 文學, 文学, n., literature, L. 25, 126

wényánwén, 文言文, 文言文, n., classical style of writing, L. 41, 216

wénzì, 文字, 文字, n., characters; writing, L. 41, 218

wénzi, 蚊子, 蚊子, n., mosquito, L. 5, 26

wěndìng, 穩定, 稳定, adj., stable, L. 22, 114

wūrǎn, 污染, 污染, n., pollution, L. 36, 187

wú, 無, 无, v., (written) there is no, L. 26, 132

wúliáo, 無聊, 无聊, adj., boring; silly; stupid, L. 39, 207

wúlùn, 無論, 无论, conj., no matter what, how, etc.; regardless of, L. 9, 46

wǔ fēn zhī yī, 五分之一, 五分之一, one fifth, L. 36, 189

wǔjiào, 午覺, 午觉, n., afternoon nap, L. 6, 28

wǔ-lóng, 舞龍, 舞龙, v.-o., Chinese dragon dance, L. 37, 196

wǔ-shī, 舞獅, 舞狮, v.-o., Chinese lion dance, L. 37, 196

wù, 勿, 勿, adv., (written) do not, L. 17, 87

wùhuì, 誤會, 误会, n./v., misunderstanding, L. 26, 132

xīběi, 西北, 西北, n., northwest, L. 43, 229

xīfàn, 稀飯, 稀饭, n., rice or millet gruel; porridge, L. 15, 76

xīguā, 西瓜, 西瓜, n., watermelon, L. 5, 25

xīhuà, 西化, 西化, n., westernization, L. 44, 238

xīlánhuā, 西蘭花, 西兰花, n., broccoli, L. 15, 79

xīnán, 西南, 西南, n., southwest, L. 43, 229

xīshōu, 吸收, 吸收, v., absorb, L. 44, 234

xīwàng, 希望, 希望, v./n., hope; wish, L. 16, 84

Xīyà, 西亞, 西亚, Western Asia, L. 44, 235

xīyǐn, 吸引, 吸引, v., attract, L. 33, 173

Xīzàng, 西藏, 西藏, Tibet, L. 43, 230

xíguàn, 習慣, 习惯, v./n., be accustomed to; be used to; habit; custom, L. 3, 12

xǐ, 洗, 洗, v., (in this context) develop (film), L. 4, 22

xǐshǒutái, 洗手台, 洗手台, n., sink (in a restroom), L. 10, 52

xǐyīfěn, 洗衣粉, 洗衣粉, n., detergent, L. 20, 103

xǐ-zǎo, 洗澡, 洗澡, v.-o., have a bath; bathe, L. 3, 12

xiārén, 蝦仁, 虾仁, n., shelled fresh shrimp, L. 15, 80

xià-chē, 下車, 下车, v.-o., get off (a car), L. 7, 36

xiàgǎng, 下崗, 下岗, v., lay off, L. 34, 174

xiàjiàng, 下降, 下降, v., descend; drop, L. 27, 136

xià-qí, 下棋, 下棋, v.-o., play chess, L. 12, 60

xiàtiān, 夏天, 夏天, n., summer, L. 6, 29

xiān.shēng, 先生, 先生, n., Mr., L. 1, 2

xiǎnrán, 顯然, 显然, adv., obviously; clearly, L. 24, 123

xiàn, 縣, 县, n., county, L. 18, 93

xiàndàihuà, 現代化, 现代化, adj./n., modern, modernization, L. 1, 5

xiànjīn, 現金, 现金, n., cash, L. 7, 38

xiànmù, 羡慕, 美慕, v., envy, L. 36, 190

xiànshí, 現實, 现实, n., reality; actuality, L. 39, 208

xiànxiàng, 現象, 现象, n., phenomenon, L. 18, 94

xiànzhì, 限制, 限制, v., limit, L. 33, 171

Xiāng, 湘, 湘, 湖南; Hunan Province, L. 15, 74

xiāngdāng, 相當, 相当, adv., quite; considerably, L. 20, 107

xiāngfǎn, 相反, 相反, adj., opposite, L. 44, 238

Xiānggǎng, 香港, 香港, Hong Kong, L. 9, 48

xiānghù, 相互, 相互, adj., mutual; each other, L. 23, 119

xiāngtóng, 相同, 相同, adj., alike; the same; identical, L. 14, 73

xiāngxìn, 相信, 相信, v., believe, L. 26, 135

xiāngyān, 香煙, 香烟, n., cigarette, L. 28, 147

xiāngyìng, 相應, 相应, v., corresponding; relevant, L. 13, 62

xiāngzi, 箱子, 箱子, n., chest; trunk; baggage, L. 1, 3

xiǎngfāngshèfǎ, 想方設法, 想方设法, v., conjure up all kinds of methods, L. 28, 144

xiǎngshòu, 享受, 享受, v., enjoy, L. 19, 101

xiǎngshòu, 享受, 享受, n., ease and comfort; enjoyment, L. 36, 188

xiǎngxiàng, 想像, 想象, v./n., imagine; imagination, L. 1, 5

xiàng, 向, 向, prep., from; towards, L. 6, 31

xiàng, 向, 向, prep., toward, L. 35, 181

xiàngshàng, 向上, 向上, v., make progress; go upward, L. 17, 86

xiàng.shēng, 相聲, 相声, n., traditional Chinese comic dialogue, L. 35, 185

xiàngzhēng, 象徵, 象征, v., symbolize, L. 42, 224

xiāofèi, 消費, 消费, v./n., consume; consumption, L. 29, 149

xiāofèipǐn, 消費品, 消费品, n., consumer goods, L. 29, 150

xiāohào, 消耗, 消耗, v., consume; expend; exhaust, L. 29, 150

xiāomiè, 消滅, 消灭, v., eliminate; abolish; exterminate; wipe out, L. 43, 231

xiāoshī, 消失, 消失, v., disappear, L. 37, 196

xiǎochī, 小吃, 小吃, n., snack; refreshments, L. 11, 56

xiǎohái, 小孩, 小孩, n., kid; children, L. 28, 143

xiǎo.jiě, 小姐, 小姐, n., Miss; also used for married professional women, L. 4, 18

xiǎokāng, 小康, 小康, adj., (said of a family or society) comparatively well-off, L. 29, 148

xiǎolǎo.pó, 小老婆, 小老婆, n., mistress; concubine, L. 37, 195

xiǎoshuō, 小說, 小说, n., fiction; novel, L. 25, 127

xiǎotān, 小攤, 小摊, n., vendor's stand; stall, L. 16, 85

xiǎoxué, 小學, 小学, n., elementary school, L. 17, 86

xiàoróng, 笑容, 笑容, *n.*, smile; smiling expression, L. 20, 104

xiàoshùn, 孝順, 孝顺, *v.*, show filial obedience, L. 30, 158

xiàoyuán, 校園, 校园, *n.*, campus, L. 2, 9

xiēhòuyǔ, 歇後語, 歇后语, *n.*, a two-part allegorical saying, L. 21, 108

xiétiáo, 協調, 协调, *adj.*, coordinate; harmonious, L. 35, 183

xiéyì, 協議, 协议, *n.*, agreement, L. 23, 119

xiézi, 鞋子, 鞋子, *n.*, shoes, L. 19, 98

Xīnjiāpō, 新加坡, 新加坡, Singapore, L. 33, 172

Xīnjiāng, 新疆, 新疆, Xinjiang, L. 43, 230

xīnshǎng, 欣賞, 欣赏, *v.*, appreciate; enjoy, L. 35, 184

xīnwén, 新聞, 新闻, *n.*, news, L. 18, 95

xīnxiān, 新鮮, 新鲜, *adj.*, new; novel, fresh, L. 14, 72

xìnfēng, 信封, 信封, *n.*, envelope, L. 4, 23

xìnxī, 信息, 信息, *n.*, information; message, L. 17, 89

xìnxīn, 信心, 信心, *n.*, confidence, L. 42, 227

xìnyǎng, 信仰, 信仰, *n.*, faith; belief; conviction, L. 43, 230

xìnzhǐ, 信紙, 信纸, *n.*, letter paper, L. 4, 23

xīngfèn, 興奮, 兴奋, *adj.*, excited, L. 1, 5

xīngqǐ, 興起, 兴起, *n./v.*, rise; spring up, L. 40, 215

xíngchéng, 形成, 形成, *v.*, form; take shape, L. 44, 240

xíngrén, 行人, 行人, *n.*, pedestrian, L. 10, 51

xíngshǐ, 行駛, 行驶, *v.*, (of a vehicle, ship, etc.) go; travel, L. 35, 184

xíngshǐ, 行使, 行使, *v.*, perform; exercise, L. 42, 222

xíngshì, 形式, 形式, *n.*, form, L. 26, 135

xǐng, 醒, 醒, *v.*, wake up; sober up, L. 3, 14

xìngmíng, 姓名, 姓名, *n.*, full name, L. 4, 23

xìngqù, 興趣, 兴趣, *n.*, interest, L. 24, 121

xiū.xí, 休息, 休息, *v.*, rest; have a rest, L. 5, 24

xiūxián, 休閑, 休闲, *adj.*, recreational, L. 12, 59

xūyào, 需要, 需要, *v./n.*, need; want; require, L. 3, 14

xuānchuán, 宣傳, 宣传, *n./v.*, propaganda; propagandize, L. 18, 97

xuǎnzé, 選擇, 选择, *v.*, select; choose, L. 15, 76

xué, 學, 学, *v.*, imitate; mimic, L. 6, 30

xué-huì, 學會, 学会, *v.-c.*, learn, L. 3, 17

xuéshù, 學術, 学术, *n.*, learning; academic, L. 23, 117

xuéwèi, 學位, 学位, *n.*, academic degree; degree, L. 40, 211

xuéxí, 學習, 学习, *v.*, study, L. 2, 9

xuézhě, 學者, 学者, *n.*, scholar; learned man, L. 25, 126

xùnliàn, 訓練, 训练, *n./v.*, training, train, L. 24, 121

yā, 鴨, 鸭, *n.*, duck, L. 15, 78

yālì, 壓力, 压力, *n.*, pressure, L. 30, 155

Yāpiàn Zhànzhēng, 鴉片戰爭, 鸦片战争, the Opium War, L. 42, 223

Yàzhōu, 亞洲, 亚洲, Asia, L. 38, 202

yán, 嚴, 严, *adj.*, strict; severe; stern, L. 1, 3

yánjiū, 研究, 研究, *v.*, consider; discuss, study, L. 13, 64

yánjiūshēng, 研究生, 研究生, *n.*, graduate student, L. 33, 170

yánjiūshēng yuàn, 研究生院, 研究生院, *n.*, graduate school, L. 33, 171

yánlùn, 言論, 言论, *n.*, opinion on public affairs; speech, L. 25, 129

yánsù, 嚴肅, 严肃, *adj.*, serious; solemn, L. 25, 127

yányòng, 沿用, 沿用, *v.*, continue to use (an old method, etc.), L. 41, 220

yánzhòng, 嚴重, 严重, *adj.*, (said of illness, situation) serious, L. 7, 35

yàn, 硯, 砚, *n.*, ink stone; ink slab, L. 40, 213

yáng, 洋, 洋, *adj.*, western; foreign, L. 44, 236

yángbù, 洋布, 洋布, *n.*, foreign cloth, L. 44, 236

yánghuǒ, 洋火, 洋火, *n.*, (informal) matches; 火柴 huǒchái, L. 44, 236

yángrén, 洋人, 洋人, *n.*, foreigner (opposite of Chinese), L. 44, 236

yāoguǒ, 腰果, 腰果, *n.*, cashew, L. 15, 80

yāoqiú, 要求, 要求, *n./v.*, request; demand, L. 13, 63

yàoburán, 要不然, 要不然, *conj.*, otherwise; or else, L. 21, 111

yī.fú, 衣服, 衣服, *n.*, clothes; clothing, L. 19, 98

yījiǔsìjiǔ, 1949, 1949, 1949, L. 9, 46

yīkào, 依靠, 依靠, *v.*, depend on, L. 27, 137

yī shí zhù xíng, 衣食住行, 衣食住行, *idm.*, "food, clothing, shelter and transportation" -- basic necessities of life, L. 35, 183

yīyuàn, 醫院, 医院, *n.*, hospital, L. 5, 27

yíbù yíbù, 一步一步, 一步一步, *adv.*, step by step, L. 13, 64

yídà, 一大 n., 一大 n., one big ..., L. 29, 153

yídìng, 一定, 一定, *adj.*, given; particular; certain, L. 13, 64

Yíhéyuán, 頤和園, 颐和园, the Summer Palace, L. 12, 58

yíqiè, 一切, 一切, *n.*, all; every; everything, L. 2, 6

yíxiàng, 一向, 一向, *adv.*, always; all along, L. 30, 158

yízài, 一再, 一再, *adv.*, again and again; repeatedly, L. 14, 69

yǐ, 乙, 乙, *n.*, the second of ten Heavenly Stems, the second person, L. 8, 40

yǐ, 以, 以,; 用; use, L. 38, 198

yǐ...wéi..., 以A爲B, 以A为B, take A as B; regard A as B, L. 30, 159

yǐjí, 以及, 以及, *conj.*, and (used in writing), L. 28, 147

yǐshàng, …以上, …以上, *postp.*, above (a given point or line), L. 29, 148

yǐwéi, 以爲, 以为, *v.*, mistakenly think, L. 3, 17

yǐxià, …以下, …以下, *postp.*, under (a given point or line), L. 39, 209

yìbān, 一般, 一般, *adj.*, general; common, L. 29, 151

yìbān láishuō, 一般來說, 一般来说, *adv.*, generally speaking, L. 3, 15

yìbānshuōlái, 一般說來, 一般说来, 一般来说, L. 15, 75

zhùzhòng, 注重, 注重, v., lay stress on; pay attention to, L. 30, 155

zhùzuò, 著作, 著作, n., work; book; writing, L. 25, 127

zhuānjiā, 專家, 专家, n., expert, L. 37, 193

zhuānxīn, 專心, 专心, adv./adj., concentrate one's attention; be absorbed, L. 38, 198

zhuānyè, 專業, 专业, n., special field of study; major, L. 24, 120

zhuānyè, 專業, 专业, adj./n., professional; profession, L. 34, 177

zhuǎnxiàng, 轉向, 转向, v., 转：turn; 向：towards, L. 34, 175

zhuàn-qián, 賺錢, 赚钱, v.-o., make money, make a profit, L. 8, 42

zhuāng, 裝, 装, v., set up; install, L. 36, 188

zhuāngshì, 裝飾, 装饰, n., decoration, L. 12, 59

zhuàng, 撞, 撞, v., collide; bump against; run into, L. 16, 83

zhuàng, 幢, 幢, an., measure word for building, L. 35, 184

zhǔnbèi, 準備, 准备, n./v., preparation, prepare, L. 24, 121

zhǔnshí, 準時, 准时, adv., punctually; on time, L. 1, 2

zhuō, 桌, 桌, an., a entire table of, L. 14, 72

zhuō, 捉, 捉, v., catch; capture, L. 21, 111

zīyuán, 資源, 资源, n., natural resources, L. 19, 99

zìcóng, 自從, 自从, prep., since, L. 18, 95

zì gǔ yǐlái, 自古以來, 自古以来, since ancient times, L. 34, 177

zìjǐ, 自己, 自己, pron., oneself, L. 6, 28

zìláishuǐ, 自來水, 自来水, n., tap water, L. 6, 30

zìmù, 字幕, 字幕, n., captions (of motion pictures, etc.); subtitles, L. 18, 95

zìrán, 自然, 自然, adv./adj., naturally; natural, L. 18, 97

zìwèi, 自衛, 自卫, v., self-defense, L. 44, 239

zìxíngchē, 自行車, 自行车, n., bicycle, L. 7, 34

zìyóu, 自由, 自由, n./adj., freedom, free, L. 25, 129

zìyuàn, 自願, 自愿, adv., of one's own free will, L. 30, 156

zìzhìqū, 自治區, 自治区, n., autonomous region, L. 43, 230

zōngjiào, 宗教, 宗教, n., religion, L. 43, 230

zǒu-lù, 走路, 走路, v.-o., walk; go on foot, L. 7, 35

zú, 族, 族, n., race; nationality, L. 43, 228

zǔfùmǔ, 祖父母, 祖父母, n., grandparents, L. 30, 156

zuìhǎo, 最好, 最好, adv., had better; it would be best, L. 4, 18

zuìjìn, 最近, 最近, adv., recently, L. 6, 30

zūnjìng, 尊敬, 尊敬, v., respect a person (because of his age, status, or deeds), L. 34, 178

zūnshǒu, 遵守, 遵守, v., observe; abide by, L. 16, 84

zūnyán, 尊嚴, 尊严, n., dignity; honor, L. 30, 157

zūnzhòng, 尊重, 尊重, n., respect; value; esteem, L. 23, 119

zuǒyòu, 左右, 左右, around (used after a number), L. 43, 228

zuò, 座, 座, an., measure word for bridges, buildings, etc., L. 16, 82

zuò-rén, 做人, 做人, v.-o., be an upright person, L. 17, 87

zuòwèi, 座位, 座位, n., seat; place, L. 14, 68

zuòyòng, 作用, 作用, n., function; effect, L. 16, 84

zuòzhě, 作者, 作者, n., author; writer, L. 40, 212

English Index

A is not so much ... as B; A is less desirable than B,
與其 A, 不如 B, 与其 A, 不如B, yǔqí..., bùrú...,
conj., L. 27, 136

abbreviated form of a name, 簡稱, 简称, jiǎnchēng,
n., L. 15, 77

abbreviation of Cultural Revolution, 文革, 文革,
Wéngé, L. 37, 192

ability; capability, 本事, 本事, běn.shì, n., L. 24, 122

about the same; similar, 差不多, 差不多,
chà.bùduō, adj., L. 15, 74

above (a given point or line), ... 以上, ... 以上,
yǐshàng, postp., L. 29, 148

absolutely not, 絕不, 绝不, juébù, adv., L. 40, 211

absorb, 吸收, 吸收, xīshōu, v., L. 44, 234

academic degree; degree, 學位, 学位, xuéwèi, n.,
L. 40, 211

accept, 接受, 接受, jiēshòu, v., L. 23, 119

according to, 據, 据, jù, prep., L. 32, 167

ache; sore, painful, 疼, 疼, téng, v./adj., L. 5, 25

achieve (a goal), 達到, 达到, dádào, v., L. 29, 151

achievement, 成就, 成就, chéngjiù, n., L. 43, 232

achievement; grade, 成績, 成绩, chéngjī, n., L. 18, 95

across from; in front of, 對面, 对面, duìmiàn, postp.,
L. 4, 20

activity, 活動, 活动, huódòng, n., L. 25, 124

actually; in reality, 實際, 实际, shíjì, adv., L. 15, 81

add; increase, 增添, 增添, zēngtiān, v., L. 35, 185

add subtitles, 打, 打, dǎ, prov., L. 18, 95

address, 地址, 地址, dìzhǐ, n., L. 4, 22

adequately fed and clothed, 溫飽, 温饱, wēnbǎo,
adj., L. 29, 148

adjustment, adjust, 調整, 调整, tiáozhěng, n./v.,
L. 44, 240

adopt, 採取, 采取, cǎiqǔ, v., L. 29, 152

advertisement, 廣告, 广告, guǎnggào, n., L. 17, 88

advocate, 提倡, 提倡, tíchàng, v., L. 18, 94

advocate; maintain, 主張, 主张, zhǔzhāng, v., L. 33,
171

affirm; confirm; approve; regard as positive,
affirmation, 肯定, 肯定, kěndìng, v./n., L. 25, 129

after..., ⋯ 之後, ⋯ 之后, zhīhòu, 25, 127

after (time duration), 過 time duration, 过 time
duration, guò, v., L. 7, 35

after all, 畢竟, 毕竟, bìjìng, adv., L. 38, 202

after all (used in a question), 到底, 到底, dàodǐ, adv.,
L. 8, 41

after entering a country, follow its customs; "When in
Rome, do as the Romans.", 入境隨俗, 入境随俗,
rù jìng suí sú, idm., L. 14, 73

afternoon nap, 午覺, 午觉, wǔjiào, n., L. 6, 28

again; anew; afresh, 重新, 重新, chóngxīn, adv.,
L. 8, 41

again and again; repeatedly, 一再, 一再, yízài, adv.,
L. 14, 69

age, 年紀, 年纪, niánjì, n., L. 14, 66

age, 年齡, 年龄, niánlíng, n., L. 30, 155

agree; promise, answer, 答應, 答应, dā.yìng, v.,
L. 13, 64

agreement, 協議, 协议, xiéyì, n., L. 23, 119

agreement; approval, agree; approve, 同意, 同意,
tóngyì, n./v., L. 13, 63

agriculture, 農業, 农业, nóngyè, n., L. 37, 195

air, 空氣, 空气, kōngqì, n., L. 36, 187

air conditioning, 空調, 空调, kōngtiáo, n., L. 2, 7

air conditioning, 冷氣, 冷气, lěngqì, n., L. 26, 133

airplane, 飛機, 飞机, fēijī, n., L. 1, 2

airport, 機場, 机场, jīchǎng, n., L. 1, 2

alike; the same; identical, 相同, 相同, xiāngtóng,
adj., L. 14, 73

all, 所有, 所有, suǒyǒu, adj., L.9, 46

all; every; everything, 一切, 一切, yíqiè, n., L. 2, 6

all house happiness: a hodgepodge of ingredients
cooked together in one pot, 全家福, 全家福,
quánjiāfú, n., L. 15, 81

all kinds of, 各種各樣, 各种各样, gèzhǒng gèyàng,
adj., L. 17, 86

all kinds of, 種種, 种种, zhǒngzhǒng, adj., L. 42, 224

all the way; all along; continuously, 一直, 一直,
yìzhí, adv., L. 1, 5

all trades and professions, 各行各業, 各行各业,
gèháng gèyè, n., L. 22, 115

alleviate, 減輕, 减轻, jiǎnqīng, v., L. 34, 176

almost; nearly, 差不多, 差不多, chà.bùduō, adv.,
L. 1, 4

almost; nearly, 幾乎, 几乎, jīhū, adv., L. 22, 113

along with; in the wake of, 隨著, 随着, suízhe, adv.,
L. 23, 119

always; all along, 一向, 一向, yíxiàng, adv., L. 30,
158

amount, 分量, 分量, fēn.liàng, n., L. 29, 150

analyse, analysis, 分析, 分析, fēnxī, v./n, L. 24, 121

ancient; age-old, 古老, 古老, gǔlǎo, adj., L. 1, 5

ancient name for Shandong, 齊魯, 齐鲁, Qí Lǔ,
L. 15, 77

ancient painting, 古畫, 古画, gǔhuà, n., L. 8, 41

ancient times, 古代, 古代, gǔdài, n., L. 12, 59

and, 與, 与, yǔ, conj., L. 18, 94

and (used in writing), 以及, 以及, yǐjí, conj., L. 28,
147

and so on; and what not, 什麼的, 什么的, shénmede,
L. 15, 79

and so on; etc., 等等, 等等, děngděng, L. 17, 89

angle; point of view, 角度, 角度, jiǎodù, n., L. 3, 17

another name for Guangdong Province, 粵, 粤, Yuè,
L. 15, 77

answer, 回答, 回答, huídá, n./v., L. 13, 63

antique, 古董, 古董, gǔdǒng, n., L. 8, 40

any; whichever; whatever, 任何, 任何, rènhé, adj.,
L. 12, 58

be willing, 願意, 愿意, yuànyì, v., L. 30, 158

be worth; deserve, 值得, 值得, zhí.dé, v., L. 17, 91

bean curd, 豆腐, 豆腐, dòu.fǔ, n., L. 15, 78

bear; have, 帶, 带, dài, v., L. 17, 88

become, 變成, 变成, biànchéng, v., L. 26, 133

become fat; fat, 胖, 胖, pàng, v./adj., L. 28, 142

bedding, 床鋪, 床铺, chuángpù, n., L. 2, 8

beef, 牛肉, 牛肉, niúròu, n., L. 15, 80

beeper, BP機, BP机, BP jī, n., L. 32, 167

beginning of, 初, 初, chū, n., L. 25, 126

Beijing, 北京, 北京, Běijīng, L. 1, 2

Beijing Opera, 京劇, 京剧, Jīngjù, n., L. 35, 184

Beijing-Kowloon railway, 京九線, 京九线, Jīngjiǔxiàn, L. 31, 160

believe, 相信, 相信, xiāngxìn, v., L. 26, 135

benefit; gain; profit; advantage, 好處, 好处, hǎo.chù, n., L. 3, 17

besides; moreover, 此外, 此外, cǐwài, adv., L. 35, 180

between A and B, A 與 B 之間, A 与 B 之间, A yǔ B zhījiān, L. 18, 94

bicycle, 自行車, 自行车, zìxíngchē, n., L. 7, 34

big melting pot, 大熔爐, 大熔炉, dà rónglú, n., L. 43, 233

bill; receipt, 發票, 发票, fāpiào, n., L. 7, 36

body; health, 身體, 身体, shēntǐ, n., L. 3, 14

Boeing, 波音, 波音, Bōyīn, L. 31, 162

boil, cook, 煮, 煮, zhǔ, v., L. 15, 78

boiled water, 開水, 开水, kāishuǐ, n., L. 6, 30

boring; silly; stupid, 無聊, 无聊, wúliáo, adj., L. 39, 207

both ... and ..., 既...又.., 既...又..., jì...yòu..., L. 10, 52

bother; put somebody to trouble, 麻煩, 麻烦, má.fán, v., L. 7, 36

bottle, 瓶, 瓶, píng, an., L. 20, 103

bowl, 碗, 碗, wǎn, n./an., L. 5, 24

brains; mental capability, 腦力, 脑力, nǎolì, n., L. 34, 177

brains; mind, 頭腦, 头脑, tóunǎo, n., L. 3, 13

braise in soy sauce, 紅燒, 红烧, hóngshāo, v., L. 15, 79

brand; trademark, 牌子, 牌子, páizi, n., L. 20, 105

brand-new, 全新, 全新, quánxīn, adj., L. 44, 240

break; smash, 打破, 打破, dǎ-pò, v.-c., L. 22, 112

bridge, 橋, 桥, qiáo, n., L. 38, 198

Britain; England, 英國, 英国, Yīngguó, L. 42, 223

broccoli, 西蘭花, 西兰花, xīlánhuā, n., L. 15, 79

browse; glance over; leaf through, 翻看, 翻看, fānkàn, v., L. 37, 192

Buddhism, 佛教, 佛教, Fójiào, L. 44, 236

Buddhist sutra, 佛經, 佛经, fójīng, n., L. 44, 237

build; construct, 建, 建, jiàn, v., L. 16, 82

building, 建築, 建筑, jiànzhù, n., L. 12, 59

bulletin board, 佈告牌, 布告牌, bùgàopái, n., L. 33, 170

burden; load, 負擔, 负担, fùdān, n., L. 30, 157

business, 生意, 生意, shēng.yì, n., L. 32, 166

businessman; merchant, 商人, 商人, shāngrén, n., L. 28, 147

busy, 忙碌, 忙碌, mánglù, adj., L. 12, 61

but; yet; however, 卻, 却, què, adv., L. 3, 14

buy and sell; trade, 買賣, 买卖, mǎimài, n., L. 29, 153

buyer, 買主, 买主, mǎizhǔ, n., L. 31, 162

by means of; by way of, 通過, 通过, tōngguò, prep., L. 38, 202

call; address; a form of address, 稱呼, 称呼, chēng.hū, v./n., L. 9, 46

call people, 呼人, 呼人, hū-rén, v.-o., L. 32, 168

calligraphy, 書法, 书法, shūfǎ, n., L. 40, 210

campus, 校園, 校园, xiàoyuán, n., L. 2, 9

candy, sugar, 糖, 糖, táng, n., L. 28, 146

cannot afford, 買不起, 买不起, mǎi.bùqǐ, v.-c., L. 8, 43

cannot catch up with, 趕不上, 赶不上, gǎn.búshàng, v.-c., L. 7, 34

cannot get used to eating, 吃不慣, 吃不惯, chī.búguàn, v.-c., L. 15, 76

cannot stand (or endure), 受不了, 受不了, shòu.bùliǎo, v.-c., L. 10, 51

capital, 首都, 首都, shǒudū, n, L. 1, 2

captions (of motion pictures, etc.); subtitles, 字幕, 字幕, zìmù, n., L. 18, 95

carelessly, 隨便, 随便, suíbiàn, adv., L. 17, 91

cargo transportation, 貨運, 货运, huòyùn, n., L. 31, 160

carry on; carry out; conduct, 進行, 进行, jìnxíng, v., L. 23, 117

carry on one's person; (take) with, 隨身, 随身, suíshēn, adv., L. 10, 53

carry out; practice, 推行, 推行, tuīxíng, v., L. 18, 94

cash, 現金, 现金, xiànjīn, n., L. 7, 38

cashew, 腰果, 腰果, yāoguǒ, n., L. 15, 80

casually; informally, 隨便, 随便, suíbiàn, adv., L. 14, 66

cat, 貓, 猫, māo, n., L. 21, 111

catalogue of titles; booklist, 書目, 书目, shūmù, n., L. 25, 126

catch; capture, 捉, 捉, zhuō, v., L. 21, 111

category, 類, 类, lèi, n., L. 34, 178

cause; create; give rise to, 造成, 造成, zàochéng, v., L. 18, 94

cause; reason (generally takes a noun phrase modifier), 緣故, 缘故, yuángù, n., L. 28, 145

cede, 割讓, 割让, gēràng, v., L. 42, 223

cellular phone, 大哥大, 大哥大, dàgēdà, n., L. 32, 164

cellular phone, 手機, 手机, shǒujī, n., L. 32, 164

cement, 水泥, 水泥, shuǐní, n., L. 23, 116

center, 中心, 中心, zhōngxīn, n., L. 25, 124

Central Asia, 中亞, 中亚, Zhōngyà, L. 44, 234

century, 世紀, 世纪, shìjì, n., L. 40, 214

Chairman Mao, 毛主席, 毛主席, Máo Zhǔxí, L. 17, 86

challenge, 挑戰, 挑战, tiǎozhàn, n./v., L. 34, 174

developed; flourishing, 發達, 发达, fādá, *adj.*, L. 25, 127

developing, 發展中, 发展中, fāzhǎnzhōng, *adj.*, L. 19, 100

dialect, 方言, 方言, fāngyán, *n.*, L. 18, 93

dialogue; conversation, 對話, 对话, duìhuà, *n.*, L. 14, 68

diced chicken, 雞丁, 鸡丁, jīdīng, *n.*, L. 20, 104

difference; divergence, 差異, 差异, chāyì, *n.*, L. 23, 118

differentiate; distinguish, 辨識, 辨识, biànshí, *v.*, L. 18, 96

difficult; difficulty, 困難, 困难, kùn.nán, *adj./n.*, L. 3, 13

dignity; honor, 尊嚴, 尊严, zūnyán, *n.*, L. 30, 157

dime, 毛, 毛, máo, *n.*, L. 4, 22

dining hall, 食堂, 食堂, shítáng, *n.*, L. 2, 10

diplomacy; foreign affairs, 外交, 外交, wàijiāo, *n.*, L. 23, 116

directly, 直接, 直接, zhíjiē, *adv.*, L. 6, 30

disadvantageous; harmful, 不利, 不利, búlì, *adj.*, L. 33, 171

disappear, 消失, 消失, xiāoshī, *v.*, L. 37, 196

disco, 迪斯科, 迪斯科, dísīkē, *n.*, L. 12, 60

discuss, 討論, 讨论, tǎolùn, *v.*, L. 33, 172

dispatch; send, 派, 派, pài, *v.*, L. 1, 2

distance, disparity, 距離, 距离, jùlí, *n.*, L. 31, 161

distant; far, 遠, 远, yuǎn, *adj.*, L. 4, 18

distant place, 遠處, 远处, yuǎnchù, *n.*, L. 11, 54

distribute; allot; assign, 分配, 分配, fēnpèi, *v.*, L. 22, 114

distribute in rations, allocate, 配給, 配给, pèijǐ, *v.*, L. 29, 150

district; area, 地區, 地区, dìqū, *n.*, L. 31, 161

divide; seperate; part, 分, 分, fēn, *v.*, L. 9, 47

divide into, 分成, 分成, fēnchéng, *v.-c.*, L. 34, 177

divorce, 離婚, 离婚, lí-hūn, *v.-o.*, L. 27, 136

do; manage; handle, 辦, 办, bàn, *v.*, L. 4, 21

do (colloguial), 幹, 干, gàn, *v.*, L. 34, 176

do not (written), 勿, 勿, wù, *adv.*, L. 17, 87

dollor; buck, 塊, 块, kuài, *n.*, L. 4, 22

domestically made, 國產, 国产, guóchǎn, *adj.*, L. 20, 106

double room, 雙人房, 双人房, shuāngrénfáng, *n.*, L. 2, 7

draw a snake and add feet to it--ruin the effect by adding something superflous, 畫蛇添足, 画蛇添足, huà shé tiān zú, *idm.*, L. 21, 110

drawing; painting, 繪畫, 绘画, huìhuà, *n.*, L. 40, 212

dress; apparel, 穿著, 穿着, chuānzhuó, *n.*, L. 44, 240

drink a toast, 乾杯, 干杯, gān-bēi, *v.-o.*, L. 14, 70

drive a car, train, etc., 開車, 开车, kāi-chē, *v.-o.*, L. 11, 54

driver, 司機, 司机, sījī, *n.*, L. 7, 32

dubb; synchronize, 配音, 配音, pèiyīn, *v.-o.*, L. 35, 185

duck, 鴨, 鸭, yā, *n.*, L. 15, 78

dumpling, 餃子, 饺子, jiǎozi, *n.*, L. 15, 75

dynasty, 朝, 朝, cháo, *n.*, L. 35, 181

dynasty, 朝代, 朝代, cháodài, *n.*, L. 44, 234

e-mail, 電子郵件, 电子邮件, diànzǐ yóujiàn, *n.*, L. 32, 164

each; every, 各 *n.*, 各 *n.*, gè, *adj.*, L. 6, 31

each has his own strong points, 各有所長, 各有所长, gè yǒu suǒ cháng, *idm.*, L. 36, 186

earn; make (money), 賺錢, 赚钱, zhuàn-qián, *v.-o.*, L. 8, 42

ease and comfort; enjoyment, 享受, 享受, xiǎngshòu, *n.*, L. 36, 188

east, south, west, and north; every direction, 東南西北, 东南西北, dōngnánxīběi, L. 31, 162

economy, 經濟, 经济, jīngjì, *n.*, L. 19, 101

edition, 版本, 版本, bǎnběn, *n.*, L. 25, 126

education, 教育, 教育, jiàoyù, *n.*, L. 24, 121

effective, 有效, 有效, yǒuxiào, *adj.*, L. 18, 96

eggplant, 茄子, 茄子, qiézi, *n.*, L. 15, 79

eight treasures (choice ingredients of certain special dishes), 八寶, 八宝, bābǎo, *n.*, L. 15, 81

elementary school, 小學, 小学, xiǎoxué, *n.*, L. 17, 86

eliminate; abolish; exterminate; wipe out, 消滅, 消灭, xiāomiè, *v.*, L. 43, 231

eliminate through selection or competition, die out; fall into disuse, 淘汰, 淘汰, táotài, *v.*, L. 30, 156

embody; incarnate; reflect, 體現, 体现, tǐxiàn, *v.*, L. 24, 122

emphasize; stress, 強調, 强调, qiángdiào, *v.*, L. 24, 123

empty; hollow; devoid of content, 空洞, 空洞, kōngdòng, *adj.*, L. 18, 92

end; last stage, 末, 末, mò, *n.*, L. 25, 125

endure; bear, 忍受, 忍受, rěnshòu, *v.*, L. 27, 139

endure hardships, tortures, rough conditions, etc.; have a hard time, 受罪, 受罪, shòu-zuì, *v.-o.*, L. 6, 29

enjoy, 享受, 享受, xiǎngshòu, *v.*, L. 19, 101

enrich, 豐富, 丰富, fēngfù, *v.*, L. 44, 236

enter; get into, 進入, 进入, jìnrù, *v.*, L. 24, 120

enter a higher school, 升學, 升学, shēng-xué, *v.-o.*, L. 30, 155

enterprise; facilities, 事業, 事业, shìyè, *n.*, L. 25, 126

entertainment, 娛樂, 娱乐, yúlè, *n.*, L. 39, 206

enthusiasm; zeal; warmth, 熱情, 热情, rèqíng, *n.*, L. 14, 69

entire table of, 桌, 桌, zhuō, *an.*, L. 14, 72

entrance examination for colleges and universities, 高考, 高考, gāokǎo, *n.*, L. 24, 120

envelope, 信封, 信封, xìnfēng, *n.*, L. 4, 23

envy, 羨慕, 羡慕, xiànmù, *v.*, L. 36, 190

equal; equality, 平等, 平等, píngděng, *adj./n.*, L. 9, 48

equipment; facilities, 設備, 设备, shèbèi, *n.*, L. 23, 116

era; times, 時代, 时代, shídài, *n.*, L. 20, 104

especially, 尤其, 尤其, yóuqí, *adv.*, L. 13, 62

especially; special, 特別, 特别, tèbié, *adv./adj.*, L. 2, 7

establish, 設立, 设立, shèlì, *v.*, L. 22, 112

establish; set up, 建立, 建立, jiànlì, v., L. 43, 231

Europe, 歐洲, 欧洲, Ōuzhōu, L. 19, 100

even, 連, 连, lián, conj., L. 7, 34

even, 甚至, 甚至, shènzhì, adv., L. 16, 85

even, 甚至於, 甚至于, shènzhìyú, conj., L. 32, 164

even though; even if, 即使, 即使, jíshǐ, conj., L. 27, 138

evening; dusk, 傍晚, 傍晚, bàngwǎn, t.w., L. 12, 60

everywhere; at all places, 到處, 到处, dàochù, adv., L. 17, 86

evident; obvious, 明顯, 明显, míngxiǎn, adj., L. 29, 149

exactly alike, 一模一樣, 一模一样, yìmú yíyàng, adj., L. 8, 45

example, 例子, 例子, lìzi, n., L. 26, 134

exceed, 超過, 超过, chāoguò, v., L. 37, 194

excellent quality at low prices-a bargain buy, 價廉物美, 价廉物美, idm., jiàlián wùměi, L. 19, 101

except for; aside from, 除了…以外, 除了…以外, chúle...yǐwài, L. 3, 15

excessively; over-, 過分, 过分, guòfèn, adv., L. 24, 123

exchange; interaction, 交流, 交流, jiāoliú, v., L. 23, 117

excited, 興奮, 兴奋, xīngfèn, adj., L. 1, 5

excuse, 藉口, 借口, jièkǒu, n., L. 2, 11

execute; carry out, 執行, 执行, zhíxíng, v., L. 42, 225

exercise, 運動, 运动, yùndòng, v., L. 36, 191

exert; exhaust, 盡, 尽, jìn, v., L. 30, 155

exist, 存在, 存在, cúnzài, v., L. 18, 93

exist simultaneously, 並存, 并存, bìngcún, v., L. 21, 109

expand, 擴展, 扩展, kuòzhǎn, v., L. 44, 239

expenses, 花費, 花费, huāfèi, n., L. 29, 149

expenses; costs, 費用, 费用, fèiyòng, n., L. 29, 150

experience, 經驗, 经验, jīngyàn, n., L. 25, 126

experienced, 有經驗, 有经验, yǒu jīngyàn, adj., L.25, 126

expert, 專家, 专家, zhuānjiā, n., L. 37, 193

explain; show, 說明, 说明, shuōmíng, v., L. 18, 93

extend; stretch, 伸展, 伸展, shēnzhǎn, v., L. 35, 181

extent; degree, 程度, 程度, chéngdù, n., L. 32, 165

extra-marital relationship, 婚外關係, 婚外关系, hūnwài guān.xì, n., L. 27, 139

extremely; exceedingly, 不得了, 不得了, bù.déliǎo, adv., L. 38, 199

extremely; to death, …死人, …死人, ...sǐrén, adv., L. 7, 33

face, 臉, 脸, liǎn, n., L. 20, 104

face; confront, 面對, 面对, miànduì, v., L. 34, 179

face; dignity, 面子, 面子, miànzi, n., L. 13, 62

factory, 工廠, 工厂, gōngchǎng, n., L. 19, 98

fair; just, 公平, 公平, gōngpíng, adj., L. 24, 122

faith; belief; conviction, 信仰, 信仰, xìnyǎng, n., L. 43, 230

fall asleep, 睡著, 睡着, shuì-zháo, v.-c., L. 1, 5

familiar, 熟, 熟, shú, adj., L. 21, 111

family; household, 家庭, 家庭, jiātíng, n., L. 20, 105

famous scenic spot, 名勝古跡, 名胜古迹, míngshèng gǔjī, n., L. 44, 237

far (in degree); by far, 遠遠, 远远, yuǎnyuǎn, adv., L. 37, 194

farmer, 農民, 农民, nóngmín, n., L. 34, 178

fast; high-speed, 快速, 快速, kuàisù, adj., L. 30, 159

fast food, 快餐, 快餐, kuàicān, n., L. 22, 113

fatty, 胖子, 胖子, pàngzi, n., L. 28, 143

fear; be afraid of, 怕, 怕, pà, v., L. 4, 21

feeling; sentiments, 情緒, 情绪, qíngxù, n., L. 37, 193

fiction; novel, 小說, 小说, xiǎoshuō, n., L. 25, 127

figure; personage, 人物, 人物, rénwù, n., L. 8, 43

fill in, 填, 填, tián, v., L. 4, 22

film, 影片, 影片, yǐngpiān, n., L. 35, 185

find; discover, 發現, 发现, fāxiàn, v., L. 3, 15

find sth. useful; need, 用得著, 用得着, yòng.dézháo, v-c., L. 32, 166

finding order in chaos, 亂中有序, 乱中有序, luànzhōng yǒuxù, idm., L. 16, 85

finish; conclude, end; conclusion, 結束, 结束, jiéshù, v./n., L. 42, 222

first of the ten Heavenly Stems; used as pronoun here meaning "the first person", 甲, 甲, jiǎ, n., L. 8, 40

fish, 魚, 鱼, yú, n., L. 15, 78

fixed; stable, 固定, 固定, gùdìng, adj., L. 44, 241

fixed amount/quantity, 定量, 定量, dìngliàng, n., L. 29, 150

flat; smooth, 平, 平, píng, adj., L. 1, 4

flushing toilet, 抽水馬桶, 抽水马桶, chōushuǐmǎtǒng, n., L. 36, 190

food, 食物, 食物, shíwù, n., L. 28, 146

food and drink, 飲食, 饮食, yǐnshí, n., L. 15, 74

food, clothing, shelter and transportation -- basic necessities of life, 衣食住行, 衣食住行, yī shí zhù xíng, idm., L. 35, 183

food prepared in a large pot, 大鍋飯, 大锅饭, dàguōfàn, n., L. 22, 115

foot-binding, 纏腳, 缠脚, chánjiǎo, v.-o., L. 37, 195

for, 為, 为, wèi, prep., L. 10, 51

for a long time, 久, 久, jiǔ, adj., L. 10, 50

for example, 好比說, 好比说, hǎobǐshuō, L. 39, 208

for example; such as, 譬如, 譬如, pìrú, L. 21, 110

for instance, 比方, 比方, bǐ.fāng, L. 10, 50

for instance; for example, 比方說, 比方说, bǐ.fāngshuō, L. 13, 63

for the most part; mostly, 大都, 大都, dàdōu, adv., L. 35, 181

for the most part; mostly, 大多, 大多, dàduō, adv., L. 6, 29

force; compel; coerce, 強迫, 强迫, qiǎngpò, v., L. 23, 119

foreign affairs office, 外事處, 外事处, wàishìchù, n., L.1, 2

foreign capital, 外資, 外资, wàizī, n., L. 37, 194

foreign cloth, 洋布, 洋布, yángbù, n., L. 44, 236

foreign country, 外國, 外国, wàiguó, n., L. 3, 17

graduate student, 研究生, 研究生, yánjiūshēng, n., L. 33, 170

grandparents, 祖父母, 祖父母, zǔfùmǔ, n., L. 30, 156

grape, 葡萄, 葡萄, pú.táo, n., L. 44, 235

gratifying; heartening, 可喜, 可喜, kěxǐ, adj., L. 25, 128

graveyard; cemetery, 墳場, 坟场, fénchǎng, n., L. 30, 154

great; mighty, 偉大, 伟大, wěidà, adj., L. 43, 231

great majority, 大多數, 大多数, dàduōshù, n., L. 36, 187

Great Wall, 長城, 长城, Chángchéng, L. 12, 58

grow up, 長大, 长大, zhǎngdà, v., L. 27, 140

grow up; be brought up, 生長, 生长, shēngzhǎng, v., L. 24, 122

gruel, 粥, 粥, zhōu, n., L. 15, 76

Guangdong Province, 廣東, 广东, Guǎngdōng, L. 15, 77

Guangming Daily, 光明日報, 光明日报, Guāngmíng Rìbào, n., L. 39, 204

guest, 客人, 客人, kèrén, n., L. 14, 68

guest of honor, 主客, 主客, zhǔkè, n., L. 14, 67

had better; it would be best, 最好, 最好, zuìhǎo, adv., L. 4, 18

hamburger, 漢堡包, 汉堡包, hànbǎobāo, n., L. 28, 146

Han Dynasty, 漢朝, 汉朝, Hàncháo, L. 44, 234

Han people, 漢人, 汉人, Hànrén, L. 43, 228

happy, 高興, 高兴, gāoxìng, adj., L. 37, 197

hard seat (on a train), 硬座, 硬座, yìngzuò, n., L. 11, 55

hard to avoid, 難免, 难免, nánmiǎn, adv./adj., L. 37, 197

harm, 害, 害, hài, v., L. 39, 208

harmful, 有害, 有害, yǒuhài, v., L. 28, 147

have a bath; bathe, 洗澡, 洗澡, xǐ-zǎo, v.-o., L. 3, 12

have a fever, 發燒, 发烧, fā-shāo, v.-o., L. 5, 25

have a traffic jam, 堵車, 堵车, dǔ-chē, v.-o., L. 7, 33

have become; became, 成了, 成了, chéngle, v., L. 9, 48

have never V-ed, 從來没 V. 過, 从来没 V. 过, cónglái méi ...guò, L. 3, 12

have no choice but to; have to, 不得不, 不得不, bùdébù, v., L. 3, 16

have received, 受了, 受了, shòule, v., L. 9, 48

have something to do with; relate to; concern, 有關, 有关, yǒuguān, v., L. 17, 87

have to; be forced to, 只好, 只好, zhǐhǎo, adv., L. 8, 43

health; physique; healthy, 健康, 健康, jiànkāng, n./adj., L. 2, 11

heaven; paradise, 天堂, 天堂, tiāntáng, n., L. 30, 154

help, 幫忙, 帮忙, bāng-máng, v.-o., L. 5, 27

help, 幫助, 帮助, bāngzhù, v., L. 31, 163

helpful, 有幫助, 有帮助, yǒu bāngzhù, adj., L. 31, 163

highway, 高速公路, 高速公路, gāosù gōnglù, n., L. 1, 4

history, 歷史, 历史, lìshǐ, n., L. 21, 108

hold (a meeting, ceremony, etc.), 舉行, 举行, jǔxíng, v., L. 24, 120

home cooking; simple meal, 家常菜, 家常菜, jiāchángcài, n., L. 14, 71

hometown, 家鄉, 家乡, jiāxiāng, n., L. 33, 172

honest, 誠實, 诚实, chéngshí, adj., L. 13, 63

Hong Kong, 香港, 香港, Xiānggǎng, L. 9, 48

Hong Kong citizens govern Hong Kong, 港人治港, 港人治港, Gǎngrén zhì Gǎng, L. 42, 225

honorable; dignity; face, 體面, 体面, tǐ.miàn, adj./n., L. 34, 178

hope; wish, 希望, 希望, xīwàng, v./n., L. 16, 84

hospital, 醫院, 医院, yīyuàn, n., L. 5, 27

host, 主人, 主人, zhǔrén, n., L. 14, 68

hostile; antagonistic, 敵對, 敌对, díduì, v., L. 23, 117

hot and suffocating; muggy, 悶熱, 闷热, mēnrè, adj., L. 12, 61

hotel, 旅館, 旅馆, lǚguǎn, n., L. 2, 9

household, 戶, 户, hù, an./n., L. 39, 205

household appliances, 家用電器, 家用电器, jiāyòng diànqì, n., L. 19, 99

housing, 住房, 住房, zhùfáng, n., L. 29, 152

how terrible; what bad luck; too bad, 糟糕, 糟糕, zāogāo, L. 7, 34

huge crowds of people, 人山人海, 人山人海, rénshān rénhǎi, idm., L. 12, 59

Hui nationality, 回族, 回族, Huízú, L. 43, 231

human labor, 人力, 人力, rénlì, n., L. 35, 183

human rights, 人權, 人权, rénquán, n., L. 23, 118

humid, 潮濕, 潮湿, cháoshī, adj., L. 12, 61

humiliation; shame, 恥辱, 耻辱, chǐrǔ, n., L. 42, 224

Hunan Province, 湖南, 湖南, Hú'nán, L. 15, 77

Hunan Province, 湘, 湘, Xiāng, L. 15, 74

hundreds of thousands, 幾十萬, 几十万, jǐshíwàn, n., L. 33, 170

husband, 丈夫, 丈夫, zhàng.fū, n., L. 27, 138

husband or wife, 愛人, 爱人, ài.rén, n., L. 14, 71

hygienic; sanitary, 衛生, 卫生, wèishēng, adj., L. 10, 51

I really don't deserve this; you flatter me, 不敢當, 不敢当, bùgǎndāng, L. 14, 67

ice cream, 冰激凌, 冰激凌, bīngjīlíng, n., L. 28, 146

ice water, 冰水, 冰水, bīngshuǐ, n., L. 6, 29

ideal, 理想, 理想, lǐxiǎng, adj./n., L. 18, 95

imagine; imagination, 想像, 想象, xiǎngxiàng, v./n., L. 1, 5

imitate; mimic, 學, 学, xué, v., L. 6, 30

imperial examinations, 科舉, 科举, kējǔ, n., L. 40, 211

Imperial Summer Residence, 避暑山莊, 避暑山庄, Bìshǔ Shānzhuāng, L. 11, 55

kilogram, 公斤, 公斤, gōngjīn, L. 28, 143

kind of traditional Chinese shadow boxing, 太極拳, 太极拳, tàijíquán, n., L. 12, 60

know; recognize, 認識, 认识, rèn.shí, v., L. 9, 47

Korean War (1950-1953), 朝鮮戰爭, 朝鲜战争, Cháoxiān Zhànzhēng, L. 38, 201

labor force, 勞動力, 劳动力, láodònglì, n., L. 19, 100

lack; be short of, 缺乏, 缺乏, quēfá, v., L. 24, 121

lady; madam, 女士, 女士, nǚshì, n., L. 9, 48

land, 土地, 土地, tǔdì, n., L. 31, 162

land; descend, 降落, 降落, jiàngluò, v., L. 1, 2

landscape painting, 山水畫, 山水画, shānshuǐhuà, n., L. 8, 41

language, 語言, 语言, yǔyán, n., L. 21, 109

large number, 大量, 大量, dàliàng, adj., L. 41, 218

largely identical but with minor differences, 大同小異, 大同小异, dàtóng xiǎoyì, idm. L. 26, 131

last phase; final phase, 末期, 末期, mòqī, n., L. 41, 217

law, 法律, 法律, fǎlù, n., L. 27, 139

lay off, 下崗, 下岗, xiàgǎng, v., L. 34, 174

lay off; fire, 解雇, 解雇, jiěgù, v., L. 34, 176

lay stress on; pay attention to, 注重, 注重, zhùzhòng, v., L. 30, 155

lead a life, 過日子, 过日子, guò rìzi, v.-o., L. 36, 188

learn, 學會, 学会, xué-huì, v.-c., L. 3, 17

learning; academic, 學術, 学术, xuéshù, n., L. 23, 117

leather suitcase, 皮箱, 皮箱, píxiāng, n., L. 19, 99

leave, 離開, 离开, líkāi, v., L. 31, 163

leg, 腿, 腿, tuǐ, n., L. 10, 50

Lei Feng (1940-1962), a soldier who died on duty and was hailed as a model for the youth of China., 雷鋒, 雷锋, L. 17, 89

leisurely and carefree, 悠閑, 悠闲, yōuxián, adj., L. 12, 61

lesson; moral, 教訓, 教训, jiàoxùn, n., L. 17, 89

letter paper, 信紙, 信纸, xìnzhǐ, n., L. 4, 23

level, 水平, 水平, shuǐpíng, n., L. 19, 101

Liberation of China (in 1949), 解放, 解放, jiěfàng, n., L. 25, 128

librarian, 圖書館員, 图书馆员, túshūguǎn yuán, n., L. 25, 126

lie in; rest with, 在於, 在于, zàiyú, v., L. 44, 241

life, 生活, 生活, shēng.huó, n., L. 6, 31

limit, 限制, 限制, xiànzhì, v., L. 33, 171

line up, 排隊, 排队, pái-duì, v.-o., L. 7, 37

listen to (radio broadcast), 收聽, 收听, shōutīng, v., L. 18, 97

literature, 文學, 文学, wénxué, n., L. 25, 126

Liulichang, 琉璃廠, 琉璃厂, Liúlíchǎng, L. 25, 125

live, 生活, 生活, shēnghuó, v., L. 11, 54

live; reside; dwell, 居住, 居住, jūzhù, v., L. 43, 229

lively; vivid, 生動, 生动, shēngdòng, adj., L. 21, 108

loan words, 外來語, 外来语, wàiláiyǔ, n., L. 41, 219

local, 地方, 地方, dìfāng, adj., L. 40, 212

local; in the locality, 當地, 当地, dāngdì, p.w., L. 6, 31

local; native, 本土, 本土, běntǔ, adj., L. 44, 238

long; long-standing, 悠久, 悠久, yōujiǔ, adj., L. 43, 231

long distance, 長途, 长途, chángtú, adj., L. 2, 11

long live, 萬歲, 万岁, wànsuì, v., L. 17, 89

look down upon; despise, 看不起, 看不起, kàn.bùqǐ, v.-c., L. 34, 177

look for; try to find; seek, 找, 找, zhǎo, v., L. 22, 113

look for an excuse, 找藉口, 找借口, zhǎo jièkǒu, v.-o., L. 13, 63

loose; slack, 鬆, 松, sōng, adj., L. 1, 4

lose, 失去, 失去, shīqù, v., L. 27, 137

lose money (in business transactions), 賠錢, 赔钱, péi-qián, v.-o., L. 8, 42

lose one's job, 失業, 失业, shīyè, v., L. 19, 100

lose something, 丟, 丢, diū, v., L. 4, 21

love, 愛, 爱, ài, v., L. 30, 158

lover, 情人, 情人, qíngrén, n., L. 12, 61

low, 低, 低, dī, adj., L. 43, 231

low-priced; cheap, 廉價, 廉价, liánjià, adj., L. 19, 100

luckily; fortunately, 好在, 好在, hǎozài, adv., L. 1, 3

luxuries, 奢侈品, 奢侈品, shēchǐpǐn, n., L. 20, 105

luxurious; extravagant, 奢侈, 奢侈, shēchǐ, adj., L. 36, 189

machine; ... gadget, … 機, … 机, jī, suff., L. 32, 166

magazine, 雜誌, 杂志, zázhì, n., L. 1, 3

magnificent; resplendent, 華麗, 华丽, huálì, adj., L. 12, 59

main, 主要, 主要, zhǔyào, adj., L. 11, 57

mainland China, 大陸, 大陆, dàlù, L. 26, 130

maintain, 維持, 维持, wéichí, v., L. 27, 138

make a fool of oneself, 鬧笑話, 闹笑话, nào xiàohua, v.-o., L. 21, 111

make a phone call; call, 打電話, 打电话, dǎ diànhuà, v.-o., L. 2, 6

make friends, 交, 交, jiāo, v., L. 11, 57

make or become heavier; increase the weight of, 加重, 加重, jiāzhòng, v., L. 30, 157

make progress; go upward, 向上, 向上, xiàngshàng, v., L. 17, 86

make tea, 泡茶, 泡茶, pào-chá, v.-o., L. 6, 31

mal-; bad, 不良, 不良, bùliáng, adj., L. 28, 144

man of letters; scholar; literati, 文人, 文人, wénrén, n., L. 40, 213

Manchu nationality, 滿族, 满族, Mǎnzú, L. 43, 230

Manchuria, 滿州, 满州, Mǎnzhōu, L. 43, 231

Mandarin Chinese, 國語, 国语, Guóyǔ, n., L. 18, 94

manufacture; make, 製造, 制造, zhìzào, v., L. 19, 99

many-sided; in many ways, 多方面, 多方面, duōfāngmiàn, adj., L. 23, 117

market, 市場, 市场, shìchǎng, n., L. 8, 44

Shandong Province, 山東, 山东, Shāndōng, L. 15, 77

Shanxi Province, 山西, 山西, Shānxī, L. 11, 55

shelled fresh shrimp, 蝦仁, 虾仁, xiārén, *n.*, L. 15, 80

shift to an earlier time; be earlier than planned or expected, 提早, 提早, tízǎo, *v.*, L. 34, 174

shoes, 鞋子, 鞋子, xiézi, *n.*, L. 19, 98

shop sign, 招牌, 招牌, zhāo.pái, *n.*, L. 15, 76

shopkeeper; boss, 老闆, 老板, lǎobǎn, *n.*, L. 8, 44

shortcoming; defect; weakness, 缺點, 缺点, quēdiǎn, *n.*, L. 24, 123

shortcoming; weakness, 短處, 短处, duǎn.chù, *n.*, L. 36, 191

shorten, 縮短, 缩短, suōduǎn, *v.*, L. 31, 161

should, 該, 该, gāi, *aux.*, L. 5, 27

show; display, 表現, 表现, biǎoxiàn, *v.*, L. 9, 49

show; express; indicate, 表示, 表示, biǎoshì, *v.*, L. 14, 69

show (TV, radio, etc.), 節目, 节目, jiémù, *n.*, L. 39, 206

show a film, 上映, 上映, shàngyìng, *v.*, L. 35, 185

show due respect for somebody's feelings, 給面子, 给面子, gěi miànzi, *v.-o.*, L. 13, 62

show filial obedience, 孝順, 孝顺, xiàoshùn, *v.*, L. 30, 158

shredded meat, 肉絲, 肉丝, ròusī, *n.*, L. 15, 80

Sichuan Province, 川, 川, Chuān, L. 15, 74

sign, 簽字, 签字, qiān-zì, *v.-o.*, L. 7, 39

significant, 重大, 重大, zhòngdà, *adj.*, L. 31, 161

Silk Road, 絲綢之路, 丝绸之路, Sīchóu Zhī Lù, *n.*, L. 44, 234

similar, 類似, 类似, lèisì, *adj.*, L. 14, 70

simple and crude, 簡陋, 简陋, jiǎnlòu, *adj.*, L. 23, 116

simplified Chinese characters, 簡體字, 简体字, jiǎntǐzì, *n.*, L. 18, 95

simply, 簡直, 简直, jiǎnzhí, *adv.*, L. 2, 8

since, 自從, 自从, zìcóng, *prep.*, L. 18, 95

since ancient times, 自古以來, 自古以来, zì gǔ yǐlái, L. 34, 177

sincere, 誠懇, 诚恳, chéngkěn, *adj.*, L. 13, 65

Singapore, 新加坡, 新加坡, Xīnjiāpō, L. 33, 172

single room, 單人房, 单人房, dānrénfáng, *n.*, L. 2, 6

single-parent family, 單親家庭, 单亲家庭, dānqīn jiātíng, *n.*, L. 27, 140

sink (in a restroom), 洗手台, 洗手台, xǐshǒutái, *n.*, L. 10, 52

site; space, 場地, 场地, chǎngdì, *n.*, L. 38, 199

situation, 情況, 情况, qíngkuàng, *n.*, L. 19, 100

situation, 情形, 情形, qíng.xíng, *n.*, L. 36, 189

skill; craftsmanship; workmanship, 手藝, 手艺, shǒuyì, *n.*, L. 14, 71

skill; technique, 技術, 技术, jìshù, *n.*, L. 40, 210

skyscraper, 摩天大樓, 摩天大楼, mótiān dàlóu, *n.*, L. 35, 182

slogan (usually writtenon a banner or poster), 標語, 标语, biāoyǔ, *n.*, L. 17, 86

slogan; watchword, 口號, 口号, kǒuhào, *n.*, L. 18, 92

small change, 零錢, 零钱, língqián, *n.*, L. 10, 53

small in number, degree, etc., 輕, 轻, qīng, *adj.*, L. 14, 69

small number; few, 少數, 少数, shǎoshù, *adj.*, L. 38, 201

smell, 聞, 闻, wén, *v.*, L. 10, 52

smile; smiling expression, 笑容, 笑容, xiàoróng, *n.*, L. 20, 104

smooth; successful, 順利, 顺利, shùnlì, *adj.*, L. 2, 6

smooth and steady; stable, 平穩, 平稳, píngwěn, *adj.*, L. 42, 226

snack; refreshments, 小吃, 小吃, xiǎochī, *n.*, L. 11, 56

so-called, 所謂, 所谓, suǒwèi, *adj.*, L. 29, 151

social class, 階級, 阶级, jiējí, *n.*, L. 43, 233

society, 社會, 社会, shèhuì, *n.*, L. 9, 49

soft bunk (on a train), 軟臥, 软卧, ruǎnwò, *n.*, L. 11, 55

solve, 解決, 解决, jiějué, *v.*, L. 29, 153

Song Dynasty, 宋朝, 宋朝, Sòngcháo, L. 43, 231

Sony, 索尼, 索尼, Suǒní, L. 20, 106

south, 南, 南, nán, *n.*, L. 4, 19

southeast, 東南, 东南, dōngnán, *n.*, L. 43, 229

Southerner, 南方人, 南方人, nánfāngrén, *n.*, L. 15, 76

southwest, 西南, 西南, xīnán, *n.*, L. 43, 229

sovereignty, 主權, 主权, zhǔquán, *n.*, L. 42, 222

speak with a mixed accent, 南腔北調, 南腔北调, nánqiāng běidiào, *n.*, L. 18, 93

special, 特殊, 特殊, tèshū, *adj.*, L. 16, 85

special administrative region, 特別行政區, 特別行政区, tèbié xíngzhèngqū, *n.*, L. 42, 226

special field of study; major, 專業, 专业, zhuānyè, *n.*, L. 24, 120

special flavor; local flavor, 風味, 风味, fēngwèi, *n.*, L. 11, 56

special local product, 特產, 特产, tèchǎn, *n.*, L. 11, 56

speed, 速度, 速度, sùdù, *n.*, L. 44, 239

spend (money), 花錢, 花钱, huā-qián, *v.-o.*, L. 8, 45

spend (time); live (life), 過, 过, guò, *v.*, L. 28, 142

spit; expectorate, 吐痰, 吐痰, tǔ-tán, *v.-o.*, L. 17, 87

spoil, 慣壞, 惯坏, guàn-huài, *v.-c.*, L. 2, 9

spoken language, 口語, 口语, kǒuyǔ, *n.*, L. 41, 217

Spring and Autumn Period (770-476 B.C.), 春秋, 春秋, Chūnqiū, L. 41, 216

squat on one's heels, 蹲, 蹲, dūn, *v.*, L. 10, 50

stable, 安定, 安定, āndìng, *adj.*, L. 19, 100

stable, 穩定, 稳定, wěndìng, *adj.*, L. 22, 114

staff, 人員, 人员, rényuán, *n.*, L. 34, 176

staff and workers, 職工, 职工, zhígōng, *n.*, L. 34, 174

stamp, 郵票, 邮票, yóupiào, *n.*, L. 4, 23

standard; criterion, 標準, 标准, biāozhǔn, *n.*, L. 23, 119

standard; norm, 規範, 规范, guīfàn, *n.*, L. 18, 92

staple food; principal food, 主食, 主食, zhǔshí, *n.*, L. 15, 75

start school; enter school, 入學, 入学, rùxué, *v.-o.*, L. 24, 120

think highly of; value; take something seriously, 重視, 重视, zhòngshì, *v.*, L. 24, 123

thinking; thought, 思想, 思想, sīxiǎng, *n.*, L. 17, 91

third of ten Heavenly Stems, the third person, 丙, 丙, bǐng, *n.*, L. 8, 44

thought; thinking, 思維, 思维, sīwéi, *n.*, L. 44, 240

thousands upon thousands, 成千上萬, 成千上万, *idm.*, chéngqiān shàngwàn, L. 21, 109

three generations living under the same roof (part of the "big family" system in old China), 三代同堂, 三代同堂, sāndàitóngtáng, *idm.*, L. 30, 157

three kinds of fresh delicacies, 三鮮, 三鲜, sānxiān, *n.*, L. 15, 81

three-wheel cart, 三輪車, 三轮车, sānlúnchē, *n.*, L. 35, 183

Tian An Men; Gate of Heavenly Peace, 天安門, 天安门, Tiān'ānmén, L. 17, 88

Tianjin, 天津, 天津, Tiānjīn, L. 38, 198

Tibet, 西藏, 西藏, Xīzàng, L. 43, 230

ticket, 門票, 门票, ménpiào, *n.*, L. 12, 58

tight; tense; high demand (said of a financial market), 緊張, 紧张, jǐnzhāng, *adj.*, L. 29, 152

time period, 時期, 时期, shíqī, *n.*, L. 37, 193

times; -fold, 倍, 倍, bèi, *n.*, L. 36, 189

title; subject; topic, 題目, 题目, tímù, *n.*, L. 17, 91

to; toward, 對, 对, duì, *prep.*, L. 1, 3

TOEFL, 托福, 托福, Tuōfú, *n.*, L. 33, 170

toilet, 馬桶, 马桶, mǎtǒng, *n.*, L. 10, 50

toilet; restroom, 廁所, 厕所, cèsuǒ, *n.*, L. 10, 50

toilet paper, 衛生紙, 卫生纸, wèishēngzhǐ, *n.*, L. 10, 52

too; exceedingly, 過 Adj., 过 Adj., guò..., L. 34, 176

tool; instrument, 工具, 工具, gōngjù, *n.*, L. 11, 57

topic of conversation, 話題, 话题, huàtí, *n.*, L. 13, 65

toward, 向, 向, xiàng, *prep.*, L. 35, 181

towel, 毛巾, 毛巾, máojīn, *n.*, L. 2, 8

tradition, 傳統, 传统, chuántǒng, *n.*, L. 34, 177

traditional alleys in Beijing, 胡同儿, 胡同儿, hútòngr, *n.*, L. 35, 182

traditional Chinese comic dialogue, 相聲, 相声, xiàng.shēng, *n.*, L. 35, 185

traditional Chinese-style compound with rooms around a courtyard, 四合院, 四合院, sìhéyuàn, *n.*, L. 35, 182

traffic, 交通, 交通, jiāotōng, *n.*, L. 7, 35

traffic jam, 交通堵塞, 交通堵塞, jiāotōng dǔsè, *n.*, L. 7, 35

traffic lane, 車道, 车道, chēdào, *n.*, L. 36, 191

traffic light, 紅綠燈, 红绿灯, hónglǜdēng, *n.*, L. 7, 36

traffic regulations, 交通規則, 交通规则, jiāotōng guīzé, *n.*, L. 16, 84

train, 火車, 火车, huǒchē, *n.*, L. 11, 54

training, train, 訓練, 训练, xùnliàn, *n./v.*, L. 24, 121

tram, 電車, 电车, diànchē, *n.*, L. 36, 188

transit, transition, 過渡, 过渡, guòdù, *v./n.*, L. 29, 153

translate, 翻譯, 翻译, fānyì, *v.*, L. 41, 218

travel, 旅行, 旅行, lǚxíng, *v.*, L. 7, 38

traveler's check, 旅行支票, 旅行支票, lǚxíng zhīpiào, *n.*, L. 7, 39

treatment, 待遇, 待遇, dàiyù, *n.*, L. 42, 224

trousers, 褲子, 裤子, kùzi, *n.*, L. 21, 108

turn off, 關掉, 关掉, guān-diào, *v.-c.*, L. 5, 26

turn towards, 轉向, 转向, zhuǎnxiàng, *v.*, L. 34, 175

TV screen, 屏幕, 屏幕, píngmù, *n.*, L. 18, 95

two-part allegorical saying, 歇後語, 歇后语, xiēhòuyǔ, *n.*, L. 21, 108

type, 打字, 打字, dǎ-zì, *v.-o.*, L. 40, 215

type, 類, 类, lèi, *n.*, L. 1, 3

U. S. dollar, 美元, 美元, měiyuán, *n.*, L. 7, 38

under (a given point or line), … 以下, … 以下, yǐxià, *postp.*, L. 39, 209

undergraduate student, 本科生, 本科生, běnkēshēng, *n.*, L. 33, 170

underground; subterranean, 地下, 地下, dìxià, *adj.*, L. 16, 85

understand, 了解, 了解, liǎojiě, *v.*, L. 17, 91

understand; comprehend, 理解, 理解, lǐjiě, *v.*, L. 21, 110

unexpectedly, 沒想到, 没想到, méi xiǎngdào, *adv.*, L. 6, 31

unexpectedly; to one's surprise, 竟, 竟, jìng, *adv.*, L. 44, 237

unexpectedly; to one's surprise, 居然, 居然, jūrán, *adv.*, L. 11, 54

unit, 單元, 单元, dānyuán, *n.*, L. 30, 159

unite; rally, union, 團結, 团结, tuánjié, *v./n.*, L. 17, 89

unnecessary; surplus, 多餘, 多余, duōyú, *adj.*, L. 21, 109

until then; until that time, 到時候, 到时候, dàoshí.hòu, L. 13, 62

up until ..., 到 … 為止, 到 … 为止, dào...wéizhǐ, L. 11, 57

urban and rural, 城鄉, 城乡, chéngxiāng, *adj.*, L. 31, 163

urge (the guest) to drink, 勸酒, 劝酒, quàn-jiǔ, *v.-o.*, L. 14, 69

urge (the guest) to eat, 勸菜, 劝菜, quàn-cài, *v.-o.*, L. 14, 69

urgent matter, 急事, 急事, jíshì, *n.*, L. 7, 38

use, 以, 以, yǐ, L. 38, 198

use; make use of; apply, 使用, 使用, shǐyòng, *v./n.*, L. 21, 109

use (something else) instead, 改用, 改用, gǎiyòng, *v.*, L. 21, 110

used in a rhetorical question to indicate negation, 哪裏, 哪里, nǎ.lǐ, L. 14, 66

utility; material gain, 功利, 功利, gōnglì, *n.*, L. 38, 202

vague, 模糊, 模糊, mó.hú, *adj.*, L. 37, 194

van, 麵包車, 面包车, miànbāochē, *n.*, L. 1, 4

vast; wide, 廣, 广, guǎng, *adj.*, L. 43, 229

VCR, 錄像機, 录像机, lùxiàngjī, *n.*, L. 20, 105

vegetable, 青菜, 青菜, qīngcài, *n.*, L. 15, 78

vegetable, 蔬菜, 蔬菜, shūcài, *n.*, L. 29, 150

vendor's stand; stall, 小攤, 小摊, xiǎotān, *n.*, L. 16, 85

verb, 動詞, 动词, dòngcí, *n.*, L. 15, 79

vernacular writing, 白話文, 白话文, báihuàwén, *n.*, L. 41, 216

versatile; gifted in many ways, 多才多藝, 多才多艺, duōcái duōyì, *idm.*, L. 40, 213

very *adj.*, ⋯ 得很, ⋯ 得很, ...dehěn, L. 2, 9

very long time, half a day, 半天, 半天, bàntiān, *n.*, L. 7, 37

video game, 電子遊戲, 电子遊戏, diànzǐ yóuxì, *n.*, L. 37, 197

vie for; scramble for, 搶, 抢, qiǎng, *v.*, L. 14, 72

Vietnam, 越南, 越南, Yuènán, L. 37, 195

view; a way of looking at a thing, 看法, 看法, kànfǎ, *n.*, L. 23, 118

vigor; energy, 活力, 活力, huólì, *n.*, L. 35, 185

vigor; vitality, spirit, 精神, 精神, jīng.shén, *n.*, L. 6, 28

vigorous; spirited, 有精神, 有精神, yǒu jīng.shén, *adj.*, L. 6, 29

violence, 暴力, 暴力, bàolì, *n.*, L. 39, 207

visit (formally), 訪問, 访问, fǎngwèn, *v.*, L. 23, 116

visit; look around, 參觀, 参观, cānguān, *v.*, L. 11, 54

visitor (to a park, etc.); tourist, 遊客, 游客, yóukè, *n.*, L. 12, 58

vocabulary, 詞彙, 词汇, cíhuì, *n.*, L. 41, 219

vomit, 吐, 吐, tù, *v.*, L. 5, 25

wake up; sober up, 醒, 醒, xǐng, *v.*, L. 3, 14

walk (somebody); accompany; escort, 送, 送, sòng, *v.*, L. 14, 70

walk; go on foot, 走路, 走路, zǒu-lù, *v.-o.*, L. 7, 35

Wangfujing, 王府井, 王府井, Wángfǔjǐng, L. 7, 32

war, 戰爭, 战争, zhànzhēng, *n.*, L. 37, 195

warm, 暖, 暖, nuǎn, *adj.*, L. 29, 148

Warring States Period (475-221 B.C.), 戰國, 战国, Zhànguó, L. 41, 217

waste; squander, 浪費, 浪费, làngfèi, *v.*, L. 6, 28

watch, 手錶, 手表, shǒubiǎo, *n.*, L. 29, 151

watch (television), 收看, 收看, shōukàn, *v.*, L. 18, 97

watermelon, 西瓜, 西瓜, xīguā, *n.*, L. 5, 25

way; means; measure, 辦法, 办法, bànfǎ, *n.*, L. 18, 96

way; method, 方法, 方法, fāngfǎ, *n.*, L. 15, 78

way a thing or person used to look, 老樣子, 老样子, lǎoyàngzi, *n.*, L. 25, 125

weaken, weak; feeble, 衰弱, 衰弱, shuāiruò, *v./adj.*, L. 43, 232

weather forecast, 天氣預報, 天气预报, tiānqì yùbào, *n.*, L. 2, 7

weather report, 氣象報告, 气象报告, qìxiàng bàogào, *n.*, L. 32, 168

weed out the old to bring forth the new, 推陳出新, 推陈出新, tuī chén chū xīn, *idm.*, L. 44, 241

weekend, 周末, 周末, zhōumò, *n.*, L. 25, 124

welcome, 歡迎, 欢迎, huānyíng, *v.*, L. 32, 169

western; foreign, 洋, 洋, yáng, *adj.*, L. 44, 236

Western Asia, 西亞, 西亚, Xīyà, L. 44, 235

westernization, 西化, 西化, xīhuà, *n.*, L. 44, 238

wheat-based food, 麵食, 面食, miànshí, *n.*, L. 15, 75

whole; entire, 整個, 整个, zhěnggè, *adj.*, L. 24, 120

whole; entire; total, 全 N., 全 N., quán, *adj.*, L. 17, 90

whole day; all day long, 整天, 整天, zhěngtiān, *adv.*, L. 3, 14

wide, 寬闊, 宽阔, kuānkuò, *adj.*, L. 35, 182

wide; broad, 寬, 宽, kuān, *adj.*, L. 1, 4

widespread; general; common, 普遍, 普遍, pǔbiàn, *adj.*, L. 32, 167

wife, 妻子, 妻子, qīzi, *n.*, L. 27, 138

wife, 太太, 太太, tàitai, *n.*, L. 26, 130

with great effort, 努力, 努力, nǔlì, *adv.*, L. 2, 11

within..., ⋯ 之內, ⋯ 之内, zhīnèi, L. 31, 161

woman (as a collective noun), 婦女, 妇女, fùnǔ, *n.*, L. 27, 137

word; term, 詞, 词, cí, *n.*, L. 9, 49

wording, 用語, 用语, yòngyǔ, *n.*, L. 21, 109

wording; way of saying a thing, 說法, 说法, shuōfǎ, *n.*, L. 26, 134

work (colloquial), 活兒, 活儿, huór, *n.*, L. 34, 176

work; book; writing, 著作, 著作, zhùzuò, *n.*, L. 25, 127

work unit, 單位, 单位, dānwèi, *n.*, L. 34, 175

worker; workman, 工人, 工人, gōngrén, *n.*, L. 19, 100

world, 世界, 世界, shìjiè, *n.*, L. 8, 41

worriment; vexation, 煩惱, 烦恼, fánnǎo, *n.*, L. 28, 144

worry; feel anxious, 擔心, 担心, dānxīn, *v.*, L. 1, 3

worry; make anxious; make impatient, 急, 急, jí, *v.*, L. 7, 33

would rather; better, 寧可, 宁可, nìngkě, *adv.*, L. 7, 35

writing, write, 書寫, 书写, shūxiě, *n./v.*, L. 18, 96

writing brush, 毛筆, 毛笔, máobǐ, *n.*, L. 40, 214

written; in written form, 書面, 书面, shūmiàn, *adj.*, L. 41, 216

written language, 書面語, 书面语, shūmiànyǔ, *n.*, L. 41, 217

Xinjiang, 新疆, 新疆, Xīnjiāng, L. 43, 230

... years old, 歲, 岁, suì, L. 28, 143

yet; but; however, 然而, 然而, ránér, *conj.*, L. 23, 118

you (polite expression), 您, 您, nín, *pron.*, L. 7, 37

young, 年輕, 年轻, niánqīng, *adj.*, L. 9, 47
Yuan Dynasty, 元代, 元代, Yuándài, L. 35, 180
Yungang Caves, 雲崗石窟, 云岗石窟, Yúngǎng
   Shíkū, L. 11, 55

Zhang (a surname), 張, 张, Zhāng, L. 1, 2

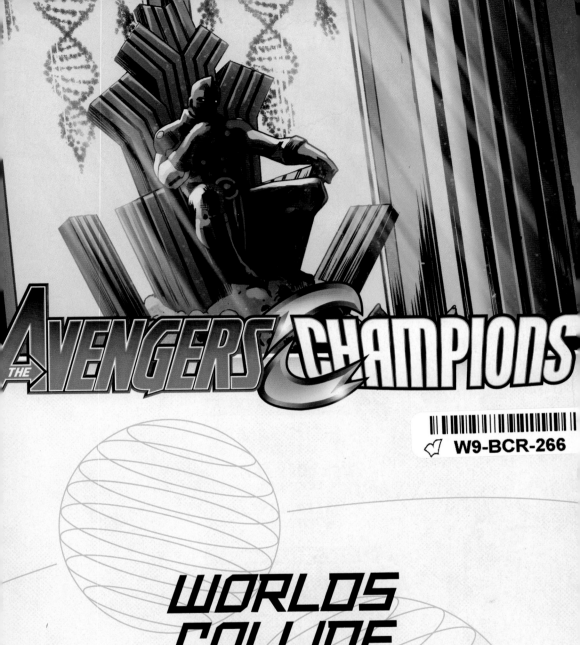

THE AVENGERS CHAMPIONS

WORLDS COLLIDE

THE AVENGERS

AVENGERS #672 & #674

JESÚS SAIZ
ARTIST

VC's CORY PETIT
LETTERER

ALEX ROSS
COVER ART

AVENGERS #673

JAVIER PINA WITH PACO DIAZ
ARTISTS

RACHELLE ROSENBERG
COLOR ARTIST

VC's CORY PETIT
LETTERER

ALEX ROSS
COVER ART

AVENGERS & CHAMPIONS: WORLDS COLLIDE. Contains material originally published in magazine form as AVENGERS #672-674 and CHAMPIONS #13-15. First printing 2018. ISBN 978-1-302-90613-9. Published by MARVE WORLDWIDE, INC., a subsidiary of MARVEL ENTERTAINMENT, LLC. OFFICE OF PUBLICATION: 135 West 50th Street, New York, NY 10020. Copyright © 2018 MARVEL No similarity between any of the names, characters, persons, an or institutions in this magazine with those of any living or dead person or institution is intended, and any such similarity which may exist is purely coincidental. **Printed in the U.S.A.** DAN BUCKLEY, President, Marvel Entertainmen JOE QUESADA, Chief Creative Officer; TOM BREVOORT, SVP of Publishing; DAVID BOGART, SVP of Business Affairs & Operations, Publishing & Partnership; DAVID GABRIEL, SVP of Sales & Marketing, Publishing; JEFF YOUNGQUIS VP of Production & Special Projects; DAN CARR, Executive Director of Publishing Technology; ALEX MORALES, Director of Publishing Operations; SUSAN CRESPI, Production Manager; STAN LEE, Chairman Emeritus. For informatio regarding advertising in Marvel Comics or on Marvel.com, please contact Vit DeBellis, Custom Solutions & Integrated Advertising Manager, at vdebellis@marvel.com. For Marvel subscription inquiries, please call 888-511-548 **Manufactured between 12/15/2017 and 1/15/2018 by LSC COMMUNICATIONS INC., KENDALLVILLE, IN, USA.**

10 9 8 7 6 5 4 3 2 1

CHAMPIONS

CHAMPIONS #13-15

HUMBERTO RAMOS
PENCILER

VICTOR OLAZABA
INKER

EDGAR DELGADO
COLOR ARTIST

VC'S CLAYTON COWLES
LETTERER

HUMBERTO RAMOS & EDGAR DELGADO
COVER ART

ALANNA SMITH
ASSISTANT EDITOR

TOM BREVOORT
EDITOR

AVENGERS CREATED BY *STAN LEE* & *JACK KIRBY*

COLLECTION EDITOR *JENNIFER GRÜNWALD* ▪ ASSISTANT EDITOR *CAITLIN O'CONNELL*
ASSOCIATE MANAGING EDITOR *KATERI WOODY* ▪ EDITOR, SPECIAL PROJECTS *MARK D. BEAZLEY*
VP PRODUCTION & SPECIAL PROJECTS *JEFF YOUNGQUIST* ▪ SVP PRINT, SALES & MARKETING *DAVID GABRIEL*
BOOK DESIGNER *JAY BOWEN*

EDITOR IN CHIEF *C.B. CEBULSKI* ▪ CHIEF CREATIVE OFFICER *JOE QUESADA*
PRESIDENT *DAN BUCKLEY* ▪ EXECUTIVE PRODUCER *ALAN FINE*

WORLDS COLLIDE **PART ONE**

...BECAUSE THEY'RE ABOUT TO SHOW YOU, THAT'S WHY!

HULK, LOOK. MAYBE I CAN'T DO THE *MATH*, BUT...

NOVA? WHY IS HULK BEING UNPLEASANT TO YOU?

THANK YOU!

HE'S GOT HIS "EIGHTH-SMARTEST-GUY-IN-THE-WORLD" HAT ON AGAIN BECAUSE, SOMEHOW, IT FITS OVER HIS *SWELLED* HEAD.

SORRY. *SORRY.* SOMETIMES I FORGET *HOW* SMART I AM.

NO, YOU DON'T.

NO, I DON'T. I'M JUST *CHUFFED.* I'D *SHOW* YOU MY CALCULATIONS, BUT I CAN'T FIND WHERE I *PUT* THEM FOR SOME REASON. IT'S LIKE THEY'VE *DISAPPEARED.* BUT--

--SEE THAT SATELLITE? ASTRONERDS HAVE BEEN WAITING FOR IT TO TAKE POSITION FOR *SIX MONTHS*...

FRONT LINE: THOR AND NOVA!

THE REST OF THE FLIERS--

REST OF THE FLIERS, *SECOND LINE.* VIV, WE'LL EACH GRAB A *SPIDER-MAN.*

SORRY, MS. M. DIDN'T MEAN TO *STEP,* BUT *TICK-TOCK.* YOU WANT TO TAKE IT FROM HERE?

HMPH.

TAKE WHAT? OT A WHOLE LOT TO DD. WE'LL GUARD THE GROUND FLOOR.

EVERYBODY ELSE, GO-GO-*GO!* HERCULES, PAY *ATTENTION!*

I *AM!* IT'S JUST--

--WHERE DID MY *CLUB* GO?

TIME TO *TRY* SOMETHING.

IF I SEED THE AIR WITH *PYM PARTICLES*, THEY SHOULD CLOUD TOGETHER LONG ENOUGH TO REDUCE THAT ROCK IN--

--SIZE--

?

DID YOU JUST SEE THAT? WHERE'D THE *METEOR* GO?

THERE'S SOMETHING *ELSE*. I FELT IT EVER SO SLIGHTLY *ABOVE*, BUT NOW IT'S MORE *PRONOUNCED*.

THE METEOR IS EMITTING A HIGH-FREQUENCY *VIBRATION*.

OH, NO.

VIV'S OUR TEAM'S *EARLY WARNING SYSTEM*. SHE'S CONNECTED TO THE *INTERNET* 24/7.

VIV, WHAT IS IT?

THAT *VIBRATION*. REPORTS ARE COMING IN...FROM AROUND THE *WORLD*...

"...ILDINGS-- *TALLEST* ...ILDINGS, ...UCH AS ...HE *BURJ* ...ALIFA*-- ...HEY'RE ...BRATING, ...TOO."

"BUT NOT *SUBTLY*."

"THEY'RE TREMBLING AS IF STRUCK BY AN *EARTHQUAKE*."

"SHANGHAI TOWER-- ONE WORLD TRADE CENTER--LOTTE WORLD TOWER IN SOUTH KOREA--

"--THEY'RE TEARING THEMSELVES *APART*, AND MANY OF THEM ARE--"

--OCCUPIED.

YOU WERE IN THE BATHROOM. IT'S A GOOD PLAN.

TELL YOU IN A SECOND, ONCE WE GET A *HANDLE* ON THIS MADNESS! NET THE PEOPLE--

--I'VE GOT THE *DEBRIS!*

GREAT. NINE DOWN, THOUSANDS TO GO. WE'VE AT LEAST GOT TO GET 'EM TO A *LOWER* LEVEL!

I...WHERE AM I...?

VIV...WHERE IS MY DAUGHTER...?

THAT *DID* TAKE A LOT OUT OF HIM! HE'S GOT *BOXER'S BRAIN!*

VISION! YOU OKAY?

I...AM. I APOLOGIZE. WHAT WAS I SAYING?

YOU CALLED OUT FOR VIV. DIDN'T REALIZE SHE WAS ON YOUR *MIND* THAT MUCH THESE DAYS.

IT'S OBVIOUS THERE'S A LOT OF FRICTION BETWEEN YOU AND YOUR DAUGHTER LATELY. DO YOU WANT T TALK IT OUT? I KNOW LOT ABOUT BOTTLING YOURSELF UP.

ME TOO!

SPIDER-MAN, YOU TALK MORE THAN ANYONE I'VE EVER *MET.*

THANK YOU, BUT OURS IS A...FAMILY AFFAIR.

THEN HOW ABOUT YOU START *TREATING* HER LIKE FAMILY, PAL...?

CYCLOPS, I DON'T SEE THE NEW YORK TEAM. DO YOU HAVE EYES ON THEM?

WE'RE APPROACHING THE *WORLD TRADE CENTER!* FALCON, VIV--GET READY FOR SOME *BACKUP!*

I CAN JOIN THEM--

NO! I NEED YOUR HELP IN *HERE!*

THAT'S THE MACHINERY THAT'S WREAKING ALL THE HAVOC! YOU'VE GOT THE *HAMMER--*

--LET'S DO SOME DEMO!

CHOOM

HEAR THAT *EXPLOSION*, BUDDY? THAT'S THE SOUND OF YOUR *BIG PLAN*, WHATEVER IT IS, GOING *KABLOOEY!*

HEH.

NO. SOMETHING'S STILL WRONG. MY SPIDER-SENSE SAYS WE'RE STILL IN *DANGER*.

IT'S IN THE *AIR*. IT'S IN THE *GROUND*. EVERYTHING FEELS...*OFF*. BUT WE SHUT DOWN THE *MACHINE*, RIGHT?

YEAH. BUT IN *TIME*...?

VIVIAN!

THERE IS NO MORE NEED FOR ALARM, FATHER.

NO CIVILIANS ARE IN PERIL--

--ONLY THE PLANET ITSELF.

EARTH IS NOW PREPARED FOR THE ASCENSION-- AND IT WILL BE UPON YOU BEFORE YOU CAN EVEN REACT.

BUILDING'S STILL SHAKING, THOUGH.

THEN WE WILL SUMMON THE OTHERS. IF THERE IS NO IMMINENT DANGER...

...IT IS IMPERATIVE THAT I SPEAK WITH MY DAUGHTER. VIVIAN, I...

...I REALIZE I HAVE BEEN MARKEDLY TENSE IN YOUR PRESENCE AS OF LATE...BUT THERE IS A REASON.

THERE IS SOMETHING VERY IMPORTANT ABOUT YOUR FUTURE WE MUST ADDRESS IF WE ARE TO WORK HARMONIOUSLY IN THIS CRISIS. SOMETHING CRITICAL.

YOU WERE *UNABLE* TO DESTROY MY MACHINERY IN TIME.

WHAT YOU NOW *SENSE*, WITH THE HELP OF THE ATTUNED BUILDINGS *WORLDWIDE*, IS A *GLOBAL SHIFT* IN EARTH'S VIBRATORY PATTERNS.

IN TIME, THAT SHIFT WILL AFFECT US *ALL*...

"...BUT NONE *SOONER* THAN THOSE LONGEST *EXPOSED* TO ITS *REMAINING SOURCE*."

VIVIAN, I AM IN DANGER OF FACING THE MOST *TRAGIC* PAIN A PARENT CAN FEEL. THERE'S SOMETHING YOU MUST *KNOW*--

VIVIAN?

FALCON! WHAT'S HAPPENING?

FATHER!

VIVIAN!

AVENGERS, DO YOU READ ME? FALCON AND VIVIAN HAVE DISAPPEARED!

WHAT IS HAPPENING?

NO MORE RIDDLES! WHERE ARE FALCON AND VIV?

FAR, FAR AWAY...

WORLDS COLLIDE PART THREE

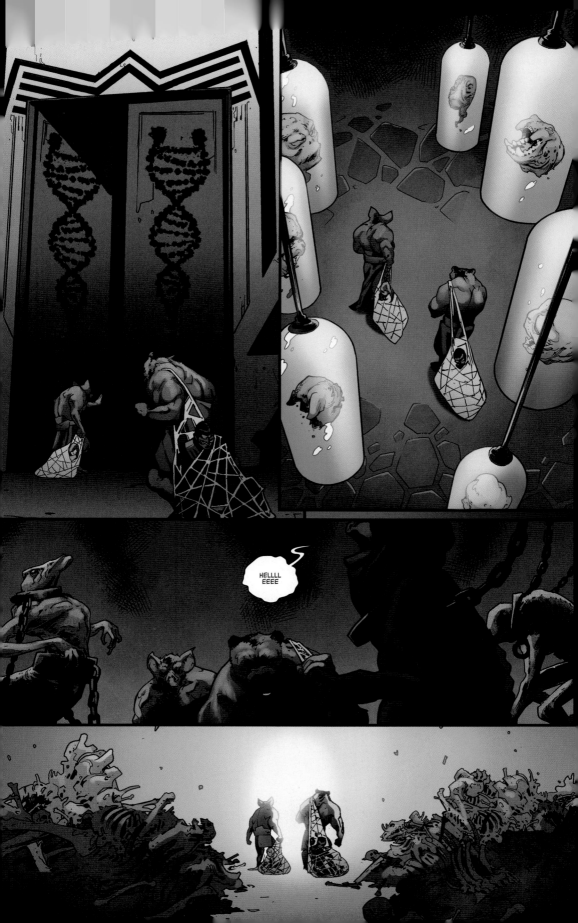

HE'S GOING TO BE IN A *REAL* RUSH TO LEAD *TWO* RIGHTEOUS TEAMS HERE TO KICK YOUR ASS!

WHATEVER YOU'RE UP TO THIS TIME, WE *WILL* SHUT YOU *DOWN.* AGAIN.

NO. MUCH IS *DIFFERENT* NOW. NONE OF YOU ARE PREPARED FOR THE SHEER SCOPE OF WHAT'S ABOUT TO OCCUR. A GOD MOVES ON A *GRAND SCALE,* SIR.

OH, YOU'RE A *GOD* NOW? ALL-POWERFUL? IMMORTAL? WHAT?

BOTH, ACTUALLY. I'VE FINALLY ALTERED MY OWN GENETIC CODE TO CONFER *ETERNAL LIFE,* SOMETHING I SHOULD HAVE DONE *AGES* AGO.

IMMORTALITY BRINGS WITH IT THE CONFIDENCE TO WORK...*LONG-TERM.*

ON WHAT?

ARTIFICIAL WINGS? HOW SLOPPY. LET'S *FIX* THAT.

TAKE HIM TO THE *LAB.*

AVENGERS ASSEMBLE!

WAIT!

THE EARTH-TO-EARTH TRANSFERS ARE RANDOM!

SO WHAT ARE THE ODDS THIS IS AN ARMY BUILT TO BATTLE US--

--AND NOT A BUNCH OF ANI-MEN JUST AS CONFUSED AS WE ARE?

I HATE TO ADMIT IT, BUT IF MY SPIDER-SENSE ISN'T TINGLING, THE KIDS ARE PROBABLY RIGHT!

I'VE HAD *ENOUGH* OF YOU!

LOOK AT YOU. BARELY A *RUNG* OR TWO UP THE EVOLUTIONARY *LADDER.*

APES YOU *WERE...*

TKK

...APES YOU *SHALL* BE AGAIN.

PULL *BACK!* *BACK!*

"ASCENSION" ISN'T ABOUT *MERGING* THE WORLDS!

FALCON SAYS THE EVOLUTIONARY CLAIMS TO BE WORKING ON A *COSMIC SCALE* NOW!

"SO THINK ABOUT WHAT HE *DOES!* HOW HE *OPERATES!*

"HE *EVOLVES* THINGS BY *BRUTE FORCE!* BY CRASHING GENES AND DNA *TOGETHER* TO MAKE SOMETHING *NEW!*

"NOW PICTURE THAT ON A *PLANETARY LEVEL!* HE'S NOT *MERGING* TWO WORLDS--

"--HE'S *COLLIDING* THEM!

"HE WANTS TO START *FRESH* WITH A BLANK-CANVAS *SUPERPLANET!*

"HE'S *IMMORTAL!* HE DOESN'T CARE AT ALL THAT IT'LL TAKE *MILLIONS OF YEARS* FOR WHAT'S LEFT TO *RECOMBINE!*

"WE'RE JUST AN EXTINCTION-LEVEL EXPERIMENT!"

THEY'RE GETTING *MUCH WORSE.* HOW MANY BEFORE *SOLID IMPACT?* TWO? THREE?

WHERE DO WE FIND THIS *VIBRATORY MACHINE?*

I THINK I CAN HELP.

WHAT COMPUTER SKILLS I HAD ARE FADING FROM *MEMORY,* BUT I REMEMBERED ENOUGH TO ACCESS A *CITADEL MAP.*

THERE'S SOMETHING *MASSIVE* DEEP UNDERGROUND. IT HAS TO BE THE *MACHINE.* I CAN TAKE US TO AN *ACCESS POINT.*

VIVIAN, YOU ARE NOT *SAFE* HERE! I TOLD YOU TO STAY WHERE YOU...

...

I AM PROUD O' YOU.

WORLDS COLLIDE PART FIVE

WAS THAT THE LAST OBSTACLE?

HAVE WE BEEN THAT LUCKY SO **FAR,** SPIDER-MAN?

WE'RE MILES AND MILES UNDERGROUND. SHOULDN'T WE HAVE **MELTED** BY THIS POINT?

OBVIOUSLY, THE HIGH EVOLUTIONARY BUILT THIS CORRIDOR WITH A VERTICAL MAGNETIC FIELD THAT ACTS AS A **HEAT SHIELD,** AND **WOW.**

IT WOULD HAVE TO BE ON A 10^6 MEGATESLA ORDER OF MAGNITUDE, WITH--

MAGNETIC FIELD. CHECK.

WE SHOULD BE NEARING OUR TARGET.

THERE IS A NATURAL POINT WHERE THE VIBRATIONAL MACHINE'S PLACEMENT WOULD BE MOST **EFFECTIVE.**

I WAS ABOUT TO SAY THAT OUR HIGH EVOLUTIONARY PAL BURIED HIS GIZMO **DEEP.**

THAT IS NOT WHAT CONCERNS ME, MS. MARVEL. WHAT **DOES** IS THAT THERE IS SOMETHING DOWN HERE ALONG **WITH** IT THAT **FRIGHTENS** HIM.

OTHERWISE, HE WOULD SIMPLY HAVE ALTERED **THIS** PLANET'S RESONANCE RATHER THAN **OURS.**

WELL, **WHATEVER** IT IS...

FORTY-EIGHT
MINUTES.

THIRTY-T

TWENTY-SIX MINUTES.

...WHO *ARE* YOU? YOU LOOK LIKE THE *EVOLUTIONARY*, BUT...

I AM BOTH MY FATHER'S GREATEST *TRIUMPH* AND HIS GREATEST *FAILURE.*

IF YOU HAVE COME WITH A *MESSAGE* FROM HIM, TAKE ONE *BACK* INSTEAD...

...THE HIGHER EVOLUTIONARY CHOOSES *NEVER* TO STOP SUFFERING FOR *HIS* CREATIONS.

IGHTEEN MINUTES.

YOU'RE CLEARLY IN AGONY. WHAT IS THIS PLACE? WHY DO YOU CALL THE EVOLUTIONARY "FATHER"?

LIKE THE ANI-MEN ABOVE, I AM A *MUTATION.* BUT I AM *UNIQUE.*

"I AM BORN OF MY FATHER'S OWN GENETIC CODE.

"HE SAID HE WAS 'TIRED' OF HIS ANI-MEN. IN ME, HE ENVISIONED A NEW SPECIES SO ADVANCED AS TO *REPLACE* THEM. BUT IN HIS CONSTRUCTION, HE MADE A TERRIBLE ERROR.

"HE FAILED TO ELIMINATE FROM ME THE ONE ATTRIBUTE HE HIMSELF HAD LONG SINCE REJECTED--

"--COMPASSION.

"THE ANI-MEN, I PLED, COULD NOT SIMPLY BE ELIMINATED--DISCARDED AS AN EXPERIMENT HE'D GROWN BORED WITH. THEY WERE LIVING BEINGS."

SIXTEEN MINUTES.

I HAD CHALLENGED HIM.

FOR THAT ACTION, HE CAST ME INTO THE STYGIAN DEPTHS OF HIS "PLANET-SIZED LABORATORY," AS HE SO CLINICALLY REFERRED TO OUR WORLD.

WHAT I DID, I DID FOR ALL HIS SUBJECTS. LOVE IS NOT A SIN!

CAN YOU IMAGINE BEING CONSTRUCTED BY YOUR FATHER--BUILT WITH HIS OWN HANDS--AND THEN BEING PUNISHED FOR EXISTING?

NO.

I'M SORRY FOR YOUR PAIN. BUT THE HIGH EVOLUTIONARY IS *GONE* NOW. AND MY FRIENDS AND I CAN *HELP* YOU.

"THAT'S WHAT WE'RE HERE TO *DO.*

"LIKE *YOU,* WE'RE HERE TO SAVE THE ANI-MEN."

IF YOU CAN GIVE US *ACCESS* TO YOUR *MACHINE*--

NO! THIS IS A *TRICK!*

TO TOUCH THE *ORBIT-ENGINE* IS TO *DESTROY US ALL!*

HE'S *BOUND* YOU TO IT--

I HAVE *CHAINED MYSELF!* I AM ITS *GUARDIAN!*

NO ONE MUST TAMPER WITH THE *HEART* OF MY *WORLD!* I WILL *NOT ALLOW* MORE *SUFFERING! LEAVE* ME!

FIVE MINUTES.

WORLDS COLLIDE PART SIX

...MINUTE BOTH PLANETS WERE STABILIZED, MY HAMMER WAS ABLE TO BREACH THE VIBRATIONAL BOUNDARIES, YES.

WE SEARCHED THE HIGH EVOLUTIONARY'S CITADEL IN HOPES OF FINDING VIV'S ORIGINAL *SYNTHEZOID FORM*, BUT IT NO LONGER EXISTS. APPARENTLY, SHE TRULY *WAS* CHANGED INTO A HUMAN BEING.

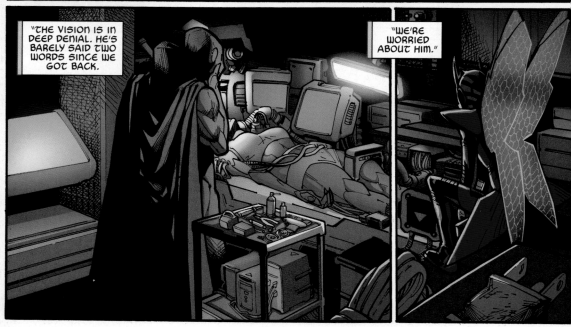

"THE VISION IS IN DEEP DENIAL. HE'S BARELY SAID TWO WORDS SINCE WE GOT BACK.

"WE'RE WORRIED ABOUT HIM."

HNNH!

YOU SOUNDED *STARTLED.* YOU WERE TELLING ME THAT VIBRATIONS FROM A *WORLDCORE* MACHINE SENT YOU HERE. IS THERE SOMETHING *ELSE?*

I JUST... I SAW MY *DAD?* MY EYES PLAYED A *TRICK...*

...MAYBE BECAUSE OF HOW YOU *REBUILT* ME? I'M NOT SURE.

WHY DO YOU DO THESE AWFUL THINGS? TRANSFORM ANIMALS, TRANSFORM *PEOPLE,* INTO *MONSTERS?*

YOU CONSIDER YOURSELF A *MONSTER* NOW? NOT A *PINOCCHIO PUPPET* TURNED INTO A *REAL GIRL?*

I WAS NEVER A *PUPPET.* YOU'RE *EVIL.*

WE GET IT! YOU'RE THE MIGHTY AVENGERS!

HIGH AND MIGHTY!

STOP!

WE SHOULD BE LEAVING ANYWAY. CHAMPIONS--

YES, WE ARE ALL ON EDGE-- BUT WHATEVER OUR DIFFERENCES, CAN WE NOT HAVE IT OUT IN A MOURNING MAN'S BACKYARD?

--LET'S TAKE THIS UP SOME OTHER TIME.

NOVA, C'MON...

IF WE'RE SO MUCH SMARTER THAN YOU--

--HOW COME YOU'RE THE ONE WHO FIGURED OUT HOW TO SAVE US FROM THE EVOLUTIONARY'S DEVOLUTION BOMB?

STAY. WE CAN'T LOSE YOU, TOO. WE CAN'T.

OKAY. I JUST MISS HER.

US, TOO.

!

ANOTHER GLIMPSE OF HOME THROUGH *UNFAMILIAR* EYES?

WHAT DID YOU MEAN, I'M NOT DATA *YET*?

WE WERE DRAWN HERE, WHEREVER *"HERE"* IS, AND IT'S BEGINNING NOT TO *MATTER*--BECAUSE *VIBRATIONS* ALTERED OUR MOLECULAR STRUCTURES.

WE WERE BROUGHT *TOGETHER* BECAUSE OUR FREQUENCIES MATCHED--WHICH WORKS *VERY* MUCH TO MY ADVANTAGE.

"AS A *LIVING SIGNAL,* I WOULD SEEM TO BE *TRAPPED* HERE BECAUSE I HAVE NO RECEIVER IN OUR REALITY.

"*YOU MIGHT,* HOWEVER. I CAN ONLY ASSUME THAT YOU HEARTBROKEN FATHER IS ATTEMPTING TO *RECONSTRUC* YOU, DON'T YOU IMAGINE?"

THAT'S WHY YOU'RE HAVING...FORGIVE ME...*VISIONS* AS IF THROUGH *"HER"* EYES. DESPITE THE *DISTANCE,* YOU MAINTAIN SOME *CONNECTION* WITH YOUR SYNTHEZOID OTHER SELF.

MEANING...

...YOU CAN TAKE US *BOTH* BACK HOME.

IF I'M TO *ESCAPE* FROM THIS PLACE, OUR FATES REMAIN *INTERTWINED*.

AND SO IT SHALL *BE*. YOU'VE NOWHERE TO *RUN*, DARLING.

NOWHERE TO *HIDE* FROM ME.

NOW, FOR THE LAST TIME...

...GIVE ME YOUR *HAND*.

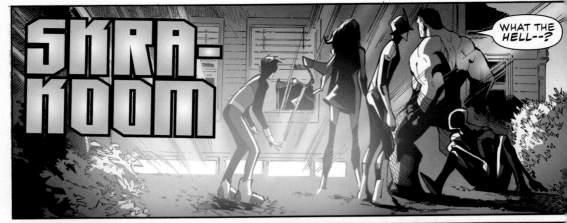

NEXT IN CHAMPIONS: DOUBLE VISION

AVENGERS #672 HOMAGE VARIANT BY *MICHAEL ALLRED & LAURA ALLRED*

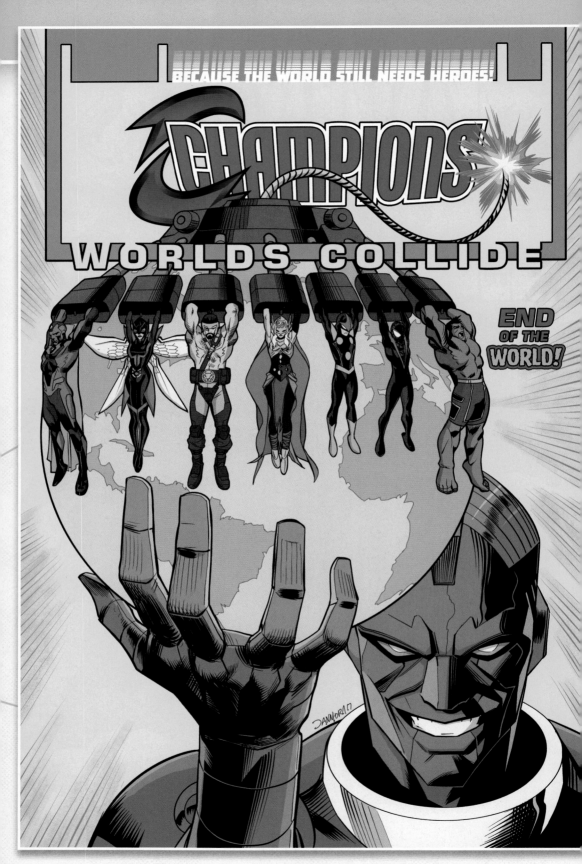

CHAMPIONS #13 HOMAGE VARIANT BY *DAN MORA* & *MEGAN WILSON*

**AVENGERS #672 1965 T-SHIRT VARIANT BY
JACK KIRBY, DON HECK, FRANK GIACOIA,
DICK AYERS & STAN GOLDBERG**

**AVENGERS #672 KIRBY 100TH ANNIVERSARY
VARIANT BY JACK KIRBY, PAUL REINMAN
& PAUL MOUNTS WITH JOE FRONTIRRE**

**CHAMPIONS #13 TRADING CARD VARIANT BY
JOHN TYLER CHRISTOPHER**

HOW TO DRAW MS. MARVEL
IN SIX EASY STEPS!
BY CHIP "CHAMP" ZDARSKY

Wow! A "sketch variant cover"! A great way to while away the time AND wreck a cover! Anyway, here's a fun and informative step-by-step guide!

1

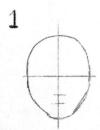

All right! First we start with the outline of her face! Give it an oval shape, but slightly boxy at the bottom! And then you can rough in the center axis for placement of her eyeline, nose and mouth!

2

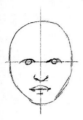

With the guides in place, draw in her eyes, roughly one eye apart, and then her nose and mouth!

3

In a nice throwback to when people thought tiny masks hid their identities, add Kamala's! Then, give her a hint of neck and body, so we can add in her hair next!

4

Now for the aforementioned hair! Add some that goes behind her body and some that goes in front! Use your eraser to get rid of guide marks, and then add her scarf and costume details!

5

Now, slightly tweak Kamala's expression to reflect the burden of being Marvel's first Muslim character with her own book and living up to the expectations that come with extra scrutiny and awards and representing an under-represented section of the populace in popular culture.

6

Now add some detail! Voila! All done!

AVENGERS #672 LEGACYHEADSHOT VARIANT BY
MIKE McKONE & RACHELLE ROSENBERG

CHAMPIONS #13 LEGACY HEADSHOT VARIANT BY
MIKE McKONE & RACHELLE ROSENBERG

AVENGERS #674 PHOENIX VARIANT BY
BRENT SCHOONOVER & NICK FILARDI

CHAMPIONS #15 PHOENIX VARIANT BY
DAVID NAKAYAMA